How to cook a galah

CELEBRATING AUSTRALIA'S CULINARY HERITAGE

LAUREL EVELYN DYSON BSc, BA, PhD, is a trained botanist, former
lecturer in Italian literature and language, and now works as an
Associate Lecturer in the Faculty of Information Technology at the
University of Technology, Sydney. Her passion for Australian
cooking began as a child in Sydney, eating at her mother's table
and quietly observing and absorbing the rituals of the kitchen.

Over many years she gathered material as she travelled
throughout Australia. From Tibooburra to Tasmania, from Broome
to Ballarat, from Cooktown to Kalgan, she tasted and collected
recipes as she went. Long hours in Sydney's Mitchell Library
poring over old cookbooks were followed by equally long sessions in
the kitchen testing recipes.

How to cook a galah

Celebrating Australia's Culinary Heritage

LAUREL EVELYN DYSON

Lothian
BOOKS

Thomas C. Lothian Pty Ltd
132 Albert Road, South Melbourne, Victoria 3205
www.lothian.com.au

National Library of Australia
Cataloguing-in-Publication data:

Dyson Laurel Evelyn.
    How to cook a galah: celebrating Australia's culinary heritage.

    Bibliography.
    Includes index.
    ISBN 0 7344 0396 8.

    1. Cookery Australian – History. 2. Food habits –
    Australia – History. 3. Food – History. I Title.
641.300994

Produced in association with Barbara Beckett Publishing Pty Ltd
14 Hargrave Street, Paddington, Sydney, Australia 2021
Design and food editing by Barbara Beckett
Printed in Australia by Advance Press

FRONT COVER: *Though not strictly a galah, this charming portrait of a king parrot performing acrobatic tricks for a few cherries was painted by Captain John Hunter in about 1788–1790.*
PAGE 1: *Pumpkin scones from an old booklet promoting self-raising flour.*
PAGES 2 AND 3: *S. T. Gill's watercolour of the kitchen in Monsieur Noufflard's House.*
PAGE 5 LOWER: *A detail of Bethany, a German village in South Australia painted by G. F. Angus.*
PAGE 5 TOP: *A detail of Aborigines hunting flying foxes and lizards in the trees.*

Contents

The ladies in this 1883 kitchen have the advantage of a gas wall-light but gas has yet to replace solid fuel in the open-grate cooking range.

Foreword

THIS book is a revelation—both fascinating and entertaining. If you are a cook, a foodie, an historian, a professional or an amateur, you will welcome the 'spirits' of the past encapsulated within these pages.

Laurel Dyson has collected food stories and recipes from wide-ranging sources. For instance, Dame Mary Gilmore describes watching her grandmother cooking in her brick baking-oven where a whole sheep could be roasted or half-a-barrow load of potatoes and pumpkins. In contrast, Barbara Hanrahan writes about the summers of her 1940s childhood and the cry of 'Ice-O!' as she danced after the iceman's cart. Recipes from the past have been rewritten for today's cook—they are delightfully evocative whether for armchair browsing or recreating in the kitchen. Where else could you find a recipe for Red-back Spider or Bush Pie?

How to cook a galah investigates our roots and considers what we could have learnt from the first Australians who enjoyed the most delicious and varied foods. Goobalathaldin in *Moon and Rainbow*, describes how the Lardil men preferred to fish together with nets at night when the tide was low. Traditional ways of cooking fish include wrapping it in paperbark or native ginger leaves.

Laurel Dyson also writes about how we have been shaped by the many immigrant communities who have settled on our shores bringing their customs, traditions, cooking and food.

The author reminds us that we have a rich culinary heritage. She links the cooking of today with those who came before us. When we gather around a barbecue or cook a damper we are following the tradition of the first Australians. But this is also a story about home cooking and how we adapted to the raw ingredients that grow so well in our variable climate.

This is a book that just had to be written. It gives us a clear picture of why Australia is now considered a force in world food.

Thank you Laurel Dyson.

MARGARET FULTON OAM

Grass is across the wagon-tracks,
and plough strikes bone across the grass,
and vineyards cover all the slopes
where the dead teams were used to pass.

O vine, grow close upon that bone
and hold it with your rooted hand.
The prophet Moses feeds the grape,
and fruitful is the Promised Land.

JUDITH WRIGHT, FROM BULLOCKY

1

'... and fruitful is the Promised Land'

Method of Climbing Trees *by the 'Port Jackson Painter' shows that young Aboriginal men were agile climbers, using footholds cut with stone axes to reach possums, flying foxes, birds, nuts and beehives.*

The Bush Food Harvest

AUSTRALIA has one of the world's oldest living cuisines, dating back more than sixty thousand years when the first human beings set foot on the northern fringe of the continent. The lifestyle of many Aboriginal Australians has changed dramatically in modern times but by tradition they are gatherers, hunters and fishers, moving in small groups purposefully and systematically over their lands according to the known availability of foods. By carefully husbanding the natural resources and limiting their population growth they succeeded in living well whatever the season or whims of climate. Even in the desert, where families used to travel widely, rarely more than half a day was spent in getting enough to eat. While food is plentiful and still fresh the custom is to have one's fill, and even now sometimes hundreds of people will gather for a feast.

Supplies are ensured by not overharvesting, by not taking undersized animals and by not wasting food. Fire-stick farming promotes the regrowth of plant foods, as well as grasses to feed game. Kangaroos are provided with soaks for drinking. Along the rivers breeding sanctuaries are kept for waterfowl and fish. Rivers and streams may be channelled to irrigate vegetables and cereals; yam tops are cut off at harvest and reset in plantations; while along the coast saplings are piled onto mud flats and left for a year to develop their crop of cobras, or mangrove worms. Apart from such practical approaches, religious rites are celebrated at places which represent the spiritual homes of various plants and animals: appeals for plenty are answered because of the ties of kinship that link the spirit beings of the land to the people and the obligations that arise from these ties.

The diet is extremely varied, more so than is typically found in a settled community, and the foods themselves often more nutritious than cultivated crops. Enormous variation occurs from one region to another. People of the desert have damper as their mainstay along with a number of staple fruits, some vegetables, supplemented by lizards, insects, small game and occasionally bigger animals such as kangaroos and emus. Beside the eastern riverways fish, waterfowl, eggs and aquatic plants combine with the kangaroo, emu and possum of the plains and woodlands. Along the coast, fish, shellfish, dugong and turtle are more important than land animals, with plenty of fruits and vegetables from the swamps. While some foods, like insects and reptiles, may seem strange to the modern diner, colonial bush cook Mina Rawson, who had herself tried many Aboriginal delicacies, affirmed that 'what they use for food you may be quite sure is the best and most wholesome'.

Food is categorised as plant or animal. It is the women's job to harvest the vegetables, fruits, nuts, grains and shellfish; they also hunt small game and fish. The men fish and hunt for large animals. Both occupations require a great deal of skill: the women have a thorough knowledge of botany, know where plants are to be found, which are safe to eat and when to harvest seasonal crops. The men understand the behaviour of the creatures they stalk, how to approach them unheeded and how to make weapons and snares. The women's contribution to the daily fare is normally at least fifty per cent, sometimes much more, chiefly because of the greater reliability of plant crops compared to the unpredictability of game. At times both sexes undertake gathering or hunting, and are able to maintain themselves independently.

Food is snacked on during the hunt or harvest and the rest brought back to camp for distribution. Most plant foods are shared within the immediate family whereas large game is always divided between all relations present according to well-defined rules. Dinner is then prepared, usually for late afternoon. There is no set breakfast or lunch as such, although leftovers from the day before may be eaten at breakfast time.

The Campfire Kitchen

The men cook the large meats and fish but most other cooking is done by the women, especially those middle-aged or older, who earn accolades for their expertise. Cookery centres around the campfire. Historically the women would carry a fire-stick from one camp to another but a new fire could be lit by the men in a couple of minutes in dry conditions. Tasmanian men struck iron pyrite with a flint to create the sparks for a fire. The Mardudjara people of the Western Desert took a split piece of dead wood rammed full of dry grass and powdered kangaroo dung, which ignited when a woomera (a spear thrower) was sawn across it vigorously. The Jirrbal men of the Far North rainforests twirled a soft fire-stick, the jiman bagar, between the palms of the hands into the notch of a flat hardwood base carved in the shape of a man: the softer wood wore away into a smouldering powder.

Since Aboriginal people are poor in material goods in contrast to the richness and complexity of their intellectual and spiritual culture, cookery utensils are for the most part light, portable and relatively few. They differ greatly across the continent. Fire tongs, dishes, buckets and pounders are constructed from wood. Carved wooden coolamons are used as mixing bowls, for carrying food and water, and for winnowing grain. Grids of sticks are useful for grilling, placed directly onto the coals or raised on four uprights. String bags and woven dillies, are employed for carrying, soaking and straining. Basketry mats keep food off the ground and free of grit. Sheets of bark are useful for kneading, serving and wrapping. Shells provide water containers and drinking vessels, spoons, knives, graters and shredders. Vegetable peelers and slicers are made from large snail shells. Knives and choppers of sharpened stone and bone are essential, and heated stones for cooking are universal across Australia. Stone mortars crush berries and crack nuts, while millstones yield flour. Nowadays, these traditional utensils are supplemented by the billy and camp oven in addition to modern kitchen equipment.

Cookery techniques vary, depending on the type of food. Many fruits, salad vegetables, nuts, eggs, shellfish and insects are eaten raw. Parching— gentle cooking in hot ash—is reserved for insects, which are then yandied in a coolamon to separate out the ash and dirt. Grilling on or over live coals is more suitable for seafood, small game, eggs, nuts and root vegetables. The fish and animals are sometimes first wrapped in a coat of clay, bark or aromatic leaves and may be cooked without cleaning and with scales, feathers or fur intact to retain the essential juices. When these are cleaned, it is through a natural opening such as the mouth or gills or by a small precise cut which allows for the least loss of moisture and flavour while cooking. Large poultry, large lizards and yams are baked in small heated ground hollows, or in leafy ground ovens which entail a certain amount of steaming and smoking. The latter are the favoured method of dealing with large animals.

Vegetables and fruits may be mashed to produce an easily digestible purée, which in turn can be made into balls and cakes. Cereals and nuts are often stoneground into flour (sometimes after poisons have been leached out in water) and then formed into small cakes or dampers. Johnny cakes and yam cakes are baked directly on hot coals or on hot, flat stones, whereas dampers are baked in the fireplace, completely covered by ash. Cress is given a full steaming in very moist ground ovens while green wattle pods and pigweed (purslane) are steam-roasted—cooked wet on hot coals. Although popular today, boiling was not a favourite traditional method of cooking but certain coastal groups used to boil food in large shells and there are reports of Northern Territory people poaching fish in water heated by hot stones.

Some of the dishes so produced are extremely sophisticated, such as the fishballs of skate, first cooked, then kneaded in changes of water to eliminate ammonia, then mixed with the raw mashed liver. Cycad cakes, with their series of leachings, pounding and roasting represent another complex food much appreciated by Aboriginal people; in the north they were kept for feasts and ceremonies. And surely the ground oven must rank as one of the world's great gastronomic experiences, with its intricate mixture of flavours from the smoke of the fire and the leaves used in the oven, the resultant meat and vegetables all moist, succulent and fragrant.

Many dishes, on the other hand, are fairly simple. Certainly the fancy sauces, garnishes and presentations of European cookery are absent. Instead, smoke from a wide range of woods and aromatic herbs are used to good effect. The game meats are for the most part highly tasty and the diversity of fruits and vegetables, coming into season in turn as the year progresses, represent an ever changing kaleidoscope of culinary experience. The freshness of the ingredients enhances their appetising qualities since the Aboriginal cook traditionally relies little on stored provisions but chooses rather the living larder of the earth around, consuming most of the harvest within a day. Aboriginal knowledge and skill ensures that this is as dependable as any modern store cupboard, whose dried, tinned and frozen goods must appear stale by comparison. The nutritiousness of many of the native foods is enhanced by the cookery techniques applied to them: frying and the use of salt was in the past unknown, and basting meats with fat is replaced by wholesome leaf-wrapping and ground-oven methods.

Despite the lack of complicated utensils, Aboriginal cooks have forged a rich cuisine of great variety and ingenuity, remarkably sympathetic to the essential nature of the raw ingredients, a cuisine in which authentic flavour rules. One colonial commentator Richard Tester, writing of a trip to the Victorian goldfields in the 1850s, described the derision shown by the Kooris in his party towards a frying pan in which fish for supper was about to be cooked. Instead, they made a gridiron of green twigs laid crossways over the fire and so grilled the fish to perfection. As Tester concluded, 'They understood cooking better than we did'.

Eating and Feasting in the Far North

The Torres Strait Islanders who settled off the tip of Cape York some ten thousand years ago are, like the coastal Aborigines, a fishing nation. Silver mullet, sardines, coral trout, schnapper, kingfish, whiting, herring, bream, whitefish and bonito are common. Lobsters, crabs, prawns, squid and octopus, pearl oysters, trochus and bailer shellfish are all part of their diet. Most sought after of all marine creatures are the dugong and turtle. Pigs and chickens are reserved for feast days and other meats are rare. There are few native land animals with the exception of some lizards and rodents, bats and birds, and the best eating of these, the Torres Strait pigeon, is uncommon nowadays. Turtle and chicken eggs are additional sources of protein.

In contrast to the mainland, the people of the Torres Strait are traditionally market gardeners. Yams, sweet potatoes, taro, cassava, corn, pumpkins and sugar cane are staple crops with bananas, mangoes, pawpaw, guavas and watermelons common fruits. The wongai, or native plum, the native almond and various lilli pillies are widely cultivated. Coconuts, whether for food, drink or flavouring, are enormously important.

Some Aboriginal cookery methods are practised by the islanders, for example grilling fish, shellfish and crustaceans on hot coals. Wrapping food in leaves and ground-oven cookery are commonplace. The banana, coconut and native almond leaves employed give far less seasoning than some of the highly aromatic leaves of the Australian mainland. Nor are the firewoods the same, so that a differently flavoured smoke is given off.

The chief point of divergence from mainland techniques is the extensive reliance on boiling, stewing and frying. Mammoth bailer shells, or nowadays oil drums, act like saucepans in which dugong, turtle, fish and shellfish as well as vegetables are cooked, often deliciously flavoured with coconut milk. Dripping, butter and peanut oil from the store, or more traditionally coconut cream, dugong and turtle oil, are utilised for frying.

Torres Strait cookery has changed much over the years from its purely Melanesian origins. Macassar seaman, in search of bêche-de-mer and mother of pearl, were the first to visit the islands from the seventeenth or early eighteenth century, bringing their curries and sambals, their dried and pickled chillies, cloves and cinnamon bark, garlic and green ginger. The British settled in the islands in the nineteenth century and established a taste for tinned and corned meat, cakes and puddings, bottled sauces and vinegar, jams and pickles, tea and lolly water. They were soon followed by Chinese storekeepers who stocked quantities of rice, flour and cornflour, dried beans and mushrooms, peanut oil and prawn paste, noodles and tins of bamboo shoots. These days potatoes have become cheaper than any of the traditional vegetables, and large quantities of flour, rice and some tinned meat forms the main diet for many people. Islanders now live on the mainland up and down the Queensland coast and their cookery includes a lot more fresh lamb and beef than is available on the islands as well as new vegetables like string beans, peas and celery.

The high point of Torres Strait cooking are still the feasts which form the main source of entertainment on most islands, always accompanied by singing and dancing. The preparations go on all day with the women making special vegetable dishes like sop-sop (page 123) and the men trying to catch a dugong or turtle or pig and then constructing the ground oven, or kup maori. Most of the food is cooked in the kup maori, with the vegetables, dampers and whole fish wrapped in banana or coconut fronds. The food is laid out on banana leaves or mats woven by the women and decorated with clusters of flowers. There are no separate courses so that fruits are presented with the main dishes, supplemented by huge bowls of custard, cakes spread with jam and tinned puddings. Mountains of rice accompany the feast and green coconuts or bottled soft drinks are the beverages.

From Hunger to Surfeit

In January 1788 a revolution in Australian life and cookery began when a group of British exiles and their keepers, about a thousand people in all, established themselves on the south-eastern rim of the continent. The first five years of settlement have been termed the 'hungry years', a time marked by shortages, nutritional imbalance and resulting ill health. The staple foods for the convicts and their marine guards were flour, rice, salt beef and pork, dried peas, ships biscuits and sometimes butter, with a spirit allowance for the marines. The rations were brought by ship from Britain, the Cape of Good Hope, Batavia and Calcutta, and were often of poor quality, the meat having been salted for up to three or four years by the time it was consumed and the rice, according to one commentator, 'a moving body from the inhabitants lodged within it'. The new settlers had little choice since it was impossible for them to learn the intricate bushcraft of the Kooris in time to fend off the scurvy and malnutrition that they soon encountered. Besides, the large numbers on the First Fleet, to be joined in 1790 and 1791 by even more people from the Second and Third Fleets, would soon have exhausted the foods available within range of Sydney.

Governor Phillip was very much aware of the need for fresh fruits and vegetables to strengthen the poor diet of those in his charge. Collecting parties were sent into the bush to gather warrigal greens, wild parsley and celery, the heart of cabbage tree palms, samphire, a small wild fig and several different berries, but the quantities were not nearly enough for the whole colony. Shooting parties were formed to supplement the salt meat ration: the odd kangaroo and emu, a few possums, ducks, crows, parrots, native pigeons and quail gave variety but were never sufficient. A supply of fish was obtained in the first few months but fell away as winter approached.

The only answer to the food crisis was farming. The first garden was at Farm Cove, with another next to the hospital to feed the sick, one on Garden Island for the crew of the ship *Sirius*, and small plots for officers. There were problems from the start with little understanding of the seasons and local conditions, insufficient agricultural implements, and ants and mice eating the seed. The convict labourers were lacking in motivation and physically weakened by their poor provisions. However, in November 1788 Phillip established a second settlement at Parramatta, west of Sydney, where the soil was more fertile. The convict James Ruse was given some land to cultivate, and other grants quickly followed when it was found that free enterprise was overtaking the low productivity of the public farms using enforced labour. The Australian climate was soon found to have its advantages: most of the familiar fruits and vegetables from Britain did well but the subtropical temperatures also favoured more exotic produce including oranges, limes, figs, grapes, guavas, watermelons and maize. On the voyage out Phillip had collected seeds and plants at Rio de Janeiro and the Cape of Good Hope and experimented with a wide range of crops. By the time he left the colony in December 1792, the settlement was no longer in danger of starvation and gradually fresh produce became plentiful as new land was opened up in the Hawkesbury area to the northwest.

Animal husbandry took a good deal longer to establish itself. The small supply of livestock which had been brought from across the oceans with so much trouble dwindled little by little. Some were slaughtered for the table, some fell prey to Koori huntsmen, dingoes, disease, even lightning strikes, and the cattle wandered off to find their own grazing land, to be rediscovered seven years later at Cowpastures on the banks of the Nepean River. Poultry was the first to thrive, followed by pigs when enough food to feed them became available. Elizabeth and John Macarthur led the way in sheep breeding by crossing their original flock of Bengal sheep with Spanish merinos in 1797, so producing the Australian merino. Once the way to the western plains was discovered, in 1813, pastoralism evolved into a major industry. The first shipments of wool to England were made in 1815 and the high prices paid gave an impetus which resulted in an oversupply of mutton by the 1840s. At that time Caroline Chisholm could boast of Australia's 'sunny sky, her rich pastures, her ships laden with wool, her cattle wild and countless on her mountains, her sheep crowding her hills, and seeking the shelter of her valleys; she can grow her own sugar, make her own wine, press her own oil, spin her own cotton, weave her own wool, grow her own corn'.

Campfire cooking at its best: a northern Australian woman proudly displays a splendid array of dampers in a shallow depression of cooling embers.

The New Australians

The colonists brought with them a mostly British attitude to eating and cookery, and probably intended to recreate their own culture in the untried land. Yet, from the beginning the new Australians adopted certain distinctly Antipodean eating habits, modifying their inherited ways to local circumstance. Their very first meal was cooked over an open fire, following a custom begun by the Aborigines and continued by the Torres Strait Islanders. Campfire cookery was an inherent part of the life of the shepherds and stockriders, drovers, swaggies and bushrangers who inhabited the bush in the pioneer days. For the colonial housewife most cooking was done over a fire for the greater part of the century. Campfire cooking has never lost its place and many Aussies of today have eaten potatoes charred in hot embers, toasted bread on a two-pronged gum twig or drunk billy tea seated on a log. In addition, certain campfire recipes were embraced by the newcomers; in particular, the great Aboriginal tradition of damper was carried through to the new society, with novel ingredients like wheaten flour being substituted for the old native grain flours.

Many of the new settlers experimented with local foodstuffs. In the first Australian cookbook, *The English and Australian Cookery Book* (1864), Edward Abbott the Younger gives directions for cooking wild duck and pigeon, wattle and mutton birds, native turkey and black swan. As well, there are notes on many of the local fish species and recipes for kangaroo pasties and steamer, roast and stewed kangaroo, kangaroo hams, and ways of preparing the brains and tail of the animal. Kangaroo meat was the food of gourmets, whose recipes vied with each other for prize medals at competitions. Mina Rawson offers game dishes for kangaroo, wallaby, bandicoots, flying fox, wild duck, parrots, quail, native turkey, water hen, snipe, ibis and brolgas. But she is even more adventurous, providing methods of cooking goanna and carpet snake, besides the classic Aboriginal recipes for witchetty grubs, cobras and grasshoppers. Native fruits and vegetables were important to many people isolated in the bush and Mrs. Rawson gives instructions for boiled pigweed (purslane), pigweed with cheese, pigweed salad, boiled wild fig shoots, wild raspberry jam, lilli pilli jelly, and she recommends native currants and lilli pillies for making summer drinks.

However, not all the new settlers appreciated the native foods and some hankered after their accustomed fare. In 1844 author and artist Louisa Anne Meredith noted the preference of well-to-do Sydneysiders for imported fish over the local product: 'I never saw any native fish at a Sydney dinner-table—the preserved or cured cod and salmon from England being served instead, at a considerable expense, and, to my taste, it is not comparable with the cheap fresh fish, but being expensive, it has become "fashionable".' Most foodstuffs consumed by white settlers were, indeed, exotic in origin but not all came from Europe. Tropical crops thrived, including pineapples, bananas, passion-fruit and grenadilla, pawpaw, mangoes, custard apples, guavas, rosellas, chokoes, sweet potatoes, sugar cane and peanuts. These foods rapidly became a feature of colonial cookery and distinguished it from both European and traditional Aboriginal cuisine.

A major contribution of the Europeans were pots and pans. The new settlers brought with them their frying pans, quart pots, kettles, griddles, cauldrons and Dutch ovens. When no frying pan was to be had a greased shovel did as well. In time, the colonists invented genuinely Australian utensils, specifically designed for the campfire: the billy, the camp oven of cast iron, and its derivative the Bedourie oven of unbreakable pressed steel. These obviously meant a departure from Aboriginal culinary techniques: boiling and stewing, frying, baking and pot roasting all became common.

Colonial Dining

The division of meals into breakfast, lunch and dinner was an inheritance from Europe with morning and afternoon tea part of the regimen. Following the British custom, breakfast assumed the form of quite a substantial meal;

because of the abundance of meat in Australia, here it centred around an ample helping of grilled or fried meat. Chops, steaks and sausages were described by colonial cookery writers as the 'eternal trio' of the breakfast table. With the addition of bacon, eggs or tomato, toast, crumpets or Johnny cakes and perhaps a plateful of porridge, all washed down with copious quantities of tea, the white settler was ready for the physical toil of colonial house or station work.

Lunch and dinner, the latter often called 'tea', were both substantial repasts featuring similar sorts of dishes. Edward Curr the Younger, taking part in an all-male squatters' hunt on the Murray River in 1849, was treated to a dinner of mutton and damper, potatoes, cabbage and dough-boys, followed by pipes, grog and 'conversation fast and somewhat uproarious'. Caroline Chisholm's description of a family Sunday dinner in the bush during the 1840s included a roast hindquarter of pork and a boiled round of beef (both large), a plentiful supply of potatoes, peas and greens, a peach pie, an orange tart and custard, all accompanied by a cup of tea. On New Year's Day 1841 Victorian settler Katharine Kirkland dined on kangaroo soup, stuffed roast turkey, a boiled leg of mutton, a carrot pie, potatoes and green peas, a plum pudding and strawberry tart with cream. A dinner party at the home of Lieutenant-Governor Sir Maurice O'Connell in June 1846 featured wallaby-tail soup, boiled schnapper with oyster sauce, a haunch of kangaroo venison, a wing of wonga-wonga pigeon with bread sauce, and for dessert, bananas, loquats, guavas, mandarins, pomegranates and custard apples. Despite differences in individual menus, most meals followed the pattern of a main course of meat in plenty and vegetables as available, followed by at least one pudding or dessert. Soup or fish might precede the main course, particularly at a dinner party, and poultry was normally only present on special occasions.

Much of the food was served hot, regardless of the season. Caroline Chisholm's advice was that 'Every woman who values her husband's health and comfort will give him a hot meal every day'. Before the advent of refrigeration many of the cooler dishes which are taken for granted today, like jellies and ice creams, were difficult to prepare. In a hot climate, with the added problem of flies, the safest course of action to reduce the risk of bacterial contamination was to cook the meal and serve it up immediately after it was taken off the fire. Left-overs from the many baked and boiled joints could be kept for a short time in a meat safe and, if necessary, cooked up again later in one of the numerous made-over recipes of the time. Most meat was cooked until well-done following the British custom, but also to minimise the chance of infection. Undoubtedly, dealing with perishable food was the greatest problem facing the colonial cook.

Most of the new settlers continued to cook many of the European dishes they had been used to back home. But inevitably the necessity of using native and tropical foods for which they had no established recipes, and of consuming the large quantities of meat produced by the pastoral industry, the different requirements of campfire cooking, and the problems of preparing food in a hot climate resulted in a departure from the European model. The rigours of bush life, in particular, encouraged cooks to great inventiveness with their limited resources. One shearers' cook, writing to domestic economist Fanny Fawcett Story in 1897, 'implored that some recipes might be sent to him for dishes which required neither eggs, butter, beef, vegetables, or fresh milk for their composition!' His would not have been an isolated case. Bush cookery is still one of the most interesting areas of our culinary heritage and has maintained a strong link with the Aboriginal tradition and with Aboriginal cooks who, as they encountered white people, gradually adopted many white foods and created unique approaches to cooking them.

The strengths and weaknesses of modern Australian cookery speedily emerged during the colonial period. Inventive meat dishes and superb puddings, desserts and cakes became its hallmark. Unfortunately, vegetables, one of the chief foods of Aboriginal and Torres Strait people, were to suffer. Many white bushmen had little time to worry about them, certainly not beyond the basic pumpkin, potatoes, onions, cabbage or tomatoes, although generally the bush housewife would cultivate a small vegetable and herb garden and try to give a more balanced diet. Where vegetables were more readily available, such as in the cities, they were often boiled to death. Only a minority of cooks seem to have treated them imaginatively.

Cookbooks and Courses

Another problem was a decline in culinary expertise. Though Australia continued to produce many excellent cooks, some young matrons, isolated as they were from female relatives left behind in Europe, obviously had difficulties. In the new egalitarian society there were few trained cooks or kitchen maids for hire so that middle class women suddenly found they had to manage their own cooking. Moreover, many immigrant men had to do for themselves initially because of the shortage of wives. The abbreviated nature of recipes given in most cookery books of the time did not help. Lady Barker, who lived for a time firstly in New Zealand and later in Western

Australia, complained bitterly about cookbooks: 'They are not the least use in the world, until you know how to cook, and then you can do without them'.

The first cookbooks used in Australia were probably British and, though popular in the colonies, had restricted application to Australian foodstuffs and conditions. In order to address this situation Caroline Chisholm's small pamphlet 'Bush Cookery' was printed in London in 1852 as part of a larger book of advice to emigrants, and Edward Abbott published his cookbook twelve years later. Mrs Chisholm's work, despite its practicality, had limitations owing to its few recipes, a mere seven in all. Abbott's work, though much more ambitious and full of interesting information on local dishes, seems not to have taken Australia by storm, perhaps because of its old-fashioned style and primitive presentation of recipes. Nor did Alfred J. Wilkinson's 1876 *Australian Cook* gain much popularity.

Only in 1878 did the housewife at last receive the sort of cookbook she needed with the publication in Queensland of the first of several volumes by Mina Rawson. This paved the way for a golden era of cookery writing in the 1880s and 1890s with Sydney home economist Harriet Wicken the most prolific. The best books of these two women are true masterpieces and still make excellent reading today. Harriet Wicken wrote more for town use whereas Mina Rawson and another country housewife Jean Rutledge aimed their books directly at the women of the bush. The cookbooks of hotelier Hannah Maclurcan and home economists Fanny Fawcett Story and Margaret J. Pearson lie somewhere in between with, on the one hand, various bush game dishes and, on the other, fish recipes more suitable for coastal dwellers. The 1890s likewise saw the publication of the first charitable fund-raising cookbooks, consisting of recipes collected from ordinary housewives—a good reflection of cookery at the time. The new cookbooks had a significant number of Australian recipes making them more practical than overseas books.

Simultaneous with this flowering of culinary writing, cookery exhibitions were being staged, special lectures given, and newspapers and magazines ran articles on domestic matters. In 1884 formal cookery courses were introduced, firstly at Sydney Technical College and then in the New South Wales public schools, both under the able direction of educator and activist Annie Fawcett Story. The other states followed in setting up similar courses to educate young women in their life's work and to train teachers for the purpose, with classes beginning in Melbourne in 1887 at the Working Men's College. Both cookery instruction and writing were becoming increasingly precise, founded on the new science of domestic economy.

The Table of the Commonwealth

The colonial era came to a close on 1 January 1901 when the six colonies federated to become the Commonwealth of Australia. Books such as *The Australasian Cookery Book*, published in 1913, continued to carry numerous recipes for native meats and native poultry, and others like Annie J. King's *Australian Missionary Cookery Book* of 1915 went on dispersing local recipes with colourful names to match. However, Australia was soon to see the end of many of the great colonial classic dishes and the end of native foods. The failure of Australian farmers to grow and market indigenous foodstuffs meant that an increasingly city-based population had no access to them. The extensive clearing and cultivation of the land for exotic crops and stock meant that even many bush people had difficulty in harvesting from the wild. Indigenous eatables were perhaps seen as too parochial for the new nation which was soon to take her place alongside other nations in World War I. The war as well as modern transportation and communication opened Australians to the wider world and favoured a more international mode of cooking and eating. The one exception were fish and shellfish. The obvious superiority of fresh seafood over preserved resulted in the acceptance of these native foods.

Yet, despite the general movement away from colonial mores cooks still continued to create Australian dishes in response to the conditions of the new century. New research into food values and vitamins, following the isolation of niacin in 1911, of vitamins A and B in 1915 and 1917, and vitamins C, D and E in the 1920s, led to important changes in the Australian diet by the 1930s. There was a greater emphasis on fruits, fruit juice and cereal at breakfast time, and salads and fruit desserts at dinner. As more people worked away from home in offices and factories the concept of a hot lunch was replaced by sandwiches or rolls, often with nutritious fillings of cheese, salad, cold meat, and the national 'health' spread Vegemite. Magazines promoted the new foods and cookbooks of the era published food tables and advice on menu planning founded on nutritional principles. Many new Australian dishes based on vegetables and fruits appeared at this time.

The full impact of vitamin research on cookery was only made possible by the advent of ice chests and domestic refrigeration. The Coolgardie safe, working on the principle of evaporation of moisture from its hessian-covered sides kept wet by a drip mechanism from a water tank above, began to be replaced in the mid 1870s when commercial refrigeration companies initiated delivery of ice blocks to the home. Town dwellers started to keep their food in the ice box, an insulated wooden or metal box, or in the more elaborate ice chest, an insulated cabinet with a compartment for the ice block at the top and shelves beneath on which the food was stored. Domestic refrigeration became a reality when Sir Edward Hallstrom commenced manufacture of kerosene-operated fridges, called Silent Knights, in 1923. These were particularly appreciated by people on the land who had limited access to ice and ice chests. Electric models soon followed with the importation of the first American-made Kelvinator in 1926. Not everyone could afford to buy one immediately (in the 1930s they cost about ten times the average male weekly wage) and it was not until the 1950s that refrigerators finally ousted ice chests. By 1960 nine out of ten Australian homes owned a fridge compared with only two out of ten in 1945.

Refrigeration is the single most important technological innovation in twentieth century cooking, especially significant in Australia's hot climate. It meant that many of the customary preservation techniques, such as salting meat, were no longer necessary. Shopping could be done less often since the ice chest or refrigerator would store food for a period of time. It also meant that the housewife could serve up cold meat and be sure that it was fresh and wholesome. The natural accompaniments to cold meat were the salads promoted by the nutritionists. Soups and hot puddings, so much in favour in colonial times, were relegated to the winter months, puddings replaced by a whole new range of cold desserts.

Apart from the refrigerator, many other changes were occurring in the Australian kitchen. Modern gas and electric stoves replaced the old solid-fuel stoves and a streamlined kitchen with benches, built-in cupboards and time-saving electrical appliances appeared. Ironically, these innovations happened against the backdrop of the Great Depression and two world wars. Inflation of food prices in World War I, poverty for many people in the thirties, and food rationing during World War II resulted in the creation of a myriad of economical dishes based on starches such as flour, potatoes, sago, tapioca and oats, and on the cheaper meats like rabbit, chops and mince.

The Heritage of Diversity

Up until World War II Australia's immigrants came mainly from the British Isles with significant minorities from Germany and China, fewer from other nations. Though the British dominated by virtue of their numerical and political superiority, non-English-speaking migrants also made a significant contribution to Australian food. The Chinese, who had come to make their fortunes in the gold rushes, stayed on to work on market gardens and banana plantations, opened Chinese restaurants and tea rooms, and worked as station cooks, storekeepers and fishermen. Germans founded the Barossa Valley wineries and were prominent in smallgoods manufacture, bakeries and flour mills in that area, with many becoming industrious small farmers. South Sea Islanders served as domestic cooks and laboured in the sugar-cane fields, later replaced by Italians, who also worked the fishing boats, owned greengroceries and manufactured pasta. The Greeks were leaders in the fishing industry, and ran fish shops, cafés, refreshment rooms and milk bars. The Japanese involved themselves in rice growing and market gardening and the brewing of soy sauce, while Danes were outstanding in butter and cheese making. The French provided chefs and winemakers.

The influence of these groups varied: some like the Germans had a significant impact, but in a narrow locality, while the enterprise of other communities was restricted to the produce level and therefore contributed little to the overall style of Australian cookery. Those who were employed as domestic cooks or operated eateries often felt constrained to serve conventional fare. Whatever their creativity in the kitchen, it remains shrouded in a pall of silence imposed largely by their inability to write English.

The end of World War II marked a new era in Australian cooking with mass migration from the Mediterranean, the Baltic, Holland, Germany and central Europe, Latin America, and later, the Middle East, Asia and South Africa. The greatly increased numbers of new immigrants had a far-reaching impact. Many opened restaurants offering new flavours and dishes which the average Australian had never encountered before. Many ran delicatessens and greengroceries which sold exotic cheeses and smallgoods, continental breads, and vegetables which were entirely new. Increasing affluence allowed Australians to be adventurous: we had plenty of money to try the strange foods, to go out to the new restaurants and also to travel overseas and broaden our culinary experiences still further. The result was a complete re-education of the Australian palate. Our tastes and what we considered acceptable to eat widened immensely. Coffee consumption more than doubled at this time, oil replaced dripping, stir-fry and pasta appeared regularly on the dinner table. Wine was drunk with the meal and used in cooking along with garlic and liberal quantities of herbs and spices. Vegetables acquired a new status whilst the overdependence on meat declined. Despite the striving by some cooks for an authenticity which risked turning their kitchens into museum pieces, altars to a tradition frozen in time, gradually the new migrant cuisines began adapting to local conditions as British cooking had done before, producing exciting new dishes and enriching our pre-existing cookery with a new vigour and vitality that it had never previously known.

Fast Food, Easy Food

In contrast to the multicultural food experience has been the onslaught of convenience foods, beginning as far back as 1870 with jams, pickles, sauces and cordials bottled on a commercial scale. In Newcastle William Arnott moved from biscuit shop to factory in 1870, and Rosella produced its first tomato sauce in 1899. Canning technology was developed at this time but received a big boost during World War I for feeding armies. Artificially flavoured jelly crystals achieved widespread acceptance when ice chests and fridges became a feature of the kitchen, with the Aeroplane Jelly Company founded in 1928. From the 1950s on, frozen foods formed part of the meal with the advent of supermarkets and freezers: the food went straight from the deep freezer at the store to the freezer of the household. Convenience foods really came into their own in the post-war era: people had more money to spend and they appealed to women who were increasingly a part of the paid workforce and had less time to prepare meals than before. Packaged foods assumed greater sophistication with whole meals enclosed in hygienic wrappers that required merely heating and serving.

Lagging somewhat behind convenience foods was the rise in consumption of fast foods. Traditional Australian take-aways included meat pies, steak sandwiches, sausage rolls, pasties, fish and chips, potato scallops, and battered saveloys. These were joined in the 1930s by hamburgers, and later in 1951 by the chiko roll. The real assault on the national digestive system came from 1968 with Australian franchises of American take-away outlets, selling fried chicken, pizzas and hamburgers. Though convenience and fast foods serviced a need in the community for quick meals they inevitably presented standardised, often bland flavours and textures; for an increased cost the nutrition provided was rarely equal to home cookery, and the food was completely unresponsive to season or place.

Migrant foods and other international cuisines were promoted heavily by the food manufacturers and fast-food outlets, partly to fill a demand by the consumer but also in an attempt to move cooking out of the home and increase dependence on the industrial sector. If the householder could be persuaded that a different cuisine should be served every night, it would then be necessary for the family to dine out more frequently, to buy in meals, or to cook with the various manufactured sauces, patent spice mixes and packet additives. The traditional skills of the home cook, whether born in Australia or overseas, would be insufficient for the new, constantly changing menu. In most cases the manufacturers presented a parody of the ethnic cuisines they promoted, reducing them down to a handful of dishes, often poorly executed.

Expanding Tastes

The last years of the twentieth century were characterised by a continued expansion of the Australian taste. Joining with the older migrant cuisines, a range of new, mostly Asian cookery styles, emerged including Thai, Vietnamese, Japanese, Malaysian and Singaporean. Even Chinese cookery, so long dominated by that perennial favourite, Cantonese, expanded into Sichuan, Beijing and Shanghai. This broader interest in Asian food was inspired by Australia's proximity to Asia and part of an increased cultural and political focus on the region. However, it was also representative of a world-wide fashion in which oriental cooking methods, ingredients and presentations found their way into kitchens everywhere. As East met West, dishes moved beyond narrow definitions of nationality and achieved a blending of different styles, ingredients and techniques.

Not only were Australian taste buds opened to a whole world of international dining, but there was also a renewed interest in our own indigenous foodstuffs, an interest which, outside the Aboriginal community, had lain dormant for the larger part of the century. Spurred on by some adventurous restaurant chefs, providores and bush-tucker experts, many Australians were encouraged to dine on kangaroo fillet or emu steak, to buy cheeses flavoured with Tasmanian pepper or Anzac biscuits spiced with ground wattle seed, and to grow lilli pillies in their backyards in expectation of the berry harvest. All too often, however, their curiosity was thwarted by the continuing limited range of bush foods available on the general market. Moreover, there was often a problem with poor understanding of the ingredients and how to deal with them, since a knowledge of Aboriginal cookery methods was not widespread and colonial experience with native foods had been largely forgotten, except in the bush.

Cookbooks proliferated at this time and many probably ended up on the coffee table and bookshelves rather than in the kitchen. In addition to cookbooks, articles on cookery in food and travel magazines and in the weekend newspapers flourished. Some authors went further, writing whole books analysing and discussing Australian cooking: its history, philosophy, motivations, strengths and weaknesses. Symposia and food festivals were organised in different parts of the country to discuss and celebrate. Gastronomy became a hot topic of study and conversation.

A noticeable change at this time was the rise in influence of restaurant chefs. Previously all the popular Australian cookbooks had been written by home cooks or home economists. Since 1968 the most influential of these had been Margaret Fulton, who through regular articles in the *Woman's Day* and *New Idea* as well as through a range of best-selling practical, home-style cookbooks had become a household name throughout Australia. Now her works were joined by cookbooks from the chefs, some of whom even had their own television shows and so rapidly achieved a high profile.

The worst of these celebrity chefs relied largely on showy presentation, garnish and stylistic tour de force. However, the top chefs promoted interesting new flavours and brought a renewed emphasis on high-quality produce, contributing significantly to the rebirth of native foodstuffs and the awakening interest in new salad greens, farmhouse cheeses, cold-pressed oils and fine vinegars. They fostered Australia's ever-maturing wine industry, and joined the call for organic produce and free-range meats. They helped create a demand for new foods, which filtered down to the broader marketplace and set up the conditions under which small, highly specialised growers could flourish. The chefs promoted these foods overseas, earning a name for Australia's fine produce.

Food for the New Millenium

During this period the traditional home-cooked Australian meal has suffered. Attacked by mass-produced food, often overwhelmed by the dazzling array of new cuisines, many Australians, especially those living in the cities, have almost forgotten their own fine culinary heritage. When in 1958 Melbourne writer Arthur Phillips coined the phrase 'cultural cringe' he was describing an attitude that sees Australian culture as inherently inferior to that from overseas, an attitude that has dogged our cookery for the last two centuries and reached a peak in the post-war era. The Australian cuisine has had to suffer from a continual barrage of criticism from those food snobs who would have us abandon our ways of eating in favour of French, Mediterranean, Thai or whatever happens to be the current fashion. They call our food British, ignoring the multitude of genuinely Australian recipes that have evolved since 1788. Moreover, they disregard at least sixty thousand years of our history when the Indigenous people laid the firm foundations of our nation.

It is in the hope of reminding Australians of their rich and lively culinary heritage, in the hope of giving some definition to a too long neglected area of our culture, that I have written this book. I have chosen to include only dishes which I believe to have been developed in Australia and not merely brought in from overseas. For the most part I have chosen recipes which are the invention of home cooks, since it is in the home kitchen and by the campfire that Australian cookery has seen its true flourishing. Furthermore, I have used the knowledge gained from years of research into Australian cookery to rewrite the recipes for today's kitchens, to put them in a form that is accessible to people cooking with today's ingredients and on today's modern gas or electric stoves. Threaded through the recipes are the reflections of Australians from all walks of life, giving voice to their own personal experiences of what it is to cook, eat and live in this land.

Despite the changes, there is a continuity in our culinary tradition which links the cooks of today with those who have preceded us. When I bake a damper I am repeating a ritual that thousands of generations of Australian women have performed before me; and my male compatriot, barbecuing his steaks or kebabs of a weekend, is following the tradition of the first Australian men as they grilled their catch on the fire. Today's campers, making a meal in the bush, are continuing an Australian custom that has been with us since the very beginning.

The future of the Australian cuisine will be built on its traditions, on an acceptance of our great Aboriginal and Torres Strait inheritance, on a rediscovery of our colonial culture, and an imaginative and genuinely Australian use of our new migrant foods. The need for bush foods is obvious and this will only be satisfied when random gathering gives way to selective breeding, cultivation and widespread marketing, all too long overdue. At the same time, an over-conscious nationalism must be avoided since this can be almost as limiting and detrimental as the snobbery that it replaces.

Yet our cookery has been and will continue to be, as Australian as our history, our literature, our lifestyle and our accents. The Australian cuisine is, at heart, a cookery of the people, a cookery which meets the needs of ordinary women and men trying unselfconsciously to do their best with the ingredients the Australian environment has provided, a cookery over which the necessities and conditions of place inevitably exert their influence as they have done in the development of all national cultures, of all cuisines, and as they have done in the Australian continent for over sixty thousand years.

2

'Fit for a king'

SOUPS

...but, nevertheless [kangaroo soup], is full of rich brown gravy, and certainly makes most delicious soup; so does its nether appendage, which, from its containing a considerable quantity of glutinous matter, bears a great resemblance to, but far outrivals in quality, the celebrated ox-tail.

GEORGE LLOYD, WRITING IN
THIRTY-THREE YEARS IN TASMANIA AND VICTORIA 1862

Sydney Parkinson's picture of a kangaroo at Endeavour River, Queensland: the finest of all Australian soups undoubtedly comes from its tail.

Soups were a familiar part of the meal during colonial times, and almost obligatory at dinner parties and among the 'fashionable' classes. However, many ordinary households failed to serve soup on a regular basis and some food writers thought it necessary to exhort their readers on the merits of this form of food. Harriet Wicken recommended soup for its nourishment and easy digestibility, its power to stimulate the digestion in winter and refresh in summer. Fanny Fawcett Story noted the blood purifying properties of the minerals contained within it, its ability to repair the daily wastage of water from the body, and even prescribed it as a 'narcotic' when taken at bedtime. C. R. Blackett, in a health lecture, described soup as 'Nature's teaching', providing a gentle excitement to the stomach which could reduce the insidious craving for artificial stimulants in the community. It was seen as invaluable for the young and the aged, the weakly and delicate, and for the busy worker.

Soup was consumed not just in the winter months but all year round. The copper or cast-iron stockpot was a feature of the well-run kitchen, simmering away on the back of the stove or suspended over the fire. Bones, scraps of meat and vegetables would be added to the pot daily and the old ones discarded. As stock was drawn off for use in soups, gravies and stews the liquid in the pot would be replenished with water or the left-over cooking liquid from vegetables and the pot itself thoroughly scrubbed out at the end of the week.

Common soups varied from hearty meat and vegetable pottages, which could make a meal by themselves, to more delicate fish soups thickened with cream or potato, garnished with peas or croûtons and suitable for dinner parties. Of the latter, oyster was the most usual although lobsters and scallops were also turned into excellent cream soups. Split peas, beans and barley were common ingredients. Of the various vegetable soups, tomato reigned supreme. Colonial cookbooks give a number of recipes, some of them simple vegetarian affairs, others with a beef-stock base. For the bush cook living away from the coast, seafood soups were normally out of the question, being replaced by soups based on 'riverfood' such as Murray cod, yellowbelly or even yabbies. Game soups made from wild duck, parrots and possums were an interesting feature of the outback repertoire and the most famous of all Australian soups, kangaroo tail, has its origins in bush cookery.

Since the coming of the refrigerator soups have gradually been relegated to the winter months and, unfortunately, tinned and packet products have tended to replace the wholesome, well-flavoured, home-made broths of our mothers and grandmothers. On the positive side, new recipes have appeared, for example, chilled soups for summer and soups with a Mediterranean or Asian flavour. Most significantly, the introduction of labour-saving devices such as the blender, food processor and the hand–held 'wand' has done away with the hair sieves, mortar and pestles—and the laborious preparation—required by many of the old recipes.

Underground Mutton Soup

SERVES 10

Australians have invented various colourful descriptive terms to define their culinary domain. All food items come under the generic description tucker, which according to Sidney Baker has been in use at least since 1852. In its wake came expressions such as tuckerbag and tuckerbox—where one keeps one's food—and bush tucker for native foods. Aboriginal languages have provided specific terms for bush tucker such as quandong, ooray, lerp, yabby, barramundi and mulloway; and Aboriginal pigeon English has contributed lollywater for soft drink, sugarbag for honey, yellabelly for Murray perch, moon food for food which requires prolonged soaking, and cheeky to describe poisonous foodstuffs.

In his book *The Australian Language*, Baker lists a number of expressions which appear to have slipped from current usage like fly bog for jam and bee-jam for honey. Murrumbidgee jam was brown sugar moistened with cold tea for spreading on damper, frog's eyes was an appropriately descriptive term for sago, ointment for custard, dynamite for baking powder, goldfish for tinned fish, bull's eyes for fried eggs and mutt eyes for corn. A bush dinner consisted of mutton, damper and tea, and a bushman's hot dinner was swagman's slang for a meal of damper spread with mustard. A duck's dinner, a term still in use, is a starvation meal of water alone, and a stockman's dinner a spit and a smoke. To bite someone's name, to sign one's hand, and to make food laugh were all expressions for eating.

Underground mutton and bush chicken are outback phrases, still heard occasionally, to describe that former staple of Australian cookery, the rabbit. In this recipe it is the basis for a hearty bush soup, thick with vegetables, barley and split peas.

1 tablespoon dripping or vegetable oil

2 onions, finely chopped

2 carrots, peeled and diced

2 potatoes, peeled and diced

1 rabbit, jointed

½ cup split peas, soaked overnight and drained

¼ cup barley

7 cups water

2 teaspoons salt

White pepper

2 tablespoons finely chopped fresh parsley

■ Melt the fat in a large saucepan over a moderate heat and fry the onions until soft, about 5 minutes. Add all the remaining ingredients except the parsley and bring to the boil. Turn the heat low and simmer, covered, for 2 hours.

■ Remove the rabbit pieces and leave until cool enough to handle. Take the meat from the bones and chop into bite-size pieces. Skim any fat from the surface of the soup with a spoon and absorbent paper. Return the rabbit meat to the saucepan and bring the soup to the boil again. Serve garnished with parsley.

Kangaroo Tail Soup

SERVES 8-10

ONE of the great classics of bush cooking, kangaroo tail soup achieved its gastronomic reputation in colonial times. George Lloyd, writing in *Thirty-Three Years in Tasmania and Victoria*, found kangaroo flesh rather coarse-grained:

…but, nevertheless, [it] is full of rich brown gravy, and certainly makes most delicious soup; so does its nether appendage, which, from its containing a considerable quantity of glutinous matter, bears a great resemblance to, but far outrivals in quality, the celebrated ox-tail.

The glutinous matter refers to the many narrow white tendons which run the length of the tail as well as to the disks of cartilage, which all go to delicious jelly in the cooking. For refined dining the bones may be discarded before serving, yet true gourmets will *always* have their soup joints and all.

There are many versions of this soup, some homely bushmen's affairs thick with vegetables, split peas and macaroni. But for true, unadulterated flavour I would recommend the following gourmet recipe.

2 tablespoons dripping or oil	500 g gravy beef or shin, sliced
2 onions, chopped	500 g ham or bacon bones
2 cloves garlic, finely chopped	6 bay leaves
1 tablespoon finely chopped fresh parsley	6 cloves
2 carrots	1½ teaspoons salt
2 parsnips	Freshly ground black pepper
2 tablespoons plain flour	8 cups water
1 kg kangaroo tail, jointed	1¼ cups red wine

▪ Heat the fat in a large soup pot or saucepan over a moderate heat and sauté the onions until soft. Add the garlic and parsley and sauté for a minute. The carrots and parsnips should be finely diced if you intend to serve them in the soup or sliced if you want a pure meat broth. Stir in the carrots, parsnips and flour, and cook for several minutes, stirring constantly. When the flour is amalgamated add all the remaining ingredients except the wine and bring to the boil. Turn the heat to a simmer and cook gently, covered, for about 2½ hours until the kangaroo meat is almost falling from the bones.

▪ With a slotted spoon lift out the beef, ham or bacon bones and bay leaves and discard. The soup may be strained and the vegetables discarded if preferred. Either serve the joints whole in the soup or discard the bones and shred the meat. Skim all the fat from the surface. Add wine before reheating.

Bush Tomato Soup

SERVES 8

THE tomato as most of us know it was brought to Australia probably in the early 1800s and was certainly thriving in our warm climate by the 1840s, long before its acceptance in Britain. Its cheapness at the markets and popularity with the home gardener led to its widespread use in soups, meat and vegetable dishes, salads, omelettes, sauces, chutneys and even jams.

Many people do not realise that Australia possesses a number of its own native tomatoes, small wild fruit about the size of marbles, important sources of vitamin C to desert Aborigines. Some are found in sufficient amounts to form a staple food and are collected in large quantities, sun dried and threaded on string or sticks for storage in trees. Bush tomatoes are sometimes available from specialty bush-food shops or gourmet food stores.

'Wild' tomatoes have a very concentrated taste and an agreeable pungency, startlingly different from their cultivated counterparts. Here both combine to create a dark red, richly flavoured soup.

1 kg tomatoes, peeled and chopped

50 g dried bush tomatoes

6 cups chicken or beef stock

1 tablespoon sugar

▪ Put the tomatoes, bush tomatoes, stock and sugar in a large saucepan. Bring to the boil over a moderate heat then turn down to a simmer. Cook, covered, for 45 minutes until the bush tomatoes are quite soft.

▪ Purée the soup in a blender or food processor. Taste and add a little salt if necessary. Reheat before serving.

Pumpkin Soup

SERVES 8

PUMPKINS flourish in Australia like few other vegetables. The German explorer Ludwig Leichhardt described them as 'the potato of the colony'. In a letter to his brother-in-law on 2nd February 1844 he related a joke common at the time:

'You can tell a currency (colonial-born) from a sterling (English-born) lass if you serve her with pumpkin and potato. The colonial girl will eat her pumpkin first, but the English girl will prefer the potato.' The pumpkins are superb, big and floury, and they keep for a long time. They grow far inland, around the stockmen's and shepherds' huts, when all other vegetables succumb to the drought.

An 1899 photograph shows a magnificently proportioned clay baking oven for breads, cakes and meats sitting a safe distance from a miner's slab hut in Lithgow.

Different varieties have come in and out of fashion over the years but the best known is the magnificent Queensland blue, which originated in the town of Beaudesert. They are vigorous growers, a couple of seeds planted in well-mulched hills sprouting runners which radiate out, bearing first the big floppy leaves and then the yellow flowers, male and female. From the latter the fruits gradually swell, the skin distending under the hot summer sun until finally they lie on the soil like great, deep-ribbed lumps, their exterior burnt hard and blue-grey in the heat, to be gathered in when the stalk withers and dies. There is no better use for these than pumpkin soup, a perennial favourite since colonial times.

30 g butter
2 onions, finely chopped
1 kg peeled and seeded pumpkin, chopped
250 g peeled sweet potato, chopped
2 cups corned beef water or stock

1 teaspoon salt
Freshly ground black pepper
¼ teaspoon ground ginger
2 cups milk
Freshly grated nutmeg

▪ Melt the butter in a large saucepan over a moderate heat and sauté the onions until soft. Add the pumpkin, sweet potato, stock, salt, pepper and ginger. Bring to the boil then turn to a simmer. Cook, covered, for 30 minutes until the vegetables are soft.

▪ Purée the soup in a blender or food processor. Thin the soup with the milk and return it to a clean saucepan. Heat through over a low heat and adjust the seasoning if necessary. Serve with a grating of nutmeg on top.

Colonial Potato Soup

SERVES 8

POTATOES have many applications in cookery but they were also employed in particularly unusual ways in colonial times. J.K. Arthur, in his book, *Kangaroo and Kauri*, describes an incident involving a circuit preacher and 'muscular Christian' Bill Bowman, who was challenged to a fight by a bully disturbing one of his meetings. Bowman, having the choice of weapons, selected for each man half a bushel of potatoes to be thrown one at a time from a distance of fifteen paces. Bowman's potatoes found their mark bursting into pieces much to the delight of the crowd until one struck the bully on the ribs, winding him: 'The desperado was taken home and put to bed, and there he stayed for more than a week before he recovered from the effects of his potato duel.'

A more productive use for potatoes is this homely yet satisfying soup flavoured with the bone from the Sunday joint and whatever scraps of meat remain on it.

COLONIAL POTATO SOUP

Remains of baked joint	6 cups water
1 onion, finely chopped	2 teaspoons salt
1 tablespoon butter or dripping	½ teaspoon white pepper
1 kg potatoes, peeled and cut in chunks	Croûtons of toast or fried bread

▪ Cut any meat from the bone and dice (about 250 g will give a good flavour). With a hammer or saw, crack or cut any large bones into two or three sections.

▪ In a large saucepan heat the butter or dripping and sauté the onion over a moderate heat until soft. Add the diced meat and bones and all the remaining ingredients. Bring to the boil and then simmer, covered, for 2 hours until the potatoes disintegrate into the soup and create a form of mealy binding.

▪ When cooked, discard the bones and skim the fat from the surface with a spoon and absorbent paper. Break up the pieces of potato roughly with a wooden spoon to distribute their flavour through the broth. Ladle into bowls and sprinkle with a few croûtons of toasted or fried bread.

Clear Soup for the Governor

IN *A Girl at Government House* Agnes Stokes describes her period of service with the Chief Justice of New South Wales in the 1890s and her sudden promotion when the cook breaks a leg. Sir Frederick approaches her:

'I say', he began, 'the Governor of New South Wales and a couple of his A.D.C.s want to come for a bit of possum shooting. They will want some dinner. What can you give us?'

I was dumbfounded. 'Oh, I can't cook for a real live Governor', I gasped.

'Of course you can! You've cooked all right for us and you can do it for them— just a simple dinner. Give us some clear soup, fried fish, a brace or two of birds, that coffee pudding of yours, and a nice savoury …'

She finishes cooking and clearing the soup at bedtime and is carefully putting it away for the next day when her candle topples into the tureen.

In the morning I packed it round with ice and skimmed the fat off in large pieces till very little liquid was left. I tasted it. Vile! It reeked of tallow. Nothing more could be done, so I made some artichoke soup instead.

'That won't do', says the butler. 'Chief's put Julien soup on the menu and Julien soup it's got to be. Don't you bother—I'll doctor it up all right—there won't be a spot left, you'll see.'

I had my doubts, but sent it in, and when the plates came out they might have been licked, they were so clean …

He came along, smiling. 'Well, that was a very nice little dinner you sent up. Very nice. We all enjoyed it. No one could have done better; but I say, that soup … That was the best soup I have tasted for many a long year'.

The butler had added half a bottle of old sherry.

Working Man's Soup

SERVES 20

THE Sydney Technical College, now the Sydney Institute of Technology, included a Department of Domestic Economy almost from its inception in the 1880s. The college spearheaded cookery instruction in Australia and the distinguished colonial home economists Annie Fawcett Story and Harriet Wicken taught there, in addition to cookbook authors Fanny Fawcett Story (Annie's daughter), Isabel Ross and Amie Monro. Cooking was consistently an extremely popular subject, drawing women from all stations of life.

In Melbourne, the Working Men's College, founded in 1887, was the chief provider of cookery instruction until 1899 when Annie Fawcett Story opened the first Victorian cooking centre in Queensberry Street State School, giving classes to teachers and school girls. In 1906, following a vigorous campaign by Mrs. Story and other prominent Victorian women, the College of Domestic Economy was opened; it was later renamed the Emily MacPherson College and in modern times forms part of the Royal Melbourne Institute of Technology.

This unpretentious but well-flavoured soup, intended for a large working class family, comes from Margaret J. Pearson, who taught at the Working Men's College in Melbourne. She graduated from the National Training School for Cookery which opened in London in 1874 and which was significant in providing, for the first time, a professional status to women cooks. She wrote two books, one on fruit cookery and another entitled *Cookery Recipes for the People*, published in 1888 and reprinted in the 1890s,

The pot of soup or stew bubbling on the fire and the sheet on the line suggests that the weather outside the cosy Victorian stockman's hut painted by S.T Gill was inclement.

which has a good selection of English and Scottish dishes as well as some recipes for local fish and game.

WORKING MAN'S SOUP

30 g butter	*250 g split peas, soaked overnight, drained*
4 onions, finely chopped	*250 g raw meat, finely chopped*
3 carrots, finely chopped	*1 teaspoon brown sugar*
½ turnip, finely chopped	*1¼ tablespoons salt*
1 head celery, finely chopped	*Freshly ground black pepper*
3.5 litres water	*¼ cup finely chopped fresh mint*

▎Melt the butter in a large saucepan over a moderate heat and sauté the onions, carrots, turnip and celery for about 15–20 minutes until softened. Add the water, peas and meat and bring to the boil. Turn the heat down and simmer gently, covered, for 3–4 hours, until the peas are soft.

▎Strain the soup through a colander or else mash it roughly with a potato masher. Stir in the seasonings and mint and serve with sippets of toasted or fried bread if preferred.

Pipi Soup

AS AN Australian who was born and has always lived by the sea, many of my earliest memories are connected with the seashore, its mysteries, its rhythms and rituals, its strange creatures. One of the most frequent inhabitants of the shore is the pipi, lying buried in the sand where the waves forever lap and recede, secreted from the prying eyes of seagulls and humans. This little organism has given rise to a well-established rite, familiar to many Australians but which might well appear odd to the uninitiated outsider: head down, the participant plants the feet close together on the sand and the whole body is then heaved into motion, the bent arms and posterior twisting energetically from side to side, propelling the feet deeper and deeper until, with any luck, the bare toes come in contact with a smooth triangular shell. Then it is a scramble to get the pipi up to the surface and into the bait bucket before the alarmed mollusc speeds away.

This method is much the same as that traditionally used by Aboriginal women, although for them the aim of the exercise is not bait but food. Pipis, despite the sand in their shells and a tendency to turn to rubber with the slightest overcooking, have an excellent flavour. Soup is perhaps the best way of preparing them: any sand will automatically fall to the bottom of the pot where it can be discarded, and the flesh is minced finely so that it will not toughen if the soup is reheated.

1 kg pipis	1½ teaspoons salt
1 onion, finely chopped	Freshly ground black pepper
1 carrot, finely chopped	1 tablespoon cornflour
1 parsnip, finely chopped	1 tablespoon lemon juice
1 swede, finely chopped	⅓ teaspoon Tabasco sauce
1 stick celery, finely chopped	Finely chopped fresh parsley
2 tablespoons barley	

▪ Wash the pipi shells. Put 2 cups of water in a saucepan and bring to a rapid boil, Put the shellfish in the water. As they open, immediately remove them with a slotted spoon to a bowl. When they are all done, carefully pour off the cooking liquid to a new saucepan, leaving the sand behind.

▪ Add another 4 cups of water to the cooking liquor. Stir in the chopped vegetables, barley, salt and pepper and simmer, covered, for 1 hour until tender.

▪ In a small bowl blend the cornflour with the lemon juice until smooth. Stir into the cooked soup with the Tabasco and simmer for a few minutes. Take the pipis from their shells and mince finely with a chef's knife or in a food processor. Add to the soup and heat through for a minute. Serve sprinkled with parsley.

Granny Smith Iced Apple Soup

SERVES 6

MARIA Ann Smith was born in England in 1800. She migrated to Australia in 1838 and settled in the Ryde district of Sydney. Because her husband was an invalid 'Granny' Smith took over much of the work on their orchard and became a familiar figure at the Queen Victoria Markets in the city selling their produce. About 1868, two years before her death, she developed the wonderful green cooking and eating apple which bears her name. Its big advantage over other apples of the day was its excellent keeping qualities which made it ideal for long storage and export.

Cold soups are not held in high favour by most Australians but this one made with Granny Smith apples, is really very refreshing.

1 kg Granny Smiths
1½ lemon
2½ cups chicken stock
1 tablespoon fresh breadcrumbs
1 teaspoon grated fresh ginger
½ teaspoon ground cinnamon
1 tablespoon honey, rosella or quince jelly

½ teaspoon salt
1½ cups white wine

GARNISH
1 lemon, shredded
Ground cinnamon

▪ Peel, core and slice the Granny Smiths and store in water acidulated with the juice of ½ lemon. Drain just before using. In a saucepan place the apples, stock, breadcrumbs, ginger, cinnamon and the finely grated rind of 1 lemon. Bring to the boil over a moderate heat then simmer, covered, for 10 minutes. Remove from the heat and stir in the juice of 1 lemon, the honey, the jelly and salt. Let cool and stir in the white wine. Purée in a blender and serve at room temperature or chilled.

▪ To garnish, remove 1 or 2 strips of rind from the remaining lemon using a vegetable peeler. Cut these into thin shreds about 3 cm long. Place in a small saucepan of water and simmer for 7 minutes. Remove with a slotted spoon. Garnish the bowls of soup with a shreds of lemon rind and cinnamon.

3

From the butter man

Milk was delivered, too, at three pence a pint, twice a day, very early in the morning and in the afternoon. The milkman used a horse and cart with a milk tank at the back, complete with two taps …

We also had a butter man called Mr Ford. He sold eggs, cheese, honey and those sorts of things.

ROSSLYN BLAY,

A LIVING HISTORY OF PARRAMATTA, 1992

Pioneers were still carving a living from the bush—in this case a dairy farm—when J. W. Lindt photographed 'Fernshaw. The Maiden all Forlorn' in 1890–92.

THERE was a shortage of dairy foods in Australia for many years after white settlement although four cows had been brought from Britain on the First Fleet. Initially, cattle were mainly bred for slaughter and it was not until thirty years after the arrival of the first cow that commercial milking began in the Illawarra region south of Sydney. Gradually a dairy industry evolved, chiefly confined to the lush coastal plains where feed was good and the distance to major markets short. The industry focused on the supply of milk and butter. The butter was salted to preserve it. It was a rich golden colour from the natrural, healthy diet of the cows, left at liberty on their green pastures for the entire year.

In colonial times the cheapness of meat reduced the demand for cheese, which had been a major source of protein for the poor of Europe. Dairy co-operatives financed by the farmers started in the 1880s and within twenty years mass processing developed. It was only then that cheese became an important item in the Australian diet, average annual consumption per person rising from 1.7 kilograms in 1901 to 8 kilograms in the 1980s. Fine cows' milk cheeses came to be made in various regions of the country, most of them fairly versatile and suitable for the table or for cooking. Tasmania and Victoria have been particularly noted for their products since their cooler climates and rich pasturage favour dairying. However, first class cheeses are produced as far north as Milanda in the Atherton Tablelands, at Caboolture and the Darling Downs in Queensland, in New South Wales, particularly on the South Coast, in the Mount Gambier area of South Australia, and at Mount Barker and Margaret River in Western Australia.

Originally most cheese was based on the cheddar model with blue vein holding a small share of the market. In the 1980s producers began to move in novel directions, responding to customer demand for greater choice. One trend was the inclusion of seasonings such as green or black peppercorns, caraway, chilli, paprika, garlic, dried tomatoes, black olives, chives, basil or mixed dried herbs. An Australian innovation during this period was the production of fruit cheeses, usually fairly mild and creamy, packed full of chopped dried fruit like apricots and sultanas, sometimes with nuts or liqueur. Their sweetness made them suitable for dessert. In addition, there has been a heartening movement towards European models, amongst the most successful being some superb bries and camemberts, but there are also French -style gruyères and washed rind cheeses, Italian gorgonzola types, Greek-style fettas, to name but a few. Many of these artisan cheeses come from especially bred herds. The goat herds of Gabriella Kervella are an outstanding example, producing a range of the finest quality. Since the 1980s, Leeton in New South Wales has produced fresh and aged cheeses from merino ewes' milk.

Eggs, unlike cheese, are a traditional food of Aboriginal and Torres Strait people and include those of reptiles, as well as many native birds. The emu egg is the largest and was also prized by the new settlers: a Diamantina cocktail was a colonial bushman's drink consisting of condensed milk, Bundaberg rum and a well-beaten emu egg. Rather than rely on native sources, most colonists raised their own poultry to ensure a good supply of fresh eggs. Gradually a poultry industry developed, usually located near the towns. Egg marketing boards came in the 1920s, and in the later 1960s battery production started to replace the old free-range farms.

Aboriginal people traditionally consume eggs raw or lightly cooked in their shells in hot sand or in the fire. White settlers preferred eggs cooked although one colonial classic, the Murrumbidgee oyster, consisted of a raw egg with pepper, salt and vinegar. Eggs come into their own at breakfast time and are good material for lunches and light meals but, most importantly, are essential in the production of the puddings, desserts, cakes and biscuits which form such a large part of the Australian culinary repertoire.

Federal Cheese Paste

MAKES ABOUT 1 ¾ CUPS

FROM 1812 the coast south of Sydney was cleared of much of its rainforest by the cedar cutters and turned into one of Australia's richest agricultural areas, dubbed the 'Garden of New South Wales'. The first land grants were issued in 1816 for grazing, potatoes and grain, with dairying becoming the principal industry from the 1840s. By the 1890s a new breed of cow, the Illawarra shorthorn, had emerged, a robust animal adapted specifically to Australian conditions with excellent heat tolerance and a capacious udder.

The early farmers had to make their own dairy products. Blanche Mitchell, daughter of Lady and Sir Thomas Mitchell, describes in her diary a visit to the family property at Stanwell Park in January 1861:

Mamma and I busy making and putting curtains to the dairy. Mamma makes plenty of butter and takes the entire charge of all appertaining to it. Such lots of delicious milk coming up every morning and evening from the cows …

Up early, made a curd cheese, which consists of simply curds tied tight up in a cloth and allowed to hang and drain a day. Then salted and placed for another twenty-four hours under a heavy press, after which time it is fit to eat.

In 1884 the first farmers' co-operative in New South Wales was founded at Kiama and butter and cheese production moved from the farms to the factory. Since it was too far to supply fresh milk to the Sydney market the coast south of Batemans Bay became the main district for cheese, producing Bodalla, Tilba, Bega and Kameruka.

A good way of using up left-overs, cheese pastes go back to early colonial times, although the following recipe dates from the era when the South Coast factories were founded.

FEDERAL CHEESE PASTE

250 g Cheddar cheese, grated
1 cup milk
2 tablespoons butter

½ teaspoon dry mustard
¼ teaspoon salt
Pinch cayenne pepper

▪ Put all the ingredients in a saucepan and bring to the boil over a medium heat, stirring constantly. Simmer for 15 minutes. Pour into an earthenware crock or into small pots. The mixture will solidify as it cools. Store covered with cling film in the refrigerator.

Burindi Savoury Slice

MAKES ABOUT 30

IN THE colonial period heat was the great enemy of the dairy and hence it was usual in Australia to put the building partially underground. A large hole would be dug, covered over with planks, sheets of bark and packed earth, with a sloping entrance left in one wall. All around inside the milk was ranged in keelers, large shallow tubs on benches until the cream rose and could be skimmed off for butter or cheese. The calves, pigs and chooks had the benefit of the left-over skim milk.

Milking was a manual operation. In *Unna You Fullas* writer Glenyse Ward recalls her milking days, growing up on Wandering Mission in Western Australia during the 1950s. The only change since colonial times was the introduction of a separating machine. Firstly the young calves were locked away and the cow bins filled with hay and mash:

Before we started milking, each girl had to wash her own cow's udder and teats. We sat on these little stools and buried our heads on one side of the cow's belly, balancing the pail between our knees. We let our knees take a firm grip, and with both hands would squeeze their teats with a striking motion, as the milk splashed from side to side.

When the pails were full, we'd carry them in to Br Victor in the Separating Room. The machine he used looked like a flying saucer with two spouts, one for the milk and one lower down for the cream.

Inside the separating machine were these disks hooked onto wire mesh running all the way round inside. On the outside Brother put real fine netting material to keep all the grime and dust out. He turned a big handle to work the machine, which made a low buzzing noise.

A tasty dish to utilise some of the cheese from the dairy is this savoury hot hors d'oeuvre from the northern New South Wales homestead of 'Burindi', whose picturesque Koori name means 'hills and valleys'. The recipe is from the 1960s fund-raising cookbook *Gunyah Gabba*.

250 g cheddar cheese, grated
250 g bacon, diced
250 g onion, finely chopped
2 cups self-raising flour

Pinch of salt
125 g butter, chilled and diced
1 egg
½ cup iced water

▪ To make the cheese filling, mix the cheese, bacon and onion together in a bowl and set aside.

▪ Sift the flour with the salt into a mixing bowl and rub in the butter with your fingertips. When the flour resembles breadcrumbs it is ready. Beat the egg with the water in a separate bowl. Stir enough of this mixture in to the flour to hold the dough together, reserving the rest for glazing. Knead a few times to amalgamate the pastry.

▪ On a floured board roll out half the pastry to form a rectangle about 20 x 30 cm. Place on a greased flat baking tray. Cover with the cheese filling. Roll out the remaining pastry, trim to fit the base and place over the filling. Press down gently to compact. Brush with the reserved glaze.

▪ Bake in a preheated oven at 230°C for 10 minutes. Reduce to 180°C and continue to cook until golden brown, about 20 minutes. Cut into bars about 3.5 x 5 cm and serve hot.

Australian Rarebit

SERVES 6

EVEN in the cities during the colonial era many families kept cows or goats to provide fresh milk, but as time went by this became impractical and townfolk relied increasingly on milk deliveries. Rosslyn Blay describes the milko of the 1920s and '30s in *A Living History of Parramatta*:

Milk was delivered, too, at three pence a pint, twice a day, very early in the morning and in the afternoon. The milkman used a horse and cart with a milk tank at the back, complete with two taps. The people left their jugs or billy-cans out and the milk was brought in to the front verandah in a measure, pint or half pint sizes. There was a thumb lever which lifted the lid to dispense the milk. When we forgot to put out the jug the milkman would call out and knock on the door.

We also had a butter man called Mr Ford. He sold eggs, cheese, honey and those sorts of things.

After the war milk came in bottles capped with silver, pasteurised but not homogenised so that the cream floated to the surface and the first glass of milk—the 'top' milk—was always really lovely, extra rich and creamy. Less fortunately, the cheese came in a plastic wrapper, destined to destroy any possibility of a nice rind, but suitable for such perennial favourites as cheese on toast, in this colonial version served with sliced hard-boiled eggs.

AUSTRALIAN RAREBIT

6 slices bread
Butter
1½ tablespoons anchovy paste
3 hard-boiled eggs

¼ teaspoons cayenne pepper
125 g cheese, grated
6 sprigs of fresh parsley, for garnish

■ Toast the bread and spread with butter, then with anchovy paste. Slice the hard-boiled eggs thinly and lay on top of the toast. Sprinkle lightly with cayenne and cover with cheese.

■ Place the rarebits on a baking tray and cook in a preheated oven at 200°C for 12–15 minutes, until puffed and golden. Serve hot, garnished with parsley.

Emu Eyes

SERVES 2

COOKED breakfasts were the norm in Australia before packaged cereal and orange juice supplanted them in many busy households. However for Glenyse Ward, writing of her childhood in *Wandering Girl*, breakfast on the mission consisted of bread with buttermilk, porridge or semolina, except on Sundays when the children received a 'treat' in the form of weeties cooked up by the nuns in big pots of boiling water until they were mushy. Sent to work as a domestic at age sixteen, she could have bread and butter, tea and plenty of weeties, but was denied the hot breakfasts by her tyrannical mistress, save when left alone in the house, able to indulge in a little culinary subversion:

Mm, just to smell the aroma of bacon and eggs cooking made my mouth water. Then I made some toast, and when everything was ready I got my old tin plate and tin mug, chucked them in the sink and took out a setting from one of her finest crockery services. I went into the dining room where she sat at the table, laid everything out, got a clean serviette, put that on my bread and butter plate, then went into the kitchen to get my breakfast out of the oven ... and then sat down to the most nourishing meal of my life.

A variation of fried eggs is emu eyes, sometimes called hole-in-one or Ned Kelly's eye, a dish of eggs fried with bread, not of Antipodean origin, but popular with bush men since colonial times.

---

2 slices of bread, cut about 2 cm thick
1½ tablespoons butter

1½ tablespoons oil
2 eggs

■ Cut a 5 cm circle out of the middle of each slice of bread with a biscuit cutter. Heat the butter and oil in a frying pan over a moderately high heat and place the slices of bread in the pan. Break the eggs into the centre of the bread and fry until the underside is golden brown and the eggs half done. Turn carefully with an egg slice and fry the other side.

Feather Fowlie Eggs

MAKES 6

THE Scots assumed a major position in Australian life from the earliest days of European settlement. A proportion of the First Fleet were Scottish and the Scots were prominent in the colonial administration, occupying three out of the first six governorships of New South Wales. Caledonians were under-represented amongst the convicts and those who came to Australia were mainly from the middle class, forced to emigrate by a scarcity of arable land at home. Large numbers entered farming and grazing, playing a significant role in dairying and stock breeding, many through their hard work and perseverance becoming wealthy squatters. The Protestant work ethic was also strong with businessmen, among them the biscuit baker William Arnott and Macpherson Robertson, founder of the MacRobertson chocolate and confectionary business.

Margaret Fulton, the author of many best-selling cookbooks and regular articles on cookery from the 1960s on, has been the most famous Scottish cook to migrate here but Scottish housewives have contributed their culinary skills to the national well-being for two centuries now. They, too, have been prominent in publishing, from 1894 to the present day, issuing a series of fund-raising cookery books for the Presbyterian Church in Queensland, New South Wales and Victoria. Many women were skilled bakers, helping to establish fine cake, biscuit and scone baking as one of the hallmarks of Australian cookery. A range of Caledonian recipes appear from time to time in Australian cookbooks: Scotch broth and Scotch eggs, baps and bannock, barley water and Edinburgh rock, Aberdeen sausage and Dundee cake, potted hough and haggis, black bun and drop scones, whisky balls and smoked haddock pies, Scotch collops and thistle fluff. Some dishes have achieved almost universal acceptance and these include scones, shortbread, porridge (usually unsalted) and orange marmalade.

Scotch eggs are a favourite picnic food, sometimes with the customary pork coating replaced by other meats like minced beef or here by chicken. If you are preparing your own minced chicken, you will need about 1.25 kilograms of chicken with the bone in.

FEATHER FOWLIE EGGS

6 hard-boiled eggs
1 tablespoon plain flour
500 g chicken meat, finely minced
½ teaspoon dried tarragon
¼ teaspoon salt

Freshly ground black pepper
1 egg, beaten
½ cup fine dry breadcrumbs
Oil for deep frying

▪ Shell the eggs and roll in the flour. In a bowl mix the chicken meat, tarragon, salt and pepper thoroughly with your hands and divide into six equal portions. Mould the mince evenly around each egg. Place the beaten egg in a bowl and the breadcrumbs in another. Dip the eggs in beaten egg and then roll them in breadcrumbs. Refrigerate for 1 hour and then re-shape so that they are well-rounded.

▪ Fill a large saucepan ⅓ full of oil and place over a high heat. Test the heat, if bread cubes colour in 1 minute when dropped in it is ready. Deep fry the eggs for a few minutes until golden brown and the chicken is cooked through. If necessary, to avoid over-crowding and absorption of too much fat, cook half at a time. Drain on absorbent paper and serve hot or let cool.

4

Gatherer's oysters

FISH AND SHELLFISH

In the colonial era some bush people continued to use Aboriginal methods when cooking fish over the campfire, adapting them to new materials such as wet newspaper instead of leaf wrappers.

Aborigines Spearing Fish *by Joseph Lycett presents an idyllic fishing scene; this favourite pastime of Australians living by the coast is also a necessary way of providing food for the table.*

Fish for the Catching

AUSTRALIA has a great wealth of seafood, the quantity and variety accentuated by the length of coastline and the range of climate from temperate to tropic. There are about two thousand different types of fish in Australian waters, of which about a tenth are commercially exploited. Most belong to the sea, with some fine fish in the big river systems although there are far fewer freshwater species than on other continents because of unpredictable rainfall and sporadic flooding. T. C. Roughley, in his authoritative book *Fish and Fisheries of Australia*, lists his favourite fish as the pearl perch, followed by John dory, Tasmanian trumpeter, Westralian dhufish, Murray cod and barramundi.

Shellfish are found in abundance, the most prized being the famous Sydney rock oyster, Tasmanian scallop and abalone although mussels and pipis are common. Of the crustaceans, prawns are consumed in the largest quantities whereas crabs and lobsters are usually too expensive except for dinner parties.

With all this profusion it is not surprising that seafood forms a customary staple of many Aboriginal groups. In South Australia alone, twenty-nine species of marine shellfish are traditionally included in the diet. Huge middens of discarded shells have been found, one on Cape York Peninsula measuring some ten metres high. Oysters, limpets and chitons, which live tightly anchored to rocks, are chiselled off at low tide, while pipis and other beach-dwellers must be scrabbled for in the sand with the feet. The greatest endurance is needed for abalone: in the past women would brave the cold southern seas, diving deep to prise off the tenacious shellfish with stone chisels, placing them in a plaited dilly bag as they swam underwater. A skilled worker could fill her bag at one dive before resurfacing.

Both women and men are keen fishers, operating from the bank, wading through the shallows, swimming powerfully across water overarm or diving under water in the pursuit of prey, or angling from canoes. Most simply, fish are grasped in the hand, collected in basketry scoops, speared or clubbed. Sometimes the water is muddied to drive the fish to the surface or narcotic plant extracts are added to 'drug' the fish. Hollow logs, dillybags and folding butterfly nets are laid in streams to trap fish, eels and yabbies. Eel traps up to 1.5 metres long and about 20 centimetres wide are woven from split lawyer canes or reeds and disguised with river grass. Elaborate baulks of logs and interlaced boughs, sometimes 30 metres in length, are constructed across rivers and small creeks, and stone traps are laid in some rivers. Fibre lines and hooks of bone, shell or hardwood are commonly used. Filet nets are made from plant fibres and attached to frames for working individually or in pairs. Seine nets as much as 300 metres long and about 1.5 metres deep, fitted with stone sinkers and paperbark floats, are trawled by large teams of people.

Torres Strait fishermen traditionally use lines of vine or vegetable fibres, hooks of turtle shell, spears and cast nets. In the Eastern Islands bamboo scoops catch small school fish like sardines. And there are immense traps called 'sei' built at the beginning of time by the legendary figures Abob and Kos, consisting of great sea fields, separated by lava-rock walls up to a metre in height, in which fish are caught by receding tides. Though not strictly fish, but seafood nevertheless, turtles and dugong are harpooned from canoes or platforms and these are so important that there is a relaxation of the normal rules forbidding the eating of totemic animals.

Into the Fire

To cook the fish a variety of techniques are used. Shellfish are consumed raw by Aboriginal people or placed on live coals until they open, the flesh inside poaching in its own juice. Crustaceans are grilled although lobsters and crabs are occasionally cooked in the ground oven. Small fish may be grilled on the fire, large ones wrapped in aromatic leaves, protective bark or clay and baked over the fire or in the ground oven where it acquires a flavour from the fuel. In addition to these methods, Torres Strait cooks prepare seafood by boiling,

Men from Melville Island show off their catch of a dugong, the prelude to a great feast.

either in water or coconut milk. This is particularly necessary for softening turtle and pearl oyster meat dried in preparation for long voyages.

In the colonial era some bush people continued to use Aboriginal methods when cooking fish over the campfire, adapting them to new materials such as wet newspaper instead of leaf wrappers. By and large though, attitudes to fish cookery changed, with frying and boiling predominant and sauces a common accompaniment. For fried fish, melted butter, anchovy, piquant and tartare sauces were recommended; for boiled fish, parsley, egg, oyster or hollandaise. Hearty fish pies, fish cakes, baked fish, fish puddings, mornays and kedgerees became popular. In those pre-refrigeration days, sousing was a good way of keeping fish.

Despite the richness of Australia's fisheries seafood was generally a much neglected article of diet. With mutton and beef so abundant and cheap, fish could never compete on a cost basis, even though today the prices appear ridiculously low: for instance, oysters sold for sixpence a dozen in the 1890s, lobsters for a shilling each.

Prior to the advent of the ice man in the 1870s, marketing of fish in the hot climate presented enormous difficulties. Isolated bush people often went without or depended on the dried and smoked product from Chinese and other coastal fishermen. For townsfolk, fish was a once-a-week affair, often consumed on Fridays for religious reasons. In polite society, a fish course preceding the meat course would have been an essential part of any elegant dinner party. Many of the dishes devised for these occasions were refined concoctions, sometimes with correspondingly fancy 'Frenchified' names, like fish à la Tasmania. Much of our knowledge of colonial fish cookery comes from Harriet Wicken who presented dozens of recipes in her cookbooks and tried to promote what she saw as 'excellent food and medicine for the brain and chest,' 'an admirable food for invalids and brain workers … for persons engaged in sedentary occupations.'

After Federation, fish continued to be the one item of native food in the diet of most Australians. Boiling went out of fashion, as did most of the colonial sauces, and plainly fried or grilled fish accompanied by lemon wedges or tartare sauce became the norm, particularly at cafés and restaurants. Some of the old homely recipes such as pies and rissoles continued on and were joined by dishes combining fish, fruit and vegetables, and in recent times tropical ingredients such as coconut, macadamias and avocado. The availability of seafood grew in the early part of the twentieth century when trawling commenced up and down the coast, and after World War II Greek fishmongers promoted squid, mussels and other delicacies previously known only to Aboriginal diners. Aquaculture, begun in the 1970s, has brought exotic varieties to the dinner table, such as trout and salmon, and widened the accessibility of the local yabbies and barramundi.

Gatherer's Oysters

SERVE 6 PER PERSON

FROM 1788 the ritual of oyster gathering, practised for millenia by the Gadigal people over the rock platforms of Sydney Harbour, was adopted enthusiastically by the new colonists. Lieutenant-Colonel Godfrey Charles Mundy, on secondment to New South Wales in the 1840s, describes the custom in *Our Antipodes*:

There is, however, connected with the shores, and islets, and coves of the harbour, one pursuit peculiarly congenial to the tastes of the people—a pastime half jaunting, half sedentary; a little sea air, a very little personal exertion, and a large amount of gastronomic recreation; I mean, oyster-eating. Every inch of rock from Sydney to the Heads is thickly colonized by these delicate shellfish; that is, every inch would be so peopled, but for the active extermination incessantly going on.

On any fine day select parties of pleasure-and-oyster-seekers may be seen proceeding by water, or land, furnished with the necessary muniments for an attack, or actively engaged in it. A hammer and a chisel, an oyster-knife, a bottle of vinegar, and the pepper-pot, with a vigorous appetite, sharpened by the almost impregnable character of the foe—such are the forces brought into the field, and the inducements to distinction. It is needless to add, that the garrison are quickly shelled out of their natural stronghold.

I enrolled myself more than once in an expedition of this kind, and only regretted that 'my great revenge had stomach' for only one-half of the luscious victims demolished by my companions.

The Sydney rock oyster grows all the way from Gladstone in tropical Queensland down to Malacoota Inlet in Victoria, cementing itself firmly to the rock platforms of every harbour and every jutting headland. The nation's preferred way of consuming them is still *au naturel*, after the fashion established in time immemorial by the Aboriginal people.

▪ Serve on special oyster plates, a bed of rock salt or on an ordinary entrée
plate. They will have a better flavour if eaten at room temperature and served
in their natural juices. If you wish, serve them with salt, black pepper and
wedges of lemon. Brown bread and butter are a fine accompaniment.

Mussels Aboriginal Style

SERVE 9 PER PERSON

THE first time I ate mussels was as a girl holidaying at Lake Conjola on the
coast south of Sydney. While swimming we had noticed a big colony of the
shiny black shellfish at the lake's entrance where the water ran out to the sea.
With a certain amount of daring (for they were regarded by ordinary
Australians at that time as funny foreign food, only eaten by newcomers to
the country) we harvested some and took them back to camp wondering
what one had to do to make them edible. With a bit of trial and error they
ended up as mussel fritters, and scrumptious they were too.

Aboriginal Australians, of course, have been eating mussels for tens of
thousands of years so they are hardly a new food in this country even if they
were new to some of us back in the sixties. The preferred Aboriginal cooking
method for shellfish involves skilfully placing them on the hot coals in such a
way that each shell forms a tiny cooking pot, retaining the precious juices,
and they are later retrieved by means of a pointed stick. At home, they can be
cooked under the griller or on a hot barbecue grill. Mussels prepared in this
manner have a real taste of the sea and I like to serve them with plenty of
crusty bread or buttered toast to soak up some of the delicious saltiness.

Allow about 9 unopened mussels per person

▪ With a small knife pull the beards off the mussels and clean the shells. Warm
your entrée plates. Place the mussels under a preheated hot griller on their
sides and grill for a few minutes until the shells open. Some will take only a
couple of minutes, others double or even triple that time. As soon as they
open remove them to the serving plates with a spoon and keep warm.
Discard any that don't open. Try to spill as little of the liquid inside the shells
as possible. Serve immediately.

Aboriginal Grilled Crab

ONE CRAB SERVES 1 PERSON

QUEENSLAND poet and civil rights activist Oodgeroo Noonuccal relates in *Stradbroke Dreamtime* the fishing and hunting which her family undertook during her childhood to supplement the meagre Aboriginal wage and rations earned by her father. About once every three months they would go in search of the male mud crabs, setting out early in the morning:

The fantastic, indescribable light that brightened the sky always made me feel I was in the presence of the Good Spirit. The colours would appear in the sky as if from nowhere and blend together as the sun peeped over the horizon. It was like a great rainbow rolled up in a huge ball, covering the eastern sky. This spectacle never failed to move me, and before the last of the colours left the sky, I had always forgiven my father for getting me out of bed at such an early hour to go crabbing.

Our boat with its chugging two-cylinder engine would finally bring us to our destination, the place where the mud crabs lurked. We had been through the crabbing drill so many times that there was never any need for Dad to give us orders. As we three girls stepped out of the boat onto the mud-flats, my younger sister would seize one bran bag and throw another to me, while my older sister took up the crab hook, which we needed for the crabs that had to be winkled out from beneath the roots of the mangrove-trees. Dad would stay on the boat and follow after us as we worked the flats.

Grilling on a barbecue or under a griller is the most flavourful way of cooking crab, or for that matter any crustacean, and is perfect for blue swimmers.

Allow one uncooked but dead crab per person   *Lemon wedges*

▪ Place the washed crabs under a preheated hot griller and cook until done, turning half-way through. As they cook, the crabs will turn vermilion on top and will sizzle as some of the juice inside escapes. Blue swimmers will not take long, about 4–5 minutes each side. Serve hot or cold, with lemon wedges. Eat with your fingers. Accompany with a dipping sauce if you prefer.

The Fishing Bounty

THE location of shellfish reefs and fishing holes was, for Aboriginal people, determined in the Dreamtime. Goobalathaldin, also known as Dick Roughsey, an artist of the Lardil people from Mornington Island in the Gulf

of Carpentaria, tells in *Moon and Rainbow* how Thuwathu, the Rainbow
Serpent, was wounded by a rival and, in his death throws, travelled over the
land carving out as he went the course of the Minya Darga River,
establishing here a large bend where he rested and there a big fishing hole
where he slept: 'He was very sick and vomited up things as he went, leaving
mud crabs here, trevalley there, then blue-fish … and sugar-bag bees … and
also left swamp turtle and water-lilies.' Eventually he died at Bugargun, where
a spring of water flows eternal from the ground, and his spirit lives on in the
river and in the sea, in every well and waterhole, while his people feast
forever on the foods left by him.

Balmain Bacon Bugs

IN EARLY to mid colonial times fish were sold at a number of doubtful
establishments, including one at Sydney's Woolloomooloo where they were
laid out on the floor in the dirt, subject to the vicissitudes of hot weather and
flies, to be inspected and poked at by customers with the point of their boots.
The lack of hygiene and the odour must surely have contributed to the low
consumption of seafood by town dwellers at the time.

With the introduction of ice-making technology the situation improved
considerably by the 1880s and nowadays only freshness exudes from the
various markets dotted along the coastline at the towns and cities which
boast a fishing fleet. Often these are merely a processing and packing shed
erected beside the wharf where the boats pull in, with a small counter at
which locals can select from the catch before the lion's share is shipped off.

Of all the fish markets in Australia, Sydney's is pre-eminent, lying on the
shores of Blackwattle Bay, an inlet of the harbour. It has huge chilling and
auction rooms, seafood eateries and a number of retailers, one specialising in
the Sydney rock oyster, another alive with aquaria of lobsters, crabs and
abalone, although most sell a great display of seafood heaped up in a glorious
and vivid mosaic of shapes, colours and patterns.

Friday is traditionally the day for buying fish but Saturday is also popular
as people often have more time then. The bustle on those two days reaches a
fever pitch during Lent with some good souls still maintaining the religious
observances, and then again in the lead up to Christmas when the hedonists
throw seafood dinner parties. As middle-aged housewives inspect the freshness
of fishy eyes and gills, customers jostle in the crush, slipping around the tiled
floors wet with drips from the icebeds, vying for the attention of the young
sales assistants.

Among the more unusual spoils are the shovel-nosed lobsters or flapjacks, christened Balmain bugs by the first trawlermen who lived in the old working-class suburb of Balmain near the market. Like their close allies the larger rock lobsters they have an exquisitely flavoured flesh, here simply wrapped in bacon and grilled. The same technique works well for cooking oysters, mussels and scallops.

1 kg green Balmain bugs (Moreton Bay bugs)   *½ grapefruit, cut in quarters*
About 7 thin rashers of bacon

- Lay the bugs on their backs and with a knife slit the leathery membrane across, where the head joins the tail. Pull the tail from the head. With a pair of kitchen scissors snip down each side of the tail underneath and remove the meat in one piece. If large, cut in two.
- Trim and discard the bacon rind and cut each rasher into three. Wrap the bugs in bacon, threading them on skewers as you go.
- Cook under a hot preheated griller or over a barbecue grill until the bacon is crisp, turning the Bacon Bugs halfway through. Serve with a wedge of grapefruit, to be squeezed generously over the bugs.

Prawns and Pineapple Boat

SERVES 8–12 AS AN APPETISER OR STARTER

PRAWNS have been netted in the estuaries which run the length of the Australian coastline since the first days of European settlement and caught by Aboriginal people well before that. T. C. Roughley describes prawning in his book *Fish and Fisheries of Australia*:

It is well known to a host of amateurs as well as professionals that the best 'runs' of prawns are taken at the estuary mouths during an outgoing tide in the dark phases of the moon. On a still summer's night at such places as the entrances to Lake Illawarra or to Tuggerah Lakes fires flicker and dance on the shore as Mum heats the water while Dad and his mate pull their hand-nets through the travelling schools of prawns that desperately seek their way to sea.

Estuarine netting was replaced commercially from 1948 by sea-trawling, leading to an enormous expansion in the industry.

A number of species are available, the banana prawn of Queensland and Western Australia, king and tiger prawns, the greasyback or greentail, even the little schoolies are excellent eating if a bit more trouble to shell. In the recipe prawns are served in pineapple shells—a popular way of serving in the 1960s.

PRAWNS AND PINEAPPLE BOAT

1 pineapple	2 tablespoons lime juice
1 kg cooked prawns	3 teaspoons horseradish relish
6 strawberries or red capsicum strips	1 teaspoon prepared mustard
COCKTAIL SAUCE	¼ teaspoon Tabasco sauce
1 egg	½ teaspoon salt
2 tablespoons tomato paste	1 cup olive oil

∎ Halve the pineapple lengthwise through the green top to the bottom and cut out and discard the core. Cut the fruit away from the skin using a grapefruit knife and dice. Reserve the pineapple shells.

∎ Shell the prawns. Devein by cutting out the intestinal tract with a small knife. Wash well and dry. Cut up if very large. With toothpicks thread the prawns and pineapple pieces together and pile into the pineapple shells. Garnish with a few strawberries or some capsicum.

∎ To prepare the sauce, place all ingredients except the olive oil in a blender or food processor. Blend the ingredients then with the motor switched on again pour in the remaining oil in a steady streama until a thick consistency, about 10–15 seconds. Place in a bowl and use as a dipping sauce.

Barbecued Yabbies

SERVES 4–6

FOR people of the inland living near rivers or waterholes there are some superb fish available for eating as well as freshwater crustaceans, and mussels the size of saucers. Dr Evelyn Crawford, teacher and one-time drover who spent all her life in outback New South Wales, recounts in *Over My Tracks* her childhood fishing expeditions:

We got crayfish—boogoli—out of the holes in the hard mud along the creek bank. You'd put your hand or foot in one hole and sort of pump it, like when you unblock a sink. You'd see where the water came up in other places, so that's where the crayfish would come out. They always come out backwards, so someone would stand over that hole while you pumped at the first hole. In the water-holes we'd catch crays and shrimps with a lump of meat on a string, and we'd scoop 'em out with a wire net. Our liveliest time was when we were findin' mussels—thilli. We'd go into the shallow

water, walk around on the mud and we'd feel the mussels, hard and lumpy. They travel
in a line, five or six behind the other. We'd dive down, pull 'em out and chuck 'em on
the bank. The smallest kids heaped them up ready to take home.

Freshwater crayfish include the River Murray cray, several land crays, as well as the little yabbies, called gilgies in Western Australia or lobbies in Queensland. Most Australians would recall catching these by the same meat-on-the-string approach as Evelyn Crawford, the only problem being how to get enough of them to fill the pot. Nowadays they are bred commercially so that you can buy as many as you want. They may be eaten plain, grilled or boiled, cooked in a creamy mornay or curry sauce, or roasted as Stephanie Alexander, one of Australia's leading chefs, does in this delicious recipe.

20 yabbies, freshly killed and chilled
Freshly ground black pepper
1 tablespoon fresh thyme leaves

½ cup extra virgin olive oil
Sea salt
Lemon wedges to serve

▪ Carefully split each yabby and its shell lengthwise, including the head, using a heavy chef's knife. Remove intestinal thread from each half. Gently wash and dry around this area. Arrange yabby halves, flesh-side up, in a single layer on an oiled baking sheet. Grind a little pepper over each; and scatter with thyme. Paint the flesh with some of the oil. Leave the yabbies at room temperature for up to 1 hour before cooking.

▪ Preheat the oven or griller to maximum. Cook the yabbies for 4 minutes until the flesh is just firm. Drizzle with a little more oil before serving with sea salt and a bowl of lemon wedges.

Gum-leaf Fish

SERVES 4

STONE fish traps were once of great economic importance to Aboriginal communities along the major inland waterways. The largest remaining is at Brewarrina on the Darling River in northern New South Wales. Ngemba history records that it was the gift of the Dreamtime figure Baiame. During a prolonged drought he set boulders in the pattern of a giant fishing net and then called on the Ngemba people to sing for rain. For several days the rain fell, bringing with it a multitude of fish which were caught in the net. This trap makes use of a natural bar of rock that forms a base for the intricate series of rock walls, channels and pens which stretch over 400 metres. The stones are set at different levels for varying river heights and allow small fish

A rare photograph, probably from the 1870s, captures a man maintaining the ingeniously arranged fish traps which straddle the Darling River at Brewarrina.

to escape while large ones are trapped. Once huge gatherings of as many as five thousand people would take place at Brewarrina, supported by the ample supply from the fisheries. The Brewarrina traps still work as Dr Evelyn Crawford discovered when raising her family by the banks of the Darling:

I could say to Rocco, 'Go down and get a fish.'
    'Righto. How big d'ya want it?'
    'About this big, or that big …' or whatever size we wanted.
    He could go down to the traps and be gone for about half an hour and come back with just that size fish. They spent that much time on those rocks, them kids, they knew where the big fish were. The boys blocked 'em up and caught 'em with their hands, and stuck a stick in the gills. I suppose they got so good at it from havin' to so we could eat.

Once caught, a widespread cooking method is to cover the fish in wet gum leaves before roasting on hot coals, good for trevally or rainbow trout.

GUM-LEAF FISH

4 x 250–350 g whole fish, gutted, scaled and   Sprigs of fresh gum leaves
  washed

▪ Wet the gum leaves and place a layer in a baking or gratin dish to form a bed. Place the fish on top. The shape of the fish will determine how many of them will fit into the tray. Lay some more gum leaves loosely over the fish to form a light covering. Place the dish in a preheated oven and bake at 190° C for 20–25 minutes.

Ginger-leaf Barramundi

SERVES 4–6

ABORIGINAL fishermen are closely in tune with the natural rhythms of the fish they hunt, the weather, the tides and the heavenly bodies. Goobalathaldin notes in *Moon and Rainbow* how the Lardil men prefer to fish when the tide is low. If low tide is at night they spend the afternoon making torches of paperbark tied into bundles 1.5 to 3 metres long and then wait for dark, studying the stars:

Buldingu, (Venus) the woman star, is first to go down in the evening. She goes to make a big fire to cook the fish which the men stars, the hunters, will be bringing home later. These men stars, Bidgingu and Gidbu Bulan, come up at ten o'clock or later. They carry on their backs Yule, the Milky Way. Yule is a road or a path for the hunters to travel on during the night …

When the old men saw Gidbu Bulan coming up, one of them would go down and look at the water. If it was right we would all get our big scoop nets, light our long torches and go down to the selected place. We would wade out until chest-deep in the water and form a big semi-circle. Two or three other men would then come wading along from further down the beach, splashing and making a lot of noise. When we saw where the fish were we would open out our nets and surround them, closing in until the fish rushed into our nets

Traditional ways of cooking fish in northern Australia include wrapping it in paperbark or in leaves of the native ginger. The flowering gingers that grow in many suburban gardens make a good substitute. An excellent method of cooking good quality fish as the leaves keep the fish beautifully moist.

Barramundi are perhaps the choicest of all Australian fish. They are the undisputed monarchs of the north, found in rivers and estuaries from Western Australia, through the Northern Territory to Queensland. In their natural environment they may reach a length of 1.5 metres but now smaller fish are available on the market, thanks to fish farming.

| *1.5 kg whole barramundi* | *6 or more fresh ginger leaves* |
| *1 teaspoon oil* | *2 lemons, wedged* |

▪ Rinse the fish inside and out and wipe dry. Starting at the tail end wrap the ginger leaves closely around the fish, tying them in place with string as you go and overlapping the leaves so that no part of the flesh is exposed. Six large leaves should be enough, more if they are small.

▪ Transfer the wrapped fish to an oiled baking dish. Cook in a preheated oven at 190°C for 45–50 minutes until done. Show your guests the fish cooked in its wrapping before removing the string and peeling back the leaves to serve. Accompany with some lemon wedges if you wish.

Fire-fire Fish

SERVES 1

THE waters of the Torres Strait teem with fish which provide the chief source of protein for the islanders. Major Roland Raven-Hart in his book *The Happy Isles* describes the fishing on one of the Eastern islands in the 1940s:

There are always fish for the catching at Mer, on the lee shore of the island: at moments the shallow water suddenly boils with agitated 'sardines', and there is the noise of breakers, vastly disconcerting if one is floating in placid contentment nearby. Mer must be one of the few places in the world where it is often quite literally possible to catch fish in a bucket or a basket or a colander … I at first perplexedly watched spearers throwing apparently at random into dense green weed in three or four feet of water, and yet bringing up sardines in twos and threes on the wires; and then saw that each throw cleared a patch in the 'weed' through which the sandy bottom became visible, and realised that the waving fronds were waving tails, so dense that they hid the sand.

Of the various methods of cooking fish, grilling on the hot coals of the fire is the simplest, called poetically fire-fire fish or urur lar.

| *1 x 250–350 g whole fish, gutted, scaled and* | *Salt and freshly ground black pepper* |
| *cleaned* | *Peanut oil* |

▪ Pat the fish dry, season with a little salt and pepper and brush with oil. Preheat the griller and brush lightly with oil. Grill the fish at a high heat until done, about 6 minutes each side, depending on the thickness of the fish. The fish is done when it flakes easily with a fork. It is better to undercook than overcook fish. It will continue to cook after it is removed from the heat.

Macadamia Fish

SERVES 4

TO THE true lover of fish the fishmonger's shop is a source of constant fascination. Journalist Phillip Adams, writing in *The Age*, describes the typical Australian fish shop when he was growing up in Melbourne in the late 1940s:

There was the open-mouthed amazement of the flatheads. The serious start of the snapper. The streamlined silver of the bream. The apoplectic cray with eyes like exclamation points. (These days Diner's Club delicacy, then, working man's tucker.) And the flounder, flat as a pancake, and the garfish sharp as darts.

None of your squids in those days, no octopus. Just decent, respectable fish, the sort you could catch off Frankston in a row boat. Who could forget the skill of the man as he filleted and that evocative, exotic smell that conjured the sound of oars, of waves, of creaking piers.

Fish fillets are the staple of the suburban fish shop and one of the best modern ways of cooking them is in a crunchy macadamia coating.

4 fish fillets, about 175 g, washed	*Freshly ground black pepper*
Plain flour for dusting	*2 egg whites*
½ cup macadamias, finely chopped	*½ cup oil*
¼ cup cornflour	

▪ Pat the fish fillets dry and roll in flour. Shake off any excess. In a bowl combine the nuts with the cornflour and pepper. In a separate bowl beat the egg whites with a fork until frothy. Dip the fish into the egg white and then coat with macadamia mixture.

▪ Heat the oil in a frying pan over a moderate heat and fry the fish for a few minutes on both sides until golden brown and cooked through. Be careful not to burn the macadamias. Drain on absorbent paper and serve.

Fish and Chip Shops

FISH and chip shops are part of Australia's British heritage, although more often than not operated by migrants from other seafaring nations. The Greeks have been particularly prominent in the fishing industry at all levels and Athanasios Comino was probably the first Greek to open a fish and chippery, on Oxford Street in Sydney, way back in 1879. Melbourne, with the largest Greek community in Australia, naturally has its own Greek-run shops and Phillip Adams recalls those of his boyhood:

… there was that kindred species, the fish and chip shop, where the fish were never seen in their naked, metallic form, but always shrouded in wrinkled batter. Where you'd order a piece of flake, two potato cakes and six penneth of chips for a greedy, greasy and glorious lunch, having first tossed away your mother's sandwiches. There the Greek would shovel up his pale, finger-thick chips—none of your French-fried matchsticks— and lower them into the deep, dark, seething oil. And while you waited you'd look around … at the mussels in bottles (looking like pickled ears) or at the pickled onions (looking like sightless eyes). Every now and then the man would shake the wire basket until it was ready to up-end on the piece of waxed paper, surrounded by newsprint. Which you'd invariably try to read as he was salting and wrapping.

Fisherman's Garfish

SERVES 1

FISHING yarns are as much a part of the armoury of every amateur angler as hooks and lines. American adventurer Augustus Baker Peirce spent some years as captain of a paddle steamer on the Murray River from the 1860s and described, in his reminiscences *Knocking About*, the capture of a Murray cod weighing fifty-one kilos:

It was so large that it nearly pulled the man into the water, but his lusty shouts for help were answered just in time to save him a ducking. When this large fish was suspended from a capstan bar through its gills, the bar being supported on the shoulders of two men, its tail dragged on the ground. On its being opened, another cod was found in the stomach weighing six pounds and in so perfect a condition that it was eaten at dinner. This discovery caused an Irishman in the crew to exclaim in amazement: 'Begorra, and I niver knew that fishes calved! Sure, and I t'ought they laid eggs!'

Tales tall or true aside, some anglers have excellent ways of cooking their catch. The best garfish recipe I know was provided to the *Kookaburra Cookery Book*, published in Adelaide in 1914, by a fisherman, Mr Gunson. Garfish have a sweet, fine-textured flesh and make good eating except for the problem of their small bones, which here are turned to advantage by being fried to a delicious frizzle.

---

200 g garfish	*½ cup curly-leaf parsley sprigs*
2 tablespoons oil	*Salt*

▪ Make sure the garfish are properly cleaned and scaled. Wash and pat them dry. Lay them on their backs and with a sharp knife cut them right down to the tail. Turn them over and firmly press them flat so that the ventral flaps of flesh open out either side and the rib bones lie flat on the bottom.

▪ Heat the oil in a frying pan over a moderate to high heat and toss the parsley sprigs in the oil until the oil stops sizzling and the parsley is crisp. Drain well on absorbent paper and sprinkle with salt.

▪ Put the fish in the pan, rib bones down, and fry for a few minutes, without turning, until crispy round the edges, golden brown on the bottom and delicately cooked on top. Serve with the fried parsley.

King Fish with Tomatoes

SERVES 4

THE best fishing story I have heard is from Goobalathaldin, who in *Moon and Rainbow*, relates a story told him by Willy Long of the Olkula people, who was fishing on the Morehead River in north Queensland. The fish were biting well and he had caught plenty of bream, catfish and cod:

Then something really big took Willy's bait and nearly pulled him into the river. The battle was on then; Willy would nearly get the big fish up to the top of the water, only to be nearly pulled back into the water himself. He kept on fighting the fish until it tired and then with a mighty pull—'I might be nearly pullem guts out'—Willy got it up to the top and saw two big green eyes looking at him. 'I lookem eye belong him, him lookem eye belong me—look out! I bin hookem bloody Rainbow.'

Willy quickly cut the line but the Rainbow Serpent had been angered and sent a mighty thunderstorm to try to drown him.

King fish, though not as ferocious as Willy Long's catch, are still one of the larger fish on the market and a good way of cooking them is this early twentieth century recipe, flavoured with tomatoes and herbs.

1 kg king fish cutlets

1 teaspoon oil

⅓ cup finely chopped mixed herbs

250 g tomatoes, thinly sliced

2 tablespoons lemon juice

1¼ cups dry white wine

Salt and freshly ground black pepper

2 tablespoons butter

▪ Wash the fillets dry. Leave small cutlets whole, but if large cut in halves or quarters to give an equal number of pieces per person. Grease a gratin or baking dish and lay the fish in one layer. Sprinkle the herbs over the fish and cover with tomatoes. Pour over the lemon juice and then wine. Sprinkle with some salt and grind some pepper over the top. Dot with butter. Bake in a preheated oven at 180°C for 20–25 minutes until the fish is cooked through. Serve immediately.

Fish à la Tasmania

SERVES 4

AUSTRALIA'S island state Tasmania has been separated from the mainland for about twelve thousand years, in which time unique culinary customs have developed. Seals and muttonbirds, as well as the more usual native game such as kangaroo and possum, are important traditional food sources for Aboriginal Tasmanians. A beached whale was once the occasion for great feasting, and garni banyip or blackfellows' bread is considered as great a delicacy as truffles are elsewhere in the world. The trunk of the cider gum is tapped for its sweet nectar which ferments and turns alcoholic if left for a period. Rock lobsters and shellfish are abundant, including abalone, oysters and the nation's juiciest scallops, but, for reasons which are poorly understood, fish with scales were shunned by cooks in the north-west after about 2,000 B.C. Damper was little used traditionally but there are plenty of native vegetables including wild cresses, parsley and nasturtiums, hearts of grass tree, bracken fern rhizomes and potato orchids, and plenty of fruits such as cherry ballarts, native cranberries and currants, kangaroo apples and Macquarie Harbour grapes.

In 1803 the island was occupied by colonists who, along with the original inhabitants, evolved a hearty, warming cuisine suitable to the cooler weather with more emphasis on soups, hot meat dishes and steamed and baked puddings than is typical on the mainland. A rich agricultural base quickly emerged, following many of the crops and farming practices of Britain. Whereas maize flourished at the expense of wheat in the early days of Sydney's settlement, Van Diemen's Land had no difficulty with the British cereal varieties. Sheep and cattle fattened on the lush pastures, requiring a much smaller acreage than they did elsewhere. A fine dairy industry was established, producing Duck River, Mersey Valley, Lactos and King Island cheeses, and recently the fine artisan-made Heidi Gruyère. Potatoes, peas and swedes, hops, apples, pears, cherries and plums, and all the English berries flourish in the cool climate. From 1861 jam manufacturing began, based on the bountiful fruit harvests, and the jams of the Apple Isle came to be sought after throughout Australia.

With the coming of the Europeans the ancient taboo on scaly fish was lifted. Salmon and ocean trout are extensively farmed these days in addition to some excellent catches off the coast, including ling and Tasmania's best eating fish, the trumpeter—ideal for this colonial dish of fried fishballs served with anchovy sauce.

500 g ling, trumpeter or rock cod fillets
80 g bacon rashers, rind removed, diced
1 small onion, roughly chopped
⅔ cup thick white sauce
2 teaspoons anchovy sauce or 1 anchovy fillet, mashed
Freshly ground black pepper
2 eggs, beaten

About 2¼ cups fresh white breadcrumbs
Oil for deep frying

ANCHOVY BUTTER SAUCE
125 g butter
2 tablespoons anchovy sauce
¼ teaspoon cayenne pepper

■ Wash and remove any skin or bones from the fish and mince finely in a food processor with the bacon and onion. Stir in the white sauce, anchovy sauce, pepper, half of the beaten eggs and ¾ cup of the breadcrumbs. Blend lightly until smooth.

■ Shape the mixture into balls about 3 cm diameter, dip in the remaining egg and roll in the left-over breadcrumbs. Pour the oil in a large saucepan until ⅓ full and bring to a high heat. When a bread cube turns golden brown in 1 minute it is ready. Fry a batch at a time for a few minutes until cooked through and golden brown. Drain on paper towels and keep warm until all are ready to serve with the anchovy butter sauce.

■ To make the anchovy butter sauce, melt the butter over a low to moderate heat and stir in the anchovy butter sauce and cayenne pepper. Let it cook for a couple of minutes to combine the flavours.

Stuffed Flathead Fillets

SERVES 4

FLATHEAD is my favourite fish, the most frequent visitor to the Friday dinner table when I was growing up and, along with bream, our most common catch when fishing as children—not that the paltry specimens in our bucket ever came anywhere near the size of the monsters whose heads were nailed to the boat shed as grim trophies of a golden era when creatures of almost mythical dimensions inhabited the deep. No doubt the huge, fierce heads made them a curiosity to the early colonists since they are not found in European waters. The profusion of flathead keeps their price within the reach of the average person—a real egalitarian food.

In the following recipe fillets are spread thinly with seasoning and baked, a first-class dish whether you use the original breadcrumb stuffing or an alternative flavoured with prawns. From the *Australasian Cookery Book* of 1913.

4 x 175–250 g flathead fillets

HERBED BREADCRUMB STUFFING
½ cup fresh breadcrumbs
1 egg, beaten
1 tablespoon finely chopped bacon fat or suet
2 teaspoons finely chopped fresh parsley
¼ teaspoon mixed dried herbs or 1 teaspoon
   fresh herbs

ALTERNATIVE PRAWN STUFFING
200 g green prawns
1 clove garlic
2 spring onions, roughly chopped
1 tablespoon butter

TOPPING
½ cup fresh breadcrumbs
60 g butter

▪ To prepare the breadcrumb stuffing, combine all the ingredients in a bowl and mix thoroughly. Alternatively, make the prawn stuffing. Shell and devein the prawns to give about 100 g of prawn meat. To devein the prawns, remove the intestinal tract with a sharp knife, wash and pat dry. Chop to a rough paste in a food processor. Remove from the processor and set aside. Finely chop the garlic and spring onions. Melt the butter in a small saucepan and sauté the garlic and spring onions gently for a few minutes. Remove from the heat and stir in the prawn meat until thoroughly mixed.

▪ Wash and dry the fillets. Cut off the two fins located near the shoulder of each fillet. Lay the fillets skin-side down and spread a quarter of the stuffing thinly over each. Fold in two, bringing the tail up to the shoulder, and press together.

Outdoor eating, such as this picnic at Mrs Macquarie's chair on the shores of Sydney Cove, is very much a part of the city's food culture.

▌ Put the folded fillets in a greased baking or gratin dish, tail-side down. Scatter the breadcrumbs over the top and dot with butter. Bake in a preheated oven at 180°C for 30 minutes until cooked, basting once half-way through. Serve each fillet with some of the cooking juices spooned over.

Schnapper à la Sydney

SERVES 4

THE capital of New South Wales and the largest city in Australia, Sydney is dominated by its waterways: the magnificent harbour which lies at its very heart and the Pacific Ocean with its ribbon of golden beaches, blue bays and rocky headlands. It was the harbour which nourished the Gadigal people, and it was through the heads that the First Fleet sailed in 1788, bringing with them a new way of life. In their wake came the great migrant ships carrying a cargo of exotic tastes and culinary traditions, the basis of the many ethnic restaurants and food shops that lend a cosmopolitan air to the city today.

Following the Gadigal before us, seafood is of prime importance, its abundance and quality unparalleled in the world. Prawn nights and seafood buffets are offered by many clubs, and large quantities of fish are consumed at the numerous fish 'n' chipperies, fish restaurants and at the few remaining old-fashioned fish cafés. A favourite pastime on a sunny weekend is to hop on the ferry to Manly for a meal at one of the many seafood restaurants, or to eat fish and chips from their paper wrapper.

This superlative baked dish from the 1930s reflects the popularity of the local seafood in this city: fillets of schnapper are masked with a creamy sauce, garnished with prawns and Sydney rock oysters.

SCHNAPPER À LA SYDNEY

4 x 175–250 g schnapper fillets	1 lemon
1¼ cups dry white wine	1½ tablespoons butter
250 g green prawns	2 tablespoons plain flour
1 dozen oysters	Pinch salt and white pepper
1 tablespoon olive oil	¼ cup cream
1 onion, finely chopped	2 tablespoons extra butter
1 tablespoon finely chopped fresh parsley	½ cup fresh breadcrumbs

▪ Wash and pat the fish fillets dry. Place them in a frying pan and add the wine and enough water to cover. Place over a low heat and simmer gently for a few minutes until barely done. Carefully remove to a buttered oven-proof dish, placing the pieces in one layer, skin side up.

▪ Shell the prawns, reserving the heads and shells. Devein by removing the intestinal tract with a sharp knife, wash and pat dry. Chop into bite-size pieces. Drain the oysters, reserving the liquor. Scatter the oysters and prawns over the pieces of fish.

▪ To make the stock, heat the oil in a large saucepan and sauté the onion and parsley until soft. Stir in the prawn heads and shells, the oysters liquor and the liquid in which the fish was cooked. With a vegetable peeler, remove the thin yellow rind from a quarter of the lemon and add the peel to the saucepan. Simmer gently, uncovered, for 30 minutes. Remove from the stove and mash roughly with a potato masher. Strain through a sieve lined with muslin. Measure the stock and keep 1¼ cups.

▪ To make the sauce, melt the butter in a small saucepan over a moderate heat and stir in the flour until smooth. Cook for a minute and season with salt and pepper. Take the saucepan off the heat and stir in the reserved stock. Return to the heat and cook, stirring constantly until it thickens. Add the cream and remove from the heat. Taste and adjust the seasoning if necessary. Spoon the sauce over the fish in the baking dish to mask it completely.

▪ Melt the extra butter over moderate to high heat. Add the breadcrumbs and toss in the butter until lightly browned. Sprinkle them over the fish dish.

▪ Bake in a preheated oven at 190°C for 10–15 minutes until the dish is golden and bubbling and the prawns and oysters are cooked.

Mrs Wicken's Baked Schnapper

FOOD is one area of culture in which there are many taboos. Goobalathaldin, in *Moon and Rainbow*, describes some of these for the Lardil people:

One law is that land food and sea food must never be mixed, and they must not be cooked on the same fire. Land food must never be taken into the sea, and anyone eating land food such as wallaby, goanna, or sugar-bag must not go into the sea for a few hours. Thuwathu the Rainbow serpent guards this law and if anyone breaks it he gets very angry and sends the spirit of one of the mulgri, the totem creatures of that part of the country, to enter his stomach and cause terrible pain or even death.

For many, Lent was a time of restriction when fish replaced meat in the diet, and the following recipe comes from *Recipes of Lenten Dishes*.

---

1 x 1.5–1.75 kg schnapper, gutted and scaled
60 g butter, softened
8–12 green prawns

LOBSTER STUFFING
80 g cooked lobster meat, finely chopped
60 g prawn meat, finely chopped
15 g fresh breadcrumbs
15 g butter, softened
1 egg
Pinch salt and white pepper

Pinch nutmeg

PRAWN SAUCE
1 tablespoon butter
1 tablespoon plain flour
2 mashed anchovy fillets or anchovy sauce
150 ml water
60 g green prawn meat, diced
Pinch salt and white pepper
2 teaspoons extra butter

▪ Wash the fish and dry it well. Mix all the lobster stuffing ingredients together in a bowl. Stuff the schnapper and lay it in a buttered baking dish. Daub the remaining butter on top. Bake the fish in a preheated oven at 190°C for 30–40 minutes until done, basting once or twice.

▪ Shell the prawns and devein but leave the tails on. When the fish is nearly cooked place the prawns in the baking dish, turning them to coat with the butter. Cook about 4 minutes until done.

▪ To make the prawn sauce, melt the butter in a small saucepan over a moderate heat. Stir in the flour and anchovy fillets and cook for a few minutes. Add the water all at once and cook, stirring until it thickens. Add the prawn meat, salt and pepper. If using anchovy sauce, add enough at this stage to give a good flavour. Cover and let stand over a low flame for 10 minutes. Just before serving stir the extra butter into the sauce. Serve the fish garnished with the prawns; pour the sauce over or serve in a sauce boat.

Lady Mitchell's Receipt to Caveach Fish

SERVES 6

IN THE old days every literate housewife kept a handwritten recipe book to deal with ingredients and problems peculiar to her situation and not addressed by the standard cookbooks available. One of the few to survive is Mary Mitchell's 'Receipes' dated 22nd May 1827, probably a gift from her kinswomen upon her migration to Australia with husband Major Thomas Mitchell, Surveyor-General of New South Wales. Occupying a position of some social standing she employed a cook, but cooked herself when needed and so added recipes to the book in her own hand as time went by.

Examining her little book, the pages carefully numbered and the recipes indexed, one can see some old British favourites but also dishes of particular usefulness to Australian conditions such as venison made from a loin of mutton, legs of mutton hams, cakes without butter or milk for periods of shortage. To serve fish in Sydney's hot weather Lady Mitchell has added an exotic 'Caveach' or ceviche, where cutlets are fried with onions then marinated in vinegar and spices. Excellent with Tasmanian salmon.

6 fish cutlets, washed

Salt and freshly ground black pepper

¼ cup plain flour

½ cup olive oil

2 onions, sliced

2 cloves crushed garlic or sliced spring onions

1 cup good quality wine or fruit vinegar

½ cup water

½ teaspoon peppercorns

4 cloves

2 blades mace

▪ Pat the fish cutlets dry and sprinkle well with salt and pepper. Dust with flour. Heat the oil in a frypan over a moderate heat and fry the cutlets until cooked through and lightly browned, about 2–4 minutes each side depending on thickness. Remove to a shallow dish with a slotted spoon.

▪ Add the onions and garlic or shallots to the pan and fry over a moderate heat until brown. Pour over the vinegar and water, add the whole spices, and simmer, uncovered, for 5 minutes. Spoon the liquid and onions over the fish and let cool. Serve straight away or, for a better blending of flavours, refrigerate for 1–2 days.

5

Ground oven to Sunday roast

Henry Melville, in 1851, recommended kangaroo as 'the most nutritious and most easily digested of any known to man' and noted: 'The settlers, who do not like to give themselves much trouble, generally cut steaks off the hind quarters, and fry or broil them on the wood fires: they are excellent, cooked in this way, when seasoned with a bush appetite.'

HENRY MELVILLE,
AUSTRALASIA AND PRISON DISCIPLINE, 1851

From the verandah of an Australian station showing river, *by an unknown artist. By the 1840s the distinctive lifestyle of the Australian pastoralist had already evolved with a shady verandah overlooking endless paddocks of grazing sheep.*

The Hunter's Harvest

AUSTRALIANS have always been a nation of meat-eaters and meat cookery is one of the most inventive areas of our cuisine. For Aboriginal people it is traditionally the men's job to hunt down and cook the larger animals while both men and women pursue the smaller creatures. Depending on the resources of a particular locality staple meats might include possums, flying foxes, bandicoots, wombats, echidnas, dingoes or their pups, platypuses, koalas, quolls, bilbies, marsupial moles, water rats and native mice, with kangaroos and wallabies holding a special place. Dugongs and beached whales are great delicacies along the coast and seals and sea lions important in southern waters. All kinds of birds are part of the diet and reptiles are a principal food source, especially for desert families, and include goannas, blue-tongue and smaller lizards, snakes, tortoises, turtles and crocodiles. A great variety of tasty insects provide essential protein, fat, vitamins and minerals, for example green tree ants and their pupae, cicada nymphs, wasp larvae, grasshoppers, the giant wood moth and mangrove worms called cobras. Bloodwood 'apples', with their juicy grub and refreshing liquid enclosed within a gall, are consumed with relish; but most famous is the witchetty grub, dug by the women from the roots of the witchetty bush, a type of wattle, and with its rich nutty flavour a real gourmet treat.

Cookery methods vary depending on the size of the animal and the nature of its flesh. Insects may be eaten *au naturel* or parched by rolling in hot ash until they swell and the skin crisps. Snakes are cooked on hot coals with one person holding each end to stop the body twisting into a tangled mass: when the contortions cease, the sinews are cut and the reptile rolled up and grilled. Small furred animals may be baked in their skins to keep the meat moist, the innards having been hooked out through the mouth first; or else the fur is singed over a high flame for about ten minutes and then scraped off with a sharp instrument, the intestines excised and then the animal returned to roast slowly over a bed of coals before being served, juicy inside, seared on the outside. Flying foxes are eaten entrails and all, their sweet diet of nectar and fruit making them a gastronomic delicacy, with even the bones being soft and edible; only the wings and bitter gall bladder are discarded. Small birds may be grilled and larger ones wrapped in clay or bark and buried in a depression in the ground, covered over with hot coals. Big animals may be roasted on coals if a quick meal is required but generally for large animals, and the bigger birds and lizards, the ground oven is the preferred medium. This is similar to the pit-roasting practised by most Pacific Islanders, but the wood and leaves employed as well as the types of meat are different. Once done, the meat is carefully apportioned to family members according to set rules, and there are strictures against not sharing food and against wastage.

Tastes in meat vary from well-done to very rare. Reptiles are usually consumed well cooked as are small furred animals. Large animals like kangaroos and wallabies may be well-done, rare or even blue, with the flesh heated thorough but nearly raw. Sometimes large animals are partially cooked and these parts eaten, any leftovers cooked up on subsequent days. Some meats are done until very tender but others, such as the grills, are fairly chewy, a textural quality that is not despised. Most of the meats are lean and healthy.

Meat Three Times a Day

When Australia was colonised by the British the new settlers brought with them their own ideas on cookery, although bush people and campers have continued to grill meat over open campfires down to the present day and a few traditional Aboriginal dishes, like baking birds in clay, were adopted. For the most part, cooking directly on the fire was superseded by the frying pan, the billy, the camp oven and other vessels. Pot roasts, boiled joints, fries, stews, pies and meatloaves became standard fare. Roasting meat suspended over a fire was rarely practised because of the lack of roasting appliances, according to Mina Rawson, and so meat was baked instead.

White settlers continued to use native meats through the colonial period but gradually these were replaced by introduced stock. Since the early nineteenth century mutton and beef have always been cheaper than pork and veal. In 1819, with pastoralism barely established, William Charles Wentworth quoted prices as 6 pence per pound for good mutton and beef, 8 pence for veal and 9 pence for pork. Journalist Richard Twopeny, writing in 1883, noted that mutton varied from 1½ to 4 pence, beef from 2½ to 6, veal 4 to 8, and pork from 7 to 9 pence, depending on quality, seasonal conditions and so on. Then as now, Australian mutton, lamb, beef and veal were healthy free-range meats with relatively low fat and little marbling of the muscle tissue, although by the 1980s grain-lot beef began to be produced for specific sectors of the market. Since the late nineteenth century wild rabbit has also become a cheap staple; and from the 1960s consumption of chicken increased twentyfold as a consequence of battery production. The 1960s also saw lamb outstripping mutton.

'Meat three times a day' became the boast of nineteenth-century Australia and was used to encourage new migrants from the British Isles. To the poor of Britain, living largely on a diet of bread, gruel, potatoes, pease pudding and cheese, this country must certainly have seemed like paradise. Richard Twopeny writes of the prevailing attitude:

Of course meat is the staple of Australian life. A working-man whose whole family did not eat meat three times a day would indeed be a phenomenon. High and low, rich and poor, all eat meat to an incredible extent, even in the hottest weather … It is not helped in mere slices, but in good substantial hunks.

By the end of the nineteenth century Victorians were consuming 125 kg of meat per person annually, the New South Welsh 132 kg, rising to a massive 168 kg for Queenslanders. This compared to a mere 50 kg for the average Briton or 68 kg in the United States of America. Even today Australians consume about 110 kg of meat per person each year.

With meat cheap and plentiful there is naturally a great wealth of original Australian meat recipes. Many colonials, particularly those in isolated areas of the country, had a very restricted diet, living on either mutton or beef from one day to the next, with the odd piece of game. Though the plentifulness of meat was welcome, it proved a challenge to cooks who needed to invent novel ways of presentation to ease the sameness of the diet.

Most recipes are for the cheaper meats, mutton or lamb, beef and rabbit, and for the more common native game such as kangaroo. The cooking of large joints, especially in the form of baked dinners and pot roasts, is a common practice. Fruit is also plentiful and economical and hence is often combined with meat in a variety of ways, either as an accompaniment, a stuffing for joints, or an ingredient in stews, curries or minces. An interesting feature of bush cookery is the new use to which corned beef and mutton have been put. Salted meat was one of the principal rations of the First Fleet and continued to figure prominently in the lives of settlers trying to survive in a hot climate before refrigeration. Even today, when the need for pickling meat is not so urgent, it still remains a popular and tasty food.

The Aboriginal Ground Oven

GROUND ovens are one of the great classics of the Australian cuisine. The method involves cooking meat and any accompanying vegetables in a hole lined with hot stones and wet, leafy branches or grass. The food is exposed to heat, smoke and herbal aromas within the moist atmosphere of the sealed oven and a humidified baking, light smoking and herbal seasoning of the food take place simultaneously. The effect is unlike any in European cookery and a new term, perhaps 'fragrant steam-baking', is needed to describe it. The food is usually cooked till well done and turns out moist and succulent.

The size of the ground oven varies tremendously depending on the catch and may be used to cook anything from a few yams or shellfish to a dugong. The bigger ovens require a good deal of physical labour and team work. Heated stones are preferable for the prolonged cooking needed by large meats although, if unavailable, pieces of anthill or clay may be substituted, hardening like bricks in the initial fire. Old ground ovens are often re-used or raided for good stones. By the sea, discarded shells may be heated to cook shellfish. Usually the food is placed directly on the hot stones and wet leaves, but sometimes it is wrapped first like a parcel in paper-bark or large leaves before being covered in more wet leaves and more stones and finally sealed with paperbark and earth. The finished oven looks like a domed mound. Experience is needed to judge the cooking time since once the oven is opened it cannot be resealed.

Ground ovens are the preferred way of catering for large gatherings and the preferred method for cooking large game. Sometimes special dishes are prepared as accompaniments. Black soup is made by filling a cleaned kangaroo stomach with blood and fat to be cooked alongside the kangaroo in the pit. A Pitjantjatjara dish consists of an emu skin pulled carefully off the bird in one piece, stuffed with grass and feathers, skewered up and browned in the flames before being put in the ground with the prepared emu. The stuffing is, of course, discarded before serving.

For those with a backyard here are the instructions to build an oven of your own. Firstly, dig a long shallow hole in the ground slightly larger than the meat to be cooked. For a piece of beef or lamb weighing about 4.5 kg, or for 5 or 6 chickens, dig a hole about 10 cm deep, 30 cm wide and 45 cm long. Light a wood fire in the hole, avoiding woods that will give an unpleasant taste to the food. Place a number of stones in the fire to heat up or use pieces of ant-bed from which the ants have been removed.

After a couple of hours the fire should have died down and the stones should be red hot. Push half of the stones to one side, reserving them for later. Over the remaining hot stones place wet branches of eucalypt, bottle-brush, paperbark, tea-tree or other plants that will give the meat a pleasant flavour. Place the meat on the branches skin side down in one layer. If cooking poultry, split the birds down the back and place a hot stone inside. Put vegetables around the meat, such as potatoes, sweet potatoes, yams, onions and pieces of pumpkin. Place the reserved hot stones on top of the meat and cover these with more wet branches. Over everything lay a large sheet of paperbark or clean, soaked sacks, ensuring that there are no holes, otherwise the meat will get dirty. Lastly, shovel earth on top and pat this down. Add more earth if you see steam or smoke escaping.

A piece of beef 8 cm thick will cook in 1 hour. Chickens will take a little longer and a forequarter of lamb will take about 1½ hours. Allow 2 hours for a forequarter of pork. When the cooking time is up, carefully clear off the earth. Lift off the paperbark or sacks slowly and very carefully so that no dirt gets on the food. Serve immediately.

The Great Australian Baked Dinner

2 KG LAMB OR 1½ ROLLED RIB BEEF SERVES 6–8

If YOU ask an Australian what their favourite meal is, they would most likely reply a baked leg of lamb. Beef would come a close second. It is really more than just a meal but also an icon of traditional values, of families gathered together around Mum's good cooking in a ritual reaffirmation of familial bonds. The Australian baked dinner centres on the unsurpassed product of its pastoral industry, served with gravy and surrounded by potatoes, pumpkin and sweet taties, and other vegetables as desired. In America (minus the lamb) and in Britain (without pumpkin or sweet potatoes) this would be called a roast dinner; but true roasting, that is the rotation of meat in a dry atmosphere over an open fire to produce a joint with extra crisp skin, has never been a common practice in Australia's long and varied history. In my mother's and grandmothers' time the baked dinner was the norm for Sunday lunch and other special occasions and, though a less regular feature of the Australian diet nowadays, there are few meals which can surpass it.

1 leg or shoulder of lamb or
  1 rolled or standing beef rib roast
Freshly ground black pepper
Salt
Dripping or oil
Vegetables such as potatoes, pumpkin and
  sweet potatoes, onions, carrots, parsnips

GRAVY
1½ tablespoons plain flour
1½ cups water or stock
Mustard, fresh herbs or wine, optional

▪ Wipe the joint with damp absorbent paper and rub all over with pepper. Rub salt into the fatty skin. Place on a thickly greased baking dish and smear some dripping or oil over any parts of the joint unprotected by fat. Bake in the middle of a preheated oven at 200°C for 20 minutes and then reduce to 180°C for the remaining time. If the joint has little fat, baste it every half hour. Once the oven temperature has been reduced, allow 15–20 minutes per 500 g for rare meat, 30–35 minutes for well-done. To test, insert a skewer into the thickest part of the meat: the juices will be clear when well-done, redder when rare. Once cooked, place on a warm plate covered with foil and let rest for 15–20 minutes in a warm place.

▪ Meanwhile, peel the vegetables, leaving the pumpkin skin on if you prefer, and cut into large chunks. Boil the potatoes for 10 minutes and drain. Stir the potatoes vigorously in their pot to roughen up the surface. Place the vegetables around the joint of meat or, for crispy potatoes, in a separate dish with a few tablespoonfuls of dripping or oil. Make sure all are coated with fat and sprinkle over a little salt and pepper. Place on the shelf beneath the meat and bake for about 1½ hours, timing them to coincide with the serving of the meat. Turn half way through.

▪ While the joint is resting, make the gravy. Pour all the meat juices from the baking dish into a small bowl. Skim off the fat with a spoon and absorbent paper. Place 1 tablespoon of fat back in the baking dish. Put the dish over a moderate heat and stir in the flour with a wooden spoon, stirring until it turns a good nut brown but is not burnt. Gradually add the water or stock, the bowl of defatted juices and any juice that has collected under the joint as it rests, stirring well to produce a smooth liquid and scraping any residues from the pan. Add salt and pepper to taste and any flavouring ingredients you like, such as mustard, fresh herbs or a spoonful of wine. If the gravy is too thin, boil it to reduce; if too thick add a little more water.

▪ Pour the gravy into a warm gravy boat and serve with the joint, the drained baked vegetables and a boiled or steamed green vegetable as well if to your liking.

Kangaroo Tail, Aboriginal Style

SERVES 3–4

UNTIL the firm establishment of the pastoral industry in the mid 1800s kangaroo was the single most important meat in Australia. The status of men often depended on their ability to hunt kangaroo and initiation of Aboriginal boys required a successful spearing. The observance of laws laid down in the Dreamtime regarding hunting, cooking and sharing of the flesh ensured the assistance of ancestral spirits in the hunt and continued good fortune. The spear and woomera were the weapons of the hunt, carved or painted in ritual designs to enhance success, smeared with kangaroo blood, or sung. These are now often replaced by the rifle and bullet.

Hunting kangaroo involves consummate skill, powerful techniques of observation and tracking, knowledge of animal behaviour, as well as athleticism, strength and often endurance. The best times are early morning or late afternoon. Bushfires are lit to drive animals into an ambush, or groups of women, children and men beat them into nets or pits. One man may act as decoy, distracting attention from the hunters closing in from another side. Most often hunters work singly or in pairs, moving silently and communicating by a sophisticated sign language: once the kangaroo is located the hunter will circle downwind and then approach to within striking distance, using mimicry to reassure the creature if it becomes edgy. The mode of hunting which excites the greatest respect involves relentless pursuit, sleeping on the track at night and continuing the chase at first light, oblivious to hunger and thirst, until at the close of the second or perhaps third day the weary prey falls victim to its pursuer. Only a skilful hunter at the peak of manly vigour can perform this feat.

Once speared or shot a wounded animal is quickly despatched with a blow to the back of the neck. A small incision is made beneath the rib cage through which the intestines are removed, the gap then closed with a stick and piece of gut. Legs are dislocated, feet removed and fur singed off by fire before being scraped clean. Usually kangaroo is cooked whole in its hide in a ground oven for two hours or so. The offal is shared and then the hunter has the responsibility of carving the meat, apportioning cuts to all members of the clan according to their relationship, keeping for himself one of the smallest and least choice cuts. The dingoes, which may have helped in the hunt, are given the scraps and bones.

The tail is usually cooked beside the animal in the ground oven but may instead be grilled in its skin. Either way the meat is wonderfully tender and gelatinous—'real deadly'.

KANGAROO TAIL, ABORIGINAL STYLE

1 x 1 kg kangaroo tail
Oil

2–3 gum leaves or bay leaves

∎ Lay all the kangaroo tail joints together on a sheet of foil, lightly oiled, and put a couple of gum or bay leaves on top if you like. Wrap the foil around the joints and seal the edges. Bake in a preheated oven or covered barbecue at 180°C for 2 hours.

Mrs Davis's Kitchen

EVEN in the present day many Aboriginal cooks continue to employ kangaroo and other wild foods, often combining them in unorthodox ways with modern foodstuffs to produce new and exciting dishes. In *A Boy's Life* West Australian poet and playwright Jack Davis fondly recalls the kitchen of his mother back in the 1920s with its mixture of familiar dishes as well as unusual ones prepared from the bush tucker brought home by the family, including bush honey, wild berries and prickly pears, wild duck and pig, emu and kangaroo:

Although mother couldn't read or write, she was a wonderful cook. The traditional English dishes such as Yorkshire pudding and roast beef, and sometimes wild pig were a delight, and her home-made scones and bread won her many prizes at fetes and the like. Mother never worked off standard scales, but she had her own small and large containers which she marked off to her own scale for measuring ingredients.

She cooked in the old-fashioned wooden fuel stoves of the day. She could judge the heat required to practise her culinary art down to perfection …

When mother placed her huge cooking pot on the table, there would be cries of 'Good on yer mother' or 'Aw you little bewdy', especially when the dish was spaghetti and kangaroo meatballs, as on this occasion one could see the partly submerged meatballs in a sea of home-made tomato sauce. This time of the day was mother's moment, it was what she lived for, the appreciation of her culinary art and knowing that her brood could stuff themselves to the utmost.

Kangaroo Steaks 'Rosedale Station'

SERVES 4–6

MANY colonists depended on native foods while establishing themselves on the land and kangaroo was the most common native meat eaten. Recipes evolved to deal with the various cuts, the saddle, haunch, hind legs and tail being the most prized. Henry Melville in his book *Australasia and Prison Discipline*, published in 1851, recommended kangaroo as 'the most nutritious and most easily digested of any known to man.' He observes: 'The settlers, who do not like to give themselves much trouble, generally cut steaks off the hind quarters, and fry or broil them on the wood fires: they are excellent, cooked in this way, when seasoned with a bush appetite.' Many people on the land still enjoy kangaroo and this is how they cook steaks at Rosedale Station in Queensland. Recipe from the National Trust's *Cork Fork and Ladle*.

KANGAROO STEAKS 'ROSEDALE STATION'

700 g–1 kg kangaroo steak	2–3 tablespoons oil
1 cup red wine	1 tablespoon plain flour
3 cloves garlic, chopped	1 cup beef stock
Freshly ground black pepper	1 tablespoon finely chopped fresh parsley

▪ On Rosedale Station they use steaks cut from the leg although I prefer kangaroo loin for this recipe. Slice the steaks fairly thinly across the grain, about 1 cm thick. Place in a bowl and add the red wine, garlic and plenty of pepper. Marinate in the refrigerator for 12 hours, turning half-way through.

▪ Drain the steaks and pat dry with absorbent paper. Heat the oil in a large frying pan over a high heat, using the extra tablespoon of oil if you have the larger quantity of meat. Brown the steaks briefly on both sides and remove from the pan with a slotted spoon.

▪ Turn the heat to moderate, add the flour to the pan and stir it into the oil. Gradually stir in the stock, scraping the bottom of the pan well. Add the marinade and when the liquid is hot add the steaks and turn the heat to simmer. Cook slowly, gently bubbling away, for approximately 30–45 minutes till very tender and the sauce is reduced. Garnish the meat with the parsley just before serving.

Kangaroo Steamer

KANGAROO steamers were greatly prized by colonial cooks and gourmets and recipes for them recur regularly in old cookbooks. Henry Melville waxes eloquently upon the subject:

But of all the dishes ever brought to table, nothing equals that of the 'steamer'. It is made by mincing the flesh of the kangaroo, and with it some pieces of pork or bacon. The animal has not any fat, or scarcely any, in its best season; when the meat is chopped up, it is thrown into a saucepan and covered over with the lid, and left to stew or steam gently by the fire-side: it is, from this method of cooking, called 'steamer'. People generally put a spoonful of water in the pot when they place it on the fire; but this is unnecessary, as the flesh soon floats in its own rich gravy: it only requires pepper and salt to render it delicious. No one can tell what a steamer is, unless it has been tasted; it indeed affords an excellent repast.

Pan Jam or Old Timer's Hash

S E R V E S   4

AFTER the billy, the frying pan is the most useful instrument for the itinerant bushman. It comes into its own at breakfast when speed is essential but can also be used to cook meat, fish, vegetables, pancakes, fritters or fat cakes for dinner. An alternative to the standard frying pan with its long handle is the bushman's frypan, where the handle is arched high over the top in a loop which can be suspended above the fire.

The First Fleet was short on frypans but new arrivals quickly found that shovels made a good substitute and many a bushman since has followed their example. Two recent authors, Wessa and Lummo, giving instructions on how to cook a rabbit on a shovel, show a typically casual approach: 'Take your shovel and give it a few good wacks to remove any dirt, then if you're fussy wash it'. Another substitute used by bushmen who are not too fastidious is a sheet of roofing iron: left out in the scorching Australian sun it soon becomes hot enough to fry eggs without the bother of lighting a fire.

Some really delectable dishes can be got up in the frypan and one of the best is this old timer's hash of kangaroo tail collected by Edward Abbott.

1 kg kangaroo tail, jointed
250 g streaky bacon, diced
1 onion, finely chopped

250 g mushrooms, finely chopped
¼ cup finely chopped fresh parsley
Freshly ground black pepper

▪ Place the tail in a pot or large saucepan with enough water to cover. Simmer gently, covered, for about 2 hours until the meat is tender. Drain.
▪ Fry the bacon with the onion in a large frying pan over a moderate heat until the onion is soft. Stir in the mushrooms, parsley, pepper, and the joints of meat. Continue to cook for a few minutes until the mushrooms are done.

Camp-oven Cookery

ONE of the most widely used cookery utensils in colonial Australia was the camp oven, a circular flat-bottomed pot of blackened cast iron raised from the ground on three short legs. When most cooking was done over a fire the camp oven was the ideal appliance for damper, scones, cakes and baked dinners, and could also handle soups, stews, fries and puddings. Even now it is still popular with campers and stock workers. Bundjalung writer Dr Ruby Langford Ginibi in her autobiography *Don't Take Your Love to Town* describes a classic camp-oven delicacy, baked porcupine or spiny ant-eater:

Campfire cookery has always been an important part of Australian bush life; this engraving shows a gang of bushrangers cooking—and drinking—by the Nepean River.

Now to get the quills off this fella, you need a kero tin of boiling water and one tin of cold. You dunk it in the boiling water to loosen the quills, then in the cold. Hold it by the legs on a log, and use a tom-axe to knock the quills off. Cut it open from the neck to the belly. In the neck are two kernels, like gallstones, where the taste of the ants goes. Take these out or else when you cook it the meat will taste of ants. Gut and wash it. The flesh is pale, the colour of pork. You bake it in a camp oven and the skin cooks like a rind, like crackling …

I cut up potato and pumpkin and baked them beside the porcupine in the camp oven. I made the gravy. A baked dinner called for bush sweets, so I made a scone mixture and boiled doughboys. The porcupine was a feast and after we had the doughboys with Golden Syrup (cocky's joy) poured over them.

The camp oven must be looked after properly, packed carefully against breakages when travelling, and greased with a little fat after washing to prevent rust. To start cooking it is lifted onto a bed of hot coals using a set of camp-oven irons which attach to small handles either side. The same irons, like a pair of long rods terminating in a hook at the lower end and joined together at the other by a chain, manoeuvre the lid on and off. Most cooking is done with the lid on, covered with coals. This two-way heat is one of the big advantages of camp-oven cookery and the expert can manipulate the quantity of coals top and bottom to achieve the optimal temperature. The top coals give a richly coloured, browned finish to bush pies, mornays, bread, pastries, and so on, much the same effect as that sought by professional chefs using a salamander.

Bush Pot au Feu

SERVES 8

THIS recipe comes from Rosa Caroline Praed's *My Australian Girlhood* in which, from her perspective as a successful novelist living in England, she looks back at her youth in Queensland in the mid 1800s:

Have you ever tasted bush pot-au-feu? Here it is—an iron pot or a large billy slung on a forked stick over the camp fire, into which each stockman dips for his dinner. A lucky pot—a sort of fishpool from which you may land half a wild duck, a whole parrot or pigeon, a lump of kangaroo tail, a slice of salt junk as they call it—or a bit of pork through all, a miscellaneous flavouring of store salt, a pinch of pepper, a suspicion of the aromatic gum-bark or bitter leaf—for the pot should be stirred with a twig from some handy tree—maybe a bunch of wild parsley, and edible fungus—who knows what? The mess is very excellent, I assure you—when it has simmered long enough—better than the best French ragout you could get in some wayside cabaret in France, and that is saying a good deal.

Here is my version of this warming, invigorating winter dish. Wild duck may be substituted for the domesticated duck if you are fortunate enough to be able to obtain one, in which case omit the initial 30-minute roasting which renders the bird:

2 kg kangaroo tail, jointed	1 gum twig with about 5 leaves
4 litres water	1 x 1.8 kg duck
2 onions, stuck with 2 cloves each	750 g carrots
1 stick celery	500 g swedes
½ teaspoon black peppercorns	350 g mushrooms
3 teaspoons salt	2 tablespoons finely chopped fresh parsley

▪ Place the kangaroo tail in a large pot of about 11 litres capacity. Add the water, onions, celery, peppercorns, salt and gum twig. Bring to the boil over a moderate heat and skim the scum from the surface. Simmer gently, uncovered, for 1 hour.

▪ In the meantime, prepare the duck. Pull the excess fat from the duck and cut off the neck. The latter may be cooked in the pot to flavour the broth. Place the bird on a rack in a baking dish and prick all over with a skewer. Bake in a preheated oven at 260°C for 30 minutes, turning half-way through, until the fat beneath the skin has rendered. Remove from the oven and drain on absorbent paper. Add the duck to the pot and continue to simmer for 30 minutes. (Save the delectable duck fat for frying potatoes.)

▮ Peel the carrots and swedes and cut into pieces if necessary so that there is a piece for each person. Add to the pot with the mushrooms and cook for about 1 hour more until both meat and vegetables are very tender.

▮ With a slotted spoon lift out the onions, celery, gum twig and duck neck and discard. Remove the meats and vegetables to a covered dish and keep warm. Boil the broth rapidly over a high heat until reduced by a third. Add the parsley and adjust the seasonings if required. Serve the broth first, followed by the meat and vegetables presented on a platter; or serve bush style with meat, vegies and broth together in large soup bowls. Accompany with jacket potatoes and damper.

Kangaroo Kebabs

SERVES 4

THE great Aussie barbecue has its origins in Aboriginal cookery, in the game and fish grilled on hot coals or on grids of sticks suspended above the campfire. In colonial times an Australian pastime sufficiently distinctive to attract the notice of British commentators was the chop picnic: a meal of fried or grilled mutton chops or steaks eaten with potatoes boiled in the billy or roasted in the coals, washed down with billy tea. Such picnics when I was young were presided over by my father: sausages and tomato sauce accompanied the chops, big slices of buttered bread and salad vegies, cordial for us kids, all followed by tinned fruit and tinned cream—an invigorating meal held in a forest clearing, logs for seats, gums scenting the air, cicadas singing up the summer heat.

The word 'barbecue' to describe such outdoor cookery was rarely used in colonial times and seems to have gained acceptance only in the 1950s when the burgeoning suburbs, each bungalow set on its own quarter-acre block, offered ample opportunity for the erection of do-it-yourself brick or concrete barbecues topped with a steel hot plate or grill. The man of the house, released from the work place and the constraints of business suit and tie, took charge of the grilling in his shorts and thongs. It became a celebration of the great Australian weekend and, as with the Aborigines so with the denizens of the suburbs, a celebration of masculinity. The wife assisted with salads and sweets but 'he' took centre stage. Ice-cold beer from the esky replaced billy tea, outdoor furniture provided greater comfort than gum-tree logs, and gradually, with the 1970s, the food diversified into Greek salads, garlic bread, white wine, marinated meats and kebabs.

A colonial recipe for kebabs, a hunter's dish known to many bushmen, consisted of slices of lean kangaroo alternating with fat or bacon. One writer dubbed this the Australian 'kabaub', although it was called 'sticker-up' when the skewer was inserted vertically in the ground to allow the fat as it cooked to drip over and baste the meat.

---

700 g kangaroo loin *Oil*
4–5 rashers bacon *Freshly ground black pepper*

▪ Cut the kangaroo into 4 cm cubes. Remove the rind from the bacon and slice into 4 cm lengths. Thread kangaroo and bacon alternatively on skewers.
▪ Brush the kebabs and a grill lightly with oil. Preheat the griller or barbecue to a high heat and cook the kebabs for about 15 minutes, turning to cook on all sides. Grind black pepper liberally all over them before serving.

Lamb for Export

KANGAROO, the staple meat of Australians for at least sixty thousand years, ceded to sheep and cattle with the coming of the Europeans. Sheep were bred initially more for wool than meat since the fleece fetched high prices on the British market whereas the small colonial population could eat only a limited quantity of the mutton. The first corned mutton was shipped from New South Wales in 1830 and meat canning began in Sydney in 1847. However, it was only with the successful arrival in Britain of a cargo of frozen meat in 1880 that the problem of consuming all the mutton from the wool industry was solved and a way opened for expansion of cattle.

In the meantime, carcasses excess to consumption were disposed of by the boiling-down establishments which grew up in most grazing districts in the 1840s. Tallow so produced went to make soap and candles: casks of tallow were transported to England and the fleshy fibre fed to dogs or used as manure. The only parts of the carcass saved were the tongues, which were preserved for the domestic and export market, and the hind legs. Georgiana Huntly McCrae describes in her *Journal* the works established at Port Phillip by Edward Curr:

At this time, legs of mutton, denuded of fat, were to be had at the boiling-down works for 5s the dozen. Many sea-captains used them, salted, for victualling their ships, while not a few families bought legs for soups or cutlets.

Mutton Ham

2 KG LAMB SERVES 6–8

COLONIAL eating was quickly dubbed a 'muttonous diet'. Though poorer immigrants revelled in the unaccustomed luxury of meat, those from the well-to-do middle classes sometimes found cause for complaint, such as Edward Curr the Younger writing of the 1840s in *Recollections of Squatting in Victoria*: 'Around us was nothing but the same everlasting gum-trees basking in changeless sunshine, whilst the rarely-varied meal of tea, mutton, and damper made its appearance on the table three times a day with such dyspeptic regularity that I used to loathe the sight of it'. A meal of mutton and damper became known as the 'Old Thing' and housewives, possessing greater cookery skills than those of Curr's bachelor establishment, invented many tasty and varied ways of preparing it including corned mock hams. Your butcher will corn a leg for you with a couple of days notice.

1 corned leg of lamb or mutton
2 teaspoons mixed ground spice
6 cups self-raising flour, optional
2½ cups water, optional
1 tablespoon dripping or oil

1 tablespoon butter
½ cup fresh breadcrumbs
1 tablespoon brown sugar
Cloves

▪ Remove the shank bone from the end of the leg, keeping it for the soup pot, and weigh the leg. Soak it in water for 1 hour. Drain and pat dry. Rub the meat all over with mixed spice.

▪ To make the dough, place the flour in a large bowl and stir in the water with a knife. Turn out onto a floured board and knead lightly until smooth. Dust with flour and roll out about 1 cm thick. Place the leg in the middle and wrap up completely, wetting the edges to seal. Alternatively, wrap the leg well in foil.

▪ Grease a baking dish with the dripping or oil and put in the sealed lamb joint. Bake in a preheated oven at 180°C allowing 35–40 minutes per 500 g. The meat is cooked when a skewer inserted in the thickest part comes out easily. Remove from the oven and discard the dough or foil. Place the leg on a plate and clean any dough from it. Carefully peel off the skin.

- Melt the butter in a small saucepan over a moderate heat and toss the breadcrumbs in it until golden brown. Remove from the stove, let cool and then mix in the sugar. Carefully spoon over the top and sides of the lamb, pressing firmly on with the back of a spoon. Stick cloves over the top in a diamond pattern. Let cool or serve hot with a paper frill covering the end of the bone.

Colonial Goose

SERVES 6–8

THE histories of New Zealand and Australia resemble each other in many ways, both countries being colonised largely by British migrants with similar culinary backgrounds and agricultural practices. Travel between the two countries, trade in seafood, meats, cheeses, fruits and manufactured foodstuffs, and the exchange of cookery books and magazines have maintained the connection despite obvious differences in climate, native foods and indigenous cultures. Lamingtons are as widespread in New Zealand cake shops as our own, we share a common national dessert in the pavlova, and Anzac biscuits commemorate the bravery of our combined fighting forces. A common passion for baked lamb and barbecues prevails on both sides of the Tasman and in the colonial period both nations enjoyed dishes like colonial goose and colonial duck.

Generally the roast from the leg is called the goose and that done with the shoulder the duck, the main bones being replaced by a stuffing but the shank left intact to represent the head and neck of the bird. In the nineteenth century they were prepared as pot roasts, sometimes with finely chopped vegetables, wine or honey added for flavour, but by the twentieth century oven-baking took over. A truly magnificent way of serving a joint of mutton, hogget or lamb.

1 x 1½–2 kg leg of lamb	½ teaspoon dried sage
2 lamb's kidneys	¼ teaspoon dried thyme
3 rashers of bacon, diced	Freshly ground black pepper
1 onion, finely chopped	1 tablespoon dripping or oil
½ cup fresh breadcrumbs	

- With a sharp boning knife, tunnel bone the leg, leaving the skin intact. Or ask the butcher to do it. The shank should be cracked and folded back.
- To make the stuffing, soak the kidneys in a bowl of water for 30 minutes.

Remove any membrane, discard the fatty core and chop finely. Cook the bacon in a frying pan over a moderate heat for a few minutes until the fat becomes transparent. Stir in the chopped onion and cook until soft. Add the kidneys and continue to cook for a couple of minutes more until barely done. Make sure they don't toughen. Remove from the heat and combine with the breadcrumbs, sage, thyme and pepper in a bowl. Spoon the stuffing loosely into the cavity of the leg and tie up securely with string.

▮ Heat the dripping or oil in a large cooking pot or saucepan over a high heat and brown the goose all over. Lower the heat and cook gently, covered, for about 2 hours, turning half-way through. Alternatively, place the goose in a greased baking dish and cook in a preheated oven at 220°C, for 20 minutes. Reduce the temperature to 180°C and continue to cook until done to taste, allowing 20–30 minutes per 500 g once the temperature is reduced. Remove the meat to a warm plate and discard the string. Serve with gravy (page 79) if you wish.

Bush Pie

SERVES 4

IRISH immigrants played a major part in the development of Australia, coming both as free settlers and as convicts, starved out of their native land by potato famines, over-population and English landlords. At one time more than a third of white Australians were of Irish descent.

About half of the migrants were women, mostly poor and young, brought out on assisted passages to correct the imbalance between the sexes. Over ninety per cent were engaged in domestic service before marriage. They were frequently maligned by their usually Protestant, anti-Irish and class-conscious mistresses for laziness, dirtiness, incompetence and an inability to know their place; and yet many must have contributed greatly to the well-being of the household and the quality of the daily meals.

Some Irishmen were attracted to Australia by gold. Some worked as wage labourers, such as farm hands, fruit pickers and shearers, in order to earn enough to buy farms of their own and so achieve that equality and independence from authority which they so much desired. As farmers they were adaptable, taking up small acreages in the more fertile areas of Victoria and growing potatoes and other intensive crops for the Melbourne market, whereas in the drier states they undertook large-scale sheep and wheat farming. Many Irish became hoteliers, attracted to the congenial and at times rough-and-tumble atmosphere of the pub. They needed little capital since the early hotels were often no more than huts and all the family could help out.

One contribution of the Irish to our cooking was the camp oven, thought to have derived from the three-legged cauldrons used in Ireland since the Stone Age. Also, the comic naming of many bushmen's dishes may well have come from the Irish sense of humour, known for its irreverence and larrikinism. Most importantly they brought with them a certain no-nonsense approach to eating and cooking, including the predilection for meat and potatoes which lives on in the present day. These are the dominant ingredients in Irish stew, one of the few Hibernian dishes cooked in Australia. The Irish, inspired no doubt by their soda breads, were partly responsible for the adaptation of damper to wheaten flour, and both damper and Irish stew combine together to form bush pie, an outback classic.

2 large onions, sliced

1½ tablespoons butter or dripping

1 kg lamb neck or scrag chops, trimmed of fat

3 potatoes, peeled and diced

2 carrots, sliced

2 tablespoons finely chopped parsley

1 teaspoon mixed dried herbs or 1 tablespoon
  fresh chopped herbs

2 teaspoons salt

1 teaspoon white pepper

2 cups water

DAMPER CRUST

1⅓ cups self-raising flour

2 teaspoons sugar

¼ teaspoon salt

1 tablespoon butter or dripping, chilled and
  diced

½ cup milk

▮ In a frying pan sauté the onions in the butter or dripping over a moderate heat until soft. Place in a casserole dish with the lamb chops, potatoes, carrots, herbs and seasonings. Pour in the water, cover and bake in a preheated oven at 180°C until nearly cooked, about 1¼ hours.

▮ Meanwhile prepare the damper crust. Sift the flour and salt into a mixing bowl and stir in the sugar. Rub in the butter or dripping with fingers until the mixture resembles breadcrumbs. Stir in the milk with a knife. On a lightly floured board knead the dough very briefly. Pat out to form a circle large enough to cover the contents of the casserole. Skim any fat from the surface of the stew with a spoon and absorbent paper. Place the dough loosely on top of the meat and continue to bake in the oven, uncovered, for a further 20–30 minutes until the dough is risen and lightly browned.

Lamb and Sweet Potato Casserole

SERVES 4

SWEET potatoes were grown from earliest colonial times, thriving in conditions too hot for the ordinary potato. They were the staple of South Sea Islanders labouring in the cane fields and a major food of Torres Strait people. The Queensland Department of Agriculture stocked about thirty different kinds, of various shapes, colours and sizes, to supply farmers and home gardeners; while on Norfolk Island a kilo of sweet potatoes formed the largest single item in the daily diet of the convicts, followed by 750 g cornmeal, 500 g corned meat and 300 g sugar. In *A Narrative of a Visit to the Australian Colonies* Quaker missionary James Backhouse described the situation in 1835:

The more orderly prisoners are allowed to cultivate small portions of ground as gardens. They grow chiefly the Sweet Potato, Batatas edulis, *a plant of the Convolvulus tribe, producing large, tuberous roots, which are excellent for food, either roasted, boiled, or fried in slices. When prepared by frying, this root resembles sweetish cake, and sometimes supplies the place of toast at breakfast.*

Sweet potatoes are part of Australia's great debt to Latin America, a region of the world which has contributed almost nothing to our style of cookery but an enormous amount by way of raw materials. From *The Courier-Mail 100 Prize Winning Recipes*.

---

3 cooking apples
350 g sweet potatoes, peeled and boiled or steamed
¼ cup brown sugar

1 teaspoon salt
Freshly ground black pepper
1 kg lamb forequarter or best neck chops
1 tablespoon tomato sauce

▪ Peel, core and dice the apples and dice the sweet potatoes. Place alternate layers in a casserole dish and sprinkle with brown sugar, salt and pepper. Trim the fat from the chops and spread them thinly with tomato sauce. Arrange on the bed of apple and potato.

▪ Bake, covered, in a preheated oven at 180°C for 1½ hours. Remove the lid and cook for another 15 minutes to brown the chops lightly.

Slippery Bob

SERVES 6

THIS old timer's dish of brain croquettes comes from Edward Abbott the Younger who wrote Australia's first cookbook, *The English and Australian Cookery Book: COOKERY for the Many, as well as for the 'Upper Ten Thousand'*, published in 1864 when its author was in his sixties. Abbott was born in New South Wales, as a youth moving with his family to Tasmania and in time becoming a pastoralist and member of the state legislature.

Writing under the pseudonym of the 'Aristologist', meaning a student of the art of dining, Abbott presents a mixture of recipe and anecdote, with contributions from local acquaintances and quotations from gastronomic writers of the day. It is an entertaining collection and gives an admirable portrait of the Tasmanian gourmet which belies the criticisms of some commentators who would have us believe that all Australians at the time lived on a constant diet of damper and fried salt meat. As a gourmet he was appreciative of culinary refinement and so gives notes on herbs, and provides sauces and stuffings along with his meat dishes. He recommends champagne to start a banquet and wines for every course, followed by liqueurs and coffee, giving recipes for colonial grape wine and a fruit liqueur called tasmanette.

Most of Abbott's recipes are British or French but he also shows a surprisingly cosmopolitan outlook, including exotic dishes such as Spanish 'gaspacho', Portugese roast pork, German 'sour-krout', Dutch beef, 'zranzy' and 'naleskikes' from Poland, many Jewish recipes, Turkish 'kebobs', Brazilian stew, Indian chutney, New England chowder, 'pone' cake, Mississippi and West India punch. He was obviously mindful of the cookery of his native land since he offers culinary notes on local fish and a number of local recipes, mostly for game meats like kangaroo. The following is one of his kangaroo recipes which I have adapted to lambs' brains with excellent results.

---

6 lambs' brains (about 600 g)	½ teaspoon salt
2 onions, finely chopped	White pepper
2 tablespoons finely chopped fresh parsley	⅔ cup milk
1 cup self-raising flour	Oil or dripping for deep frying

▪ Soak the brains in cold water for 30 minutes. Remove the membranes if the brains have not been frozen. Drain and chop into small pieces. In a bowl mix with the onions and parsley. Sift the flour into a second bowl with the salt and pepper. Gradually beat in the milk to make a smooth batter. Stir in the brains and onions.

▮ Fill a saucepan ⅓ full of oil and place over a moderate to high heat. Heat the oil to about 190°C or until a cube of bread turns golden brown in 1 minute. Drop tablespoonfuls of the brain mixture into the hot oil and deep fry for a few minutes until golden brown and cooked through. Drain on absorbent paper and serve immediately.

Killing Days

KILLING days on colonial stations were important events, particularly for the cook whose job it was to deal with the sudden influx of fresh meat. Mina Rawson describes the atmosphere at such times:

> ... *I must say there was very great pleasure and some excitement in it. Killing is usually done in the afternoon, towards 4 or 5 o'clock, and invariably that evening's meal consists of liver and bacon, with usually the sweetbread also fried ...*
>
> *The brains make a nice breakfast dish for next morning ... There is always steak for breakfast as well, and being so fresh it is usually rather tough.*

The offal was eaten first since it would deteriorate quickly in the heat. The late time of day was chosen to avoid the clouds of flies that would otherwise descend to feast upon the carcass. Aboriginal butchers did not have the luxury of choosing their hour, not knowing when the hunt would be successful, and so would place some unwanted offal at a distance from the camp as a lure to keep the flies away, and this is still a common practice today.

The colonial cook had many inventive ways of dealing with the 'killings' as the offal was called. The head was transformed into exquisite brawn, the feet were made into jelly, a very useful article before the invention of powdered gelatine, the tripe was stewed or occasionally fried, but the most sought after were the liver, brains, kidneys, tongue and sweetbreads. Lamb's fry and bacon is a deservedly popular dish in Australia even today.

Mutton Duck

SERVES 4

THE Australian custom of a baked dinner on Sunday necessarily produced a lot of left-over meat. In summer this was often served up cold with salad and a home-made pickle or chutney for Monday night's tea, that day being devoted to washing with little time for cookery. In winter, recipes for leftovers provided good, warming dishes and yet using up cold meat, like stale bread, remained a major problem, as Harriet Wicken enunciated in 1890:

The cold meat question is always a difficult one with housekeepers. Nearly every one likes a slice from a joint, but, alas, very few care to see it a second time. Unless the family is large, the question of what shall I do with the cold meat haunts the housekeeper like a nightmare.

Most old cookery books give a few recipes although Jean Rutledge in *The Goulburn Cookery Book* has a whole section 'What to Do with Cold Meat' listing thirty-three recipes, not to mention others scattered through the rest of her book. These include fairly basic approaches like croquettes and rissoles, curries and hashes, potato and macaroni pies. Fancier options were tomatoes stuffed with cold meat bound with mayonnaise, and kromeskies, an elegant version of the croquette.

The following recipe from Mina Rawson is a particularly good way of using up leftover meat, rather like a thick-baked omelette, flavoured with onion and sage and interleaved with slices of mutton or lamb.

2 tablespoons butter
1 large onion, finely chopped
1 cup fresh breadcrumbs
1 teaspoon dried sage
½ teaspoon salt
Freshly ground black pepper

350 g cold cooked mutton or lamb, sliced and trimmed of fat
2 eggs
⅔ cup milk
2 teaspoons extra butter

▪ Melt the butter in a frying pan over moderate heat and sauté the onion until soft. Remove from the heat; stir in breadcrumbs, sage, salt and pepper.
▪ Grease an oven-proof dish and put in a layer of meat. Spoon over some of the seasoned breadcrumbs. Repeat the layers until all the ingredients are used up, finishing with breadcrumbs. Beat the eggs and milk together in a small bowl. Pour the egg-milk mixture into the dish. Dot with the extra butter.
▪ Bake in a preheated oven at 215°C for about 30 minutes until the eggs are set and the top is golden brown.

Kimberley Mutton

GOATS came to Australia with First Fleet and were important in the early years of settlement when there was a dire shortage of cows. Godfrey Charles

Mundy in *Our Antipodes* describes the situation in Sydney in the 1850s:

That picturesque animal, the goat, by-the-by, forms a conspicuous item of the Sydney street menagerie—amounting to a pest little less dire than the plague of dogs. Nearly every cottage has its goat or family of goats. They ramble about the highways and by-ways, picking up a haphazard livelihood during the day; and going home willingly or compulsorily in the evening to be milked.

Woe betide the suburban garden whose gate is left for a moment unclosed.

Goats were valued chiefly for their milk, particularly by families with young children. As the dairy industry became established they were gradually replaced, except in the outback where they could thrive on fodder too poor for dairy cows, and in the tropics where they had a superior heat tolerance.

In cattle country the meat was of value in providing variety to the diet of beef and was often disguised under the title of Kimberley mutton. In the Kimberleys the closest thing to sheep were the flocks of milk goats and their wild relatives which inhabited the hills. The best places to buy goat meat in the cities are Turkish, Lebanese and Italian butcheries.

Bush Pot

SERVES 4

IN THE old days bush butchers were often characters and many stories remain of their peculiarities. The most notorious in colonial times was the 'Butcher Baronet', a man operating from a hut in Wagga Wagga under the name of Tom Castro. He proclaimed himself Sir Roger Tichborne, who had been lost at sea in 1853, and set off to England where he persuaded many people, including Sir Roger's mother, that he was the long-lost heir to the Tichborne estates. In 1873 he was jailed for forgery and perjury.

Some of the bush butchers were itinerants, operating travelling meat waggons covered in a bed of gum leaves to keep the meat fresh. Bush housewife and airline hostess Henriette Pearce, recounting in *Two at Daly Waters* her life in the Northern Territory in the decades leading up to World War II, gives us a vivid portrait of Bill the Butcher, otherwise known as 'Take it or leave it'. The first customers on his sixteen-kilometre route had a choice of cuts but by the time he arrived at her household 'it was well not to have set one's heart on any kind of beef in particular'. One hot Christmas Day he was doing the rounds, letting his clients select their meat and sharing a Christmas drink with all of them afterwards. Having stopped at twenty camps he arrived at his last stop, very late, completely sozzled, and with only some soup bones remaining. The two old miners, who had been waiting for hours in expectation of a nice little joint, were indignant:

'Take it or leave it', said Bill the Butcher, turning to go.
  'We'll take you and leave you, too', roared the miners, and with that they seized him from behind and threw him on to a ten-foot pile of sawdust and left him there.

The following tasty dish of stewed beef and cabbage is what those old timers might have cooked up had they had a more reliable provedore.

2 tablespoons oil or dripping	¾ teaspoon thyme
1 kg chuck steak, diced	1 bay leaf
1 tablespoon water	750 g cabbage, shredded
1 teaspoon salt	125 g bacon, finely chopped
Freshly ground black pepper	

▪ Heat the fat in a pan over a high heat and brown the steak. Lower the heat, stir in water, salt, pepper and herbs and simmer gently, covered, for 1 hour.
▪ Give the beef a good stir and place a layer of cabbage on top without stirring in. Sprinkle with bacon and some pepper. Repeat the layers of cabbage and bacon, finishing with the bacon. Raise the heat under the pan to moderate and cook, uncovered, for about 10 minutes until the cabbage is steaming nicely. Lower the heat and continue for about 20 minutes till done.

Parramatta in the 1920s

WHEN Australians ate more meat than now there were a lot more butcher shops. Rosslyn Blay, in *A Living History of Parramatta*, recalls those of her youth in the 1920s and '30s:

A retired butcher told me recently that from Granville through Parramatta once had thirty five butcher shops. I can remember Mr Metcalfe on the Rivoli Hill, Tuckers, Vidlers, Carsons, Watsons, Rogers, Munros, Picketts and two Finlayson shops run by different families all situated along Church Street. Many had sawdust on the floor, ceiling fans, animal carcases hanging around on hooks and water cascading down the windows where the meat was displayed and decorated with sprays of fresh bracken fern.
  When I was a child we had moved to Harris Street, Harris Park. We did not boast an ice chest (refrigerators being unknown), so each afternoon after school I would

go around to Mr Cook's butcher shop in Marion Street for the meat for the evening meal. It was in the pan and cooked within an hour or so of leaving the shop.

Carpet Bag Steak

Serves 1

As CHOPS are the daily staple of lamb cookery so steaks are the principal cut of beef, quickly turned into a satisfying meal by the housewife or bushman. On the wallaby and out of work in Victoria in May 1871, poet and one-time farmer Joseph Jenkins describes his al fresco cooking arrangements in *Diary of a Welsh Swagman*:

I was frying a meal of mutton chops and potatoes, and went some thirty yards' distance to collect some watercress. On my return I found that nine pigs had consumed all. The pigs were owned by the local butcher, and fortunately he had witnessed the hogs feasting at the swagman's table, so he invited me into his shop and presented me with a liberal consignment of meat ... Presently I sit on a log enjoying a meal of beef steak and potatoes. Neither the Queen of England, nor the Pope in Rome, have partaken of a better repast.

For many Australian men no dinner excells a steak simply grilled. It is at its best served as a carpet bag crammed with Sydney rock oysters; this meal can be enjoyed in any good steakhouse in the country and has been on the national menu for at least a century.

1 fillet of rump or sirloin steak,
    cut 3.5 cm thick
6 oysters
Freshly ground black pepper

2 teaspoons butter, cut into dice
Canola, macadamia or olive oil
Salt

▮ With a sharp knife cut a pocket in the side of the steak about 5 cm long. Season the oysters with a little pepper and place in the pocket with 1 teaspoon of the butter. Secure the pocket opening with a short skewer or toothpicks.
▮ Brush the steak with oil and season with more pepper. Cook under a preheated hot grill or on a barbecue grill for about 5 minutes each side until medium rare. Remove the skewer, sprinkle with a little salt and top with the remaining butter. Serve immediately.

Butchers in Gold-rush Days

IN THE 1850s Australia was in the grip of gold fever with the initial finds near Bathurst, New South Wales, followed soon after by discoveries throughout Victoria. Thousands of people from all walks of life threw up their jobs and headed to the fields in hope of fortune. Noted botanical artist Ellis Rowan, in *A Flower-Hunter in Queensland and New Zealand*, describes the north Queensland gold town of Muldiva, newly established at the time of her visit in the early 1890s:

The general store is a tent on forked sticks with a wall of branches on all sides, the proprietor's name is written in huge letters upon it, and a counter with glasses and array of tins proclaim his calling.

Next comes a real bush bark hut, of which many are studded about in every direction, then another tent, a bakehouse, one or two more stores, and two shelters that call themselves hotels. A man sits under an awning in the principal street (which is still full of felled trees and stumps) with the air of an Indian potentate, guarding a keg of beer, tumblers, matches, tobacco, pipes, etc … The butcher's shop is a green arbour of boughs.

These open-air butcheries were the norm and must have had questionable hygiene standards. Ellen Clacy describes one in Victoria in *A Lady's Visit to the Gold Diggings of Australia in 1852–53*:

We passed a butcher's shop, or rather tent, which formed a curious spectacle. The animals, cut into halves or quarters, were hung round; no small joints there—half a sheep or none; heads, feet, and skins were lying about for any one to have for the trouble of picking up, and a quantity of goods of all sorts and sizes, grid-irons, saucepans, cradles, empty tea-chests, were lying scattered around in all directions ticketed 'for sale'. We quickly went on, for it was not a particularly pleasant sight.

Despite the initial privations of goldfields life, made worse by the inflated price of commodities, money was quickly earned and freely spent on the luxuries available at the good hotels and eateries that soon sprung up. A common practice for the fortunate was to host banquets on behalf of their fellow miners. At one dinner tinned oysters, cold roast sucking pig, bread and cheese, rum and bottled beer formed the menu. The farewell banquet of 'Lucky' Johnson at Beechworth had, amongst other items, plates piled with sandwiches, the fillings of which were one-pound notes!

Beef and Cashews

APART from the market garden the main contribution of Chinese immigrants to Australian food was the Chinese restaurant. These sprang up in the Chinatowns of Melbourne, Sydney, Brisbane and Bendigo but also proliferated out into the suburbs. The dominant style was Cantonese, denoting the origins of most of our Chinese citizens, but also a style which adapted well to the local palate with its emphasis on sweet dishes like honey prawns and sweet and sour fish, the combinations of meats with fruit so beloved by Australians such as pineapple or lychee duck, lemon or orange chicken and pork in plum sauce, as well as the various seafood dishes. Even quite conservative Aussies took to the diet easily and a night out at the suburban Chinese with its red flock wallpaper, dragon lanterns and other geegaws became a regular weekly event for many and often their sole encounter with exotic cookery before the opening of Italian, Greek and other ethnic eateries in the 1960s. Some of the dishes became Australianised, particularly in the suburbs, with a predominance of familiar vegetables like carrots, celery, onions and peas, few vegetarian dishes, and far more beef than one would ever see in China. Beef and cashews is a typical adaptation.

500 g rump steak
1 egg white
1 tablespoon cornflour
1 teaspoon finely grated fresh ginger
1 teaspoon soy sauce
½ teaspoon sesame oil
¼ teaspoon sugar
Oil for deep frying

SAUCE
1 tablespoon cornflour
¾ cup water
1 tablespoon oyster sauce

1 teaspoon soy sauce
1 teaspoon sherry
¼ teaspoon salt
Freshly ground black pepper

VEGETABLES
1 onion, halved and sliced lengthways
2 cloves garlic, crushed
2 sticks celery, sliced diagonally
2 lightly boiled carrots, sliced diagonally
½ cup cooked peas
¾ cup roasted cashews

▪ Slice the beef thinly into short strips and place in a bowl with the egg white, cornflour, ginger, soy, sesame oil and sugar. Mix altogether and leave to marinate at least 30 minutes.

▪ To prepare the sauce, blend the cornflour gradually with the water in a small bowl and mix with the remaining sauce ingredients.

▪ Heat a wok or large frying pan over a high heat. Pour in enough oil for deep frying and when the oil is hot add the steak gradually so that the pieces remain separate. Stir-fry very briefly until barely cooked and still tender, about 2–3 minutes. Drain on absorbent paper.

▪ Pour off most of the oil, leaving about 1 tablespoon. Turn the heat to moderate. Stir-fry the onion and garlic for 1 minute. Stir the sauce and add to the pan with the celery. Stir until it comes to the boil and the onion and celery are barely cooked. Add the carrots, peas and beef and heat through quickly, while continuing to stir-fry. Stir in the cashews and serve immediately.

Harriet Wicken's Kingswood Pie

SERVES 6

HARRIET Wicken was professionally educated at the National Training School for Cookery in London where she gained a first class diploma. She taught in London and there published her first cookbook, a slim volume of standard British dishes of the day, before migrating to Melbourne to teach. Soon after, she became head of the Department of Domestic Economy at Sydney Technical College from 1889 to 1896, at the same time giving specialist courses on invalid cookery to nurses, before moving on to Perth and finally returning to New South Wales, to East Sydney Technical College, where she taught into the second decade of the new century.

Over a span of twenty-six years Mrs Wicken published a total of seven cookbooks, a handbook on domestic economy, and also contributed the recipe section to a book on nutrition by Dr. Philip Muskett, surgeon at Sydney Hospital. Not only was she the most prolific gastronomic writer of the colonial period but her books are notable for their clarity and consistency, as well as for the reliability and general excellence of the recipes. Her recipes bear a decidedly modern aspect with precise lists of ingredients, precise quantities and a logical and easily understandable method.

Harriet Wicken was obviously vitally interested in the cuisine of her 'adopted and well loved country' since she included numerous Australian recipes. Some of these, like Lady Carrington pudding, were probably of her own invention; others such as Mittagong dumpling and Adelaide sausage, were collected from fellow Australian cooks. In contrast to Mina Rawson she was a city cook, ignorant of the Aboriginal culinary heritage, and with the exception of seafood oblivious to native foods, only rarely including a bush recipe such as damper or bushman's pudding. However, she embraced the fish and tropical fruits of her new home as well as the pumpkins, chokoes, sweet corn, tomatoes and eggplant which its warm climate yielded. She was deeply concerned with aspects of nutrition, publishing four books dealing primarily with fish, fruit and vegetables. In addition, she was responsive to the needs of the day, writing *Useful Recipes*, a book of economical and practical dishes, in the depths of the 1890s recession.

The following recipe comes from *The Kingswood Cookery Book*, the Australian editions of which represent the peak of her culinary writing. It makes a particularly sumptuous meat pie, enriched with lambs' kidneys, oysters and eggs.

HARRIET WICKEN'S KINGSWOOD PIE

4 lambs' kidneys

1 kg rump or chuck steak, cut into bite-size
   pieces

1½ tablespoons plain flour

2 tablespoons dripping or oil

3 spring onions, sliced

1 cup beef stock

2 pickled walnuts, finely chopped, optional

¼ teaspoon salt

Freshly ground black pepper

2 dozen (or 1 bottle) oysters, drained

2 hard-boiled eggs, sliced

225 g puff pastry, chilled or 2 sheets frozen
   and defrosted puff pastry, chilled

1 egg yolk

▪ Soak the kidneys in water for 30 minutes. Remove any membranes, slice in half lengthwise and discard the fatty core. Chop them finely and set aside.

▪ Dredge the steak with the flour. Heat the fat in a saucepan over a high heat and brown the meat in batches. Before returning the meat add the spring onions, reduce the heat and cook for a couple of minutes. Stir in the meat, stock, pickled walnuts, salt and pepper, and the chopped kidneys. Bring to the boil and simmer gently, covered, for 1¼ hours. Remove from the heat and let cool. When cold, place the stew in a pie dish or oven-proof dish and scatter over the oysters and sliced eggs.

▪ On a lightly floured board, roll out the pastry. Cut out a shape large enough to cover the dish. Brush the rim of the dish with a little egg yolk. Fit the pastry over the dish, pressing it firmly onto the rim, and crimp the edge between your thumb and forefinger. Decorate the pie with pastry leaves or shapes cut from the scraps and cut some slits in the crust. Thin the remaining yolk with a spoonful of water and brush over the pastry to glaze.

▪ Bake in a preheated oven at 230°C for 15 minutes. Lower the temperature to 190°C and continue to cook for another 20 minutes until a nice golden brown.

Ayers Rock Oysters

SERVES 6

MANY bush recipes have colourful bush names which reflect the dry Australian sense of humour in the face of a monotony of certain foodstuffs, while expressing an irreverent affection for those same foods. Now that we have realised that Australia's history and culture is far older and at least as meaningful as the centres of knowledge in Europe and the Middle East I am tempted to rename this dish. Uluru oysters, though, misses the bush joke, the play on words with Sydney rock oysters, and so I shall let the colonial designation stand. They make a good breakfast dish served with bacon and grilled tomatoes, rather like meaty, savoury pikelets.

2 cups self-raising flour
1 teaspoon salt
Pinch white pepper
1 egg
1 tablespoon tomato sauce
1½ cups milk

1 cup chopped roast beef
1 small onion, finely chopped
1 rasher bacon, cooked until crisp and finely chopped
Dripping or oil for shallow frying

▪ Sift the flour with the salt and pepper into a large bowl. In a separate bowl whisk the egg and beat in the tomato sauce and milk. Slowly beat the liquid into the flour until smoothly combined. Mix in the beef, onion and bacon.
▪ Place a tablespoon of dripping or oil in a frying pan and set over a moderate heat. When hot, put large spoonfuls of the mixture into the fat and cook until golden on both sides. Fry the oysters in batches, being careful not to overcrowd the pan. Drain on absorbent paper.

Camp Pie

SERVES 6

FROM the late colonial period many Australians in the bush depended on tinned food for their supplies. For Harriet Daly, living at the Darwin Residency in the 1870s, tinned meat was the staple of diet, as she relates in *Digging, Squatting and Pioneering Life*:

'Blanket', 'blanket', or, as a friend of mine terms it, 'iron-clad food', without

intermission, from one month's end to the other. Cookery books were studied, and every recipe that Soyer could suggest or Mrs Beeton advise was tried, but in vain, to disguise this much abused article of food. Curry, hash, mince, and stew, were the forms it appeared in at table, and many were the maledictions heaped upon it till the entrance of the sweets turned one's thoughts in another direction.

Camp pie has been around for many decades, the favourite of the tinned meats. The home-made version is, of course, far superior, a delicious jellied meatloaf, steamed in the billy.

CAMP PIE

750 g lean beef	*Freshly ground black pepper*
250 g bacon	*½ teaspoon dry mustard*
1 egg	*½ teaspoon grated grated nutmeg*
1 tablespoon gelatine	*¼ teaspoon ground allspice*
¼ teaspoon salt	*¼ teaspoon ground cloves*

▪ Put the beef and bacon through the finest blade of a mincer or mince in a food processor. Place in a bowl and using your hand, mix thoroughly with all the remaining ingredients.

▪ Grease a billy or large can. (If all else fails, a soufflé dish or pudding basin may be used.) Pack the meat in and replace the lid (or cover with two thicknesses of foil, tied with string). Place in a large saucepan of simmering water, cover and steam for 2½ hours. The water should come one to two thirds up the billy, check the level occasionally.

▪ Remove the billy from the saucepan of water. To press the meat, place a saucer on the meat and a weight on top of the plate. Refrigerate until completely cold. Run a knife around the edge of the billy, dip the base in hot water to loosen the meat and turn out onto a plate.

Bush Rissoles

SERVES 3 – 4

'THE great art of bush-cookery,' writes Caroline Chisholm, 'consists in giving a variety out of salt beef and flour'. Unlike Aboriginal people, who traditionally slaughter meat as required and cook it soon after, most colonial stations had a killing day once a month, some only every three months. Of the various pre-refrigeration treatments available for preserving meat Australians favoured the British method of soaking meat in brine, although sometimes drying was necessary as well. Evelyn Maunsell describes the practice in *S'pose I Die*, the record of her life in the Gulf Country managing a cattle station with her husband early in the twentieth century:

Fresh meat would not keep for more than a day in that tropical climate, so all the beef that could not be cooked and eaten at once had to be salted. It was laid out in the fly-proof meat house on a bench raised at one end, coarse salt was rubbed into it, and the brine allowed to drain into a hogshead cask under the lower end of the bench. When the salting was complete, the meat was stored in the brine for use as needed.

Before it could be carried in the musterers' pack-bags, the salt meat had to be dried by being laid out on a sheet of iron and turned constantly. Then it was smoked by being hung in the closed kitchen all night. A big log would be put in the firebox, the covers taken off the top of the stove, and by morning the whole kitchen would be as hot as an oven, and the meat smoked as hard as a board. In the sultry summer months, or when there was nobody to look after it, the meat would not keep in the brine and all of it had to be smoked.

A kero tin often replaced the wooden cask, and saltpetre (potassium nitrate) prevented discolouration of the meat. Cloves, mace, bay leaves and brown sugar were often added for flavour, with peppercorns giving it the designation 'corned', although in colonial Australia it frequently went by the name of salt junk. Soaking in fresh water helped reduce the saltiness, and beating with a rolling pin or mallet softened old dry meat before cooking.

Bush cooks had a strong motivation to invent novel ways of dealing with the daily corned beef ration and both of the recipes given here are from the bush. Many of these dishes are really good tucker and bush rissoles are a particular favourite of mine.

---

250 g cooked corned beef
1 onion
Freshly ground black pepper

⅔ cup water
1 cup self-raising flour
Dripping or oil for shallow frying

▪ Finely chop the meat and onion and mix together with the pepper in a bowl. Stir in the water. Sift the flour over the meat and stir until thoroughly combined.
▪ Pour dripping or oil in a frypan 1 cm deep. Place over a moderate heat and drop heaped tablespoonfuls of the mixture in. Fry for about 8 minutes each side until well browned and crispy. Cook in batches rather than overcrowd

By the mid 1840s, German farmers in the Barossa Valley had established a prosperous but simple self-sufficiency with salted pork and a whole range of cured meats and sausages, an important part of the diet.

the pan. Turn only the once for crispiest results. Drain on absorbent paper and serve hot.

Station Jack

SERVES 6–8

THIS recipe comes from *Bush Cookery,* Australia's first cookery publication, written probably in the early 1840s by Caroline Chisholm, the great pioneer social worker and 'immigrant's friend'. Consisting of seven corned beef recipes as well as general advice on coping with the daily meat and flour ration, in 1852 it was included in a book for migrants by one of Mrs Chisholm's supporters Eneas MacKenzie.

The recipes, composed in the terse but still intelligible style of her era, were arranged day by day: for Monday, the Queen's nightcap (a savoury pancake); for Tuesday, trout dumpling (rissoles); Wednesday, stewed goose (a boiled bush pie); on Thursday, boiled corned beef and sinkers, or dumplings; on Friday, corned beef pudding for Protestants or fish for Catholics; Saturday, corned beef à la mode; and finally Sunday's recommendation was Station Jack. Comprising mainly original Australian recipes which she had collected from bush people, it was a small yet auspicious beginning to the long line of cookery publications in this country.

Sunday's dinner is a magnificent meat pudding consisting of a piece of corned beef simmered until tender and then clothed in a jacket of damper dough. In colonial days meat puddings were an important feature of bush cooking, and corned meat and bread formed the foundation on which the great outback stations ran.

1.5 kg corned silverside
1 onion
1 carrot
2 sprigs parsley
2 tablespoons brown sugar
1 tablespoon vinegar

DOUGH
4½ cups self-raising flour
1½ tablespoons sugar
1 egg

1½ cups milk
1 teaspoon cloves, optional

ONION SAUCE
60 g butter
350 g onions, finely chopped
¼ cup plain flour
2 cups milk
⅓ teaspoon salt
¼ teaspoon white pepper

■ Trim any fat from the beef and put in a large pot or saucepan with the onion, carrot, parsley, sugar and vinegar. Add enough cold water to cover and bring to the boil over a moderate heat. Simmer gently, covered, for about 1½ hours until done (a skewer inserted into the thickest part of the meat should come out easily). Leave in the hot broth while you prepare the dough.

■ Sift the flour into a large mixing bowl and mix in the sugar. In a separate bowl beat the egg with the milk and gradually stir into the flour with the blade of a knife. Turn the dough out onto a floured board and knead very lightly. Pat the dough out with the heel of the hand to a size large enough to enclose the beef.

■ Remove the meat from the pot, pat dry and place in the middle of the dough. Gather the dough around the meat to completely cover it. Moisten the edges and press together to join, smoothing over them with a wet finger. Stud the surface with cloves. Wring out a large pudding cloth of calico or cotton sheeting in water and sprinkle with flour. Place the Jack on the cloth and wrap up loosely like a parcel. Allow enough slack inside the cloth for the dough to expand while it cooks. Tie up with string, again allowing some slack for expansion. Place a small plate or saucer on the bottom of the pot in which the meat was cooked to stop the pudding from sticking. Lower the Jack into the pot, using the old cooking liquid, and simmer, covered, for about 40 minutes until the dough has swollen up.

∎ While the Jack is cooking, prepare the sauce. Melt the butter in a saucepan over a moderate heat and stir in the chopped onions. Cook gently, covered, for about 5–10 minutes until soft but not brown. Stir in the flour and cook for a minute or two. Off the heat, gradually stir in the milk until smoothly combined. Add the salt and pepper and return to the heat. Stir until it thickens and comes to the boil. If the pudding is not ready, reduce the heat to a simmer (use a simmer mat) or place over hot water to keep warm.

∎ When the pudding is done, remove it from the pot and cut through the string. Unfold the cloth and carefully remove the Jack to a warm serving plate using a fork and with a large perforated skimmer supporting it underneath. Serve it in thick slices with the onion sauce and boiled vegetables.

Elizabeth Farm at Parramatta

IN THE earliest years of colonial Australia, sheep and cattle were in such short supply that farmers dedicated to building up their herds did not dare slaughter them. Elizabeth Macarthur, writing to England in August 1794 from Elizabeth Farm at Parramatta, lists her animals as one horse, two mares, two cows, 130 goats, at least 100 hogs, and the greatest abundance of all kinds of poultry. Four years later the numbers had increased dramatically:

Our stock of cattle is large, we have now Fifty head, a dozen Horses, & about a thousand Sheep. You may conclude from this that we kill mutton, but hitherto we have not been so extravagant. Next year, Mr Macarthur tells me, we may begin.

In the meantime, their large household of ex-convict servants and farm herds lived on a constant supply of wild duck and kangaroo, averaging about 136 kg per week, as well as plenty of pork. The pigs fattened well on the excess produce of their fruit and vegetable garden, enjoying many treats such as daily loads of peaches during the summer months.

Pork and Rabbit Brawn

SERVES 8

BRAWN and sausages were the logical sequence to killing day, ways of using the otherwise unusable scraps. Various ingredients went into sausages, pork and beef being the most common, although in *Stradbroke Dreamtime*

Oodgeroo Noonuccal remembers a dish made by her mother from dugong meat and dugong intestine, or grumpii:

She would take home the precious meat, trusting us to help her with the heavy load, but she always carried the grumpii herself … She would wash the grumpii thoroughly in salt sea-water, then place it in a pot of water to boil on the stove until it was tender. After that it was allowed to cool while Mother minced up some of the flesh, and the heart and liver. This was all pushed into the grumpii, and the ends tied tightly with string, and it was then put into a pot of water once more and boiled. We called it grumpii sausage. In later years I had the opportunity to taste Scots haggis, and found it not unlike our dugong sausage.

Like sausages, brawns were made from a variety of meats. In colonial times cooks found that a fine brawn could be obtained from kangaroo tail; but the constituent of most was pork. Sometimes it would be combined with other economical meats such as mutton or beef or, in this case, rabbit.

Half a pig's head	*6 peppercorns*
1 rabbit, jointed	*2 sprigs fresh parsley*
1 onion, stuck with 6 cloves	*1 teaspoon salt*
1 carrot	*½ teaspoon ground mace*
2 bay leaves	*½ teaspoon cayenne pepper*

▪ Place all the ingredients except the mace and cayenne in a large pot or saucepan. Cover with water and bring to the boil over a moderate heat. Skim the surface, lower the heat and simmer gently, covered, for 2½ hours.
▪ Drain the liquid from the meat and vegetables. Discard the vegetables and set the meat aside to cool slightly. Return the cooking liquid to a clean saucepan and add the mace and cayenne pepper. Boil rapidly, uncovered, until reduced to about 1 cup.
▪ Remove the meat from the bones and dice, cutting the pork rind finely. Place in a pudding basin and pour over the stock. Stir to distribute the ingredients evenly. Put a plate on top with a weight and refrigerate overnight. Dip the basin in hot water to unmould.

Rabbit-oh!

IN THE Great Depression rabbits were a staple meat of the poor and this has given them a stigma which has taken several decades to overcome. The call of the 'rabbit-oh' with his horse-drawn cart was then a familiar part of the suburban scene. Shirley Ball in *Muma's Boarding House* recalls the little gnome of a man and his black van who used to visit her Brisbane street during that era:

He would lower the rear flap and on this he piled pinkly glistening skinned rabbit carcasses from inside the van. In a stentorian bellow, at odds with his spare frame, he'd yell, 'Rabbit-oh! Rabbit-oh! Come and get your fresh killed rabbits!' As customers gathered around he'd brandish his chopping knife, intoning, 'Tuppence a half and fourpence a whole, everyone eats rabbit on the dole'.

Shooter's Fried Rabbit

SERVES 3

DOMESTIC rabbits were introduced into Australia with the First Fleet but it was only in 1859 with the importation of two dozen animals by Thomas Austin of Barwon Park near Geelong in Victoria that the great colonisation of the continent began. These were hybrids, bred with the wild English rabbit, full of hybrid vigour for Australia's diverse conditions.

The introduction of this creature to Australia was a disaster both for the farmer and for the ecology. They razed crops and degraded pastures causing soil erosion, competed with livestock and with native animals, some teetering on the brink of extinction.

Barrier fences thousands of miles long were constructed in an attempt to halt the spread of the rabbit, and bounties paid by government to trappers and shooters. Joseph Jenkins, in *Diary of a Welsh Swagman*, describes one shooting spree in Victoria, February 1887:

A public holiday has been proclaimed to encourage everybody to go into the Bush in order to reduce the rabbit population. Everybody appears to be carrying a gun, and many of them have not carried one before. It is really dangerous. They were conveyed to the Bush in buggies and coaches. They returned at dusk singing merrily because they had consumed barrels of beer. One party alone had killed 450 rabbits, and had left the carcasses in the Bush, but the ears were brought back as evidence when they claim an award from the Government, which had already paid out £7,000 for destroying the hares and rabbits.

By November of that same year the Victorian government had paid $700,000 on extermination schemes but with little effect.

It was only with the introduction from South America of the myxomatosis virus in 1950 that numbers were drastically reduced. However, because of a gradual build up in resistance to the disease farmers still spend much time and money on eradication measures. Rabbits have formed an excellent cheap food for Australians from the late colonial period on. For bush people they provide a welcome change in the diet and indeed for many Aboriginal cooks a necessary source of meat since the proliferation of rabbits has been at the expense of traditional small game animals. Desert women who once hunted the bilby now pursue rabbits, prising them from their burrows with a digging stock: a sharp twist to the neck, a fire to singe off the fur and the animal is ready for roasting on hot coals or boiling in the billy. If the rabbit is young, frying is one of the best methods of preparing it and at the same time one of the simplest.

1 young rabbit, about 800 g, jointed   *Dripping or oil for frying*
2 tablespoons plain flour

■ Dredge the rabbit pieces with flour. Heat some dripping or oil in a frying pan over moderate heat. Brown the rabbit lightly in the hot fat. Lower the heat a little and fry the rabbit gently on all sides until golden brown and cooked through, about 15 minutes. Don't overcook or it will dry out.

Australian Rabbit Pie

SERVES 5−6

MEAT pies arrived in Australia with the British and gradually developed into a national addiction. Individual hot meat pies with tomato sauce are a standard lunch for blue-collar workers and a popular snack for football and cricket fans. In colonial times the pieman was a conspicuous institution on the streets, his meat pies enclosed in a metal box on legs, kept warm by a charcoal burner. The pies were seasoned from the spout of the pieman's gravy can after a hole had been poked in the crust with his finger. The most famous of these ambulatory provedores was the Flying Pieman William F. King, who performed bizarre pedestrian feats for anyone prepared to lay a wager, at times burdened with a goat or other encumbrance to add to the spectacle. On one occasion he outpaced the Windsor to Sydney coach, arriving seven minutes before it. On another he walked from Parramatta to Windsor and back on three consecutive days in consecutively shorter times. Once he walked a thousand quarter-miles in a thousand quarter-hours. He

A kitchen about the time of World War I: gas has been employed to provide light over the mantlepiece but otherwise the kitchen, with its solid-fuel stove, timber shelves, dresser and table is quite traditional.

died in 1873 in a paupers' asylum at the age of sixty-six.

In those times mutton was a common ingredient in commercial pies but nowadays beef is almost universal, either diced or minced, sometimes with kidney, mixed vegetables, onions or mushrooms, or with a mashed potato topping. In Adelaide you may order a floater, that is a pie served in a bowl of split pea soup; and in the Northern Territory your pie and peas may come under the intriguing title of a train smash ("cos it looks like one'). In Victoria rabbit pies are still sold and, though not produced on the same scale as beef, there are few things on earth more exquisitely delectable than a well-made rabbit pie. The following superlative recipe comes from Henrietta McGowan's *Keeyuga Cookery Book* published in Victoria in 1911. Frozen shortcrust pastry may be used but nothing beats homemade.

1 rabbit, jointed
250 g bacon
¼ cup plain flour
2 onions
4 cloves
½ teaspoon dried thyme
½ teaspoon dried marjoram
Freshly ground black pepper
3 cups chicken stock
1 lemon

3 hard-boiled eggs, sliced
1 tablespoon mushroom ketchup or tomato
   sauce

SHORT CRUST PASTRY
1 cup self-raising flour
½ teaspoon salt
60 g dripping or butter, chilled
About 3 tablespoons iced water
1 tablespoon milk for glazing

▪ Remove the liver from the rabbit, chop finely and set aside. Discard the remaining innards. Blanch the bacon briefly in boiling water to remove excess saltiness, drain and cut the rashers into quarters, removing the rind if you wish. Put the rabbit joints and bacon in a bowl and toss with the flour to coat. Place in a large saucepan and add the onions stuck with the cloves, the herbs tied in muslin, the pepper and the stock. With a vegetable peeler remove the thin yellow rind from a quarter of the lemon and add the rind to the pot. Bring to the boil over a moderate heat and then simmer gently, covered, for 1½ hours until the rabbit is tender. Let cool.

▪ When cold, remove the rabbit meat from the bones and cut into bite-size pieces. Place in an oven-proof dish, lay the cooked bacon over the rabbit and cover with the hard-boiled egg slices. Scatter the chopped liver over the top. Strain the cooking liquid and measure 2 cups. Stir in the ketchup and pour over the eggs. Add extra liquid if necessary to barely cover the meat.

▪ Make the shortcrust pastry while the rabbit is cooking. Sift the flour and salt into a mixing bowl. The method is the same whether using dripping or butter, but for an authentic colonial flavour use dripping for this recipe. Rub in the dripping or butter quickly until the mixture resembles breadcrumbs. Add enough iced water to hold the dough together under light pressure. Sprinkle the water a tablespoon at a time over the flour, tossing it with a fork. Press the dough into a flattened ball, cover with cling wrap and chill for at least 20 minutes.

▪ Dust a pastry board and rolling pin lightly with flour. Roll out the dough, until about 2–3 cm thick. Cut a shape about 3 cm larger than the pie dish. Trim off a 1.5 cm strip of pastry all round. Dampen the edge of the dish and press the pastry strip onto it. Brush with water and place the circle of pastry over the pie, pressing the edges firmly to seal. Knock up the edge with the back of a knife and crimp. Slash a few steam vents and decorate with pastry leaves cut from the scraps. Brush with milk to glaze.

∎ Bake in a preheated oven at 230°C for 10 minutes. Reduce the temperature to 180°C and cook for a further 30 minutes until golden brown.

Bush Mud Birds

SERVES 4

IN *Over My Tracks* Evelyn Crawford recalls the various meats eaten over her lifetime in the outback including plenty of poultry:

> There were always lots of galah feathers because we lived on them as meat.
>
> We didn't eat cranes because they tasted too much like fish, so does a pelican. Yet it's a strange thing, the duck who lives in the water and eats the same things as the pelican and the crane, his meat tastes like meat, not fish. Crane meat is very black. We'd feed it to the dogs …
>
> Livin' just down below us were two Irishmen, real Irishmen, that talked funny. We could hardly understand 'em. The oldest feller used to come along to our camp with a big silver pot of Irish stew. We thought, 'That's only natural. Irishmen should cook Irish stew, Indians should cook curry. We eat kangaroos and emus 'cos we're Aboriginals.' He'd give us this Irish stew, and it was beautiful. We were there a long time before we found out the meat in it was galahs! We were knockin' galahs down ourselves with sticks and stewin' them and curryin' them.

Stews and curries are common nowadays amongst Aboriginal cooks, done in the billy, yet an older method is to coat birds in clay or mud, then cook them in a small heated pit with a fire on top. When done, the clay is broken away taking skin and feathers with it and leaving a succulent bird.

8 x 150 g quail or 1 x 1.5 kg chicken	*¾ cup breadcrumbs*
1 tablespoon dripping or butter	*¼ teaspoon salt*
1 small onion, finely chopped	*¼ teaspoon mixed dried herbs*
1 small potato, finely chopped	*3 kg clay*

∎ Cut the necks and wing tips off the birds, wash and pat dry. Melt the fat in a saucepan over a moderate heat and sauté the onion and potato for about 12 minutes until soft. Remove from the heat and stir in the crumbs, salt and herbs. Spoon the stuffing into the body cavity. If the birds are plucked, wrap each in a square of foil.

▪ Place the clay (available from potters' supply shops) on a clean plastic garbage bag. Push out with the heel of the hand or fingers to make rectangles of clay 15 x 23 cm for each quail, or 30 x 38 cm for a chicken. Place the bird on its back in the middle, gather up the clay, peeling off the plastic and completely enclosing the bird. Smooth and seal over the joins. Transfer to a baking dish or baking tray and cook in a preheated oven or covered barbecue at 190°C for 1½ hours for quail, 2 hours for chicken.

▪ When done, crack the clay with a mallet or hammer on the cutting board. Present the birds in their clay coats and then remove the clay and foil.

Hazards of Keeping Chooks

IN THE past poultry runs were concentrated around the cities so that the eggs could be brought to market as fresh and with as few breakages as possible. Bush folk either depended on native sources or tended their own chooks. Mary Boothby describes in *Memories of My Bush Life* the provisioning arrangements on the remote sheep station of Tintinara in South Australia from her arrival there in 1864:

> ... I also devoted many hours to the well being of a large number of fowls, ducks and geese, and a great amusement they were to me, so much so that I was on affectionately intimate terms with every cock and hen and members of the feathered tribe on the premises, having known them from the eggshell. The worst effect of which friendship was that I could never make up my mind as to which of my favourites I could best part with and sacrifice for dinner when necessary, and I often stood in the hen house at night when they had all gone to roost, in wretched indecision as to which victim should be selected while our faithful manservant Edward stood by ready to seize the leg of the unhappy object of my choice when I could quite make up my mind. But it was 'Oh, Edward, we really must not kill that grey pullet, she is such a good layer' or 'Oh, it must not be old speckly, she's such a dear old thing, or that young cock either. I couldn't eat him'. And so it went on, until poor Edward lost all patience with me, and said 'There, do go in, ma'am, just leave it to me, and I'll pick out some old hen as really wants to be killed'.

Keepers of poultry had various ways of dealing with tough old birds no longer of any use for egg production. They were usually steamed till tender or stewed or casseroled.

Paperbark Chook

SERVES 4

CONDITIONS in Australia have always lent themselves naturally to camping and campfire meals. In *Cobbers* Thomas Wood, a visitor to Australia during the Great Depression, contrasted uncomfortable memories of camping in the damp and cold of his native England with the Antipodean experience:

But here was kindly earth, heaped with gum leaves, warm and dry; dead wood which kindled at a touch of flame; boughs which burned steadily, leaving the red glow a gridiron longs for …

We drank tea straight from the billy, an amber liquid scented with the smoke of gum leaves, made as the water came to the boil. That, and fried steaks, and a slice of bread and jam; apples to finish with. A peaceful meal.

High above, among the branches, the firelight danced with the shadows as it would on the roof of a cave. It rippled along the boughs, turned leaves to flakes of glowing iron, flitted down the trunks and was gone, noiseless as the sap behind the bark.

Campfire cooks who lack the billy and frypan can manage quite well using the natural resources around them. Paperbark is known to many bush cooks, easily stripped from melaleuca trees in sheets, which can be fashioned into troughs for carrying food and water, or spread on the ground for kneading damper or laying out food. Wrapped around game birds and large fish it keeps the flesh juicy while emitting a lovely smoky fragrance.

1.5 kg chicken
3 sprigs paperbark leaves, optional

Salt and freshly ground black pepper, optional
1 sheet of paperbark, about 40 x 45 cm

▪ Wash the chicken and dry with absorbent paper. Wet the leaves and push inside the body cavity. Rub with salt and pepper if you wish.
▪ Wipe over the paperbark with a damp cloth. Rub off as many as possible of the little long fibres to leave a smooth, clean surface on one side. Patch any holes with pieces of bark, overlapping the edges. Place the chicken on its back in the middle of the bark on the smooth side. Wrap around the chicken, overlapping the edges over the breast. Tie with string in 2 or 3 places across the bird. Then fold the bark over at the ends and tie again.

▌ Put the wrapped fowl on a baking tray and cook in a preheated oven or covered barbecue at 190°C for about 1¾–2 hours until done. Remove the string and bark in front of the guests just before serving.

Chicken with Honey Barbecue Sauce

BEFORE the advent of battery production poultry was produced on farms divided into dirt yards enclosed by chicken wire, where the fowls could scratch in the earth and ruffle their feathers and feel the sun on their backs. Each yard had its corrugated iron shed where they sheltered at night or in rain, and life wasn't too bad for a chook. So I remember the farm of my Aunty Spot and Uncle Dec when I was a child and used to play amongst the sheds and chase the hens.

Chicken was expensive then and most people enjoyed it only at Christmas or other special occasions. With the exception of old boilers poultry was nearly always roasted, with a bread stuffing and a simple gravy.

By the 1970s battery production had taken over from the old free-range farms. Unfortunately both the birds' living conditions and the quality of the meat deteriorated. Joan Austin Palmer compares modern chicken with that grown on Lake Midgeon Station in *Memories of My Bush Life*:

It is hard for people now to imagine the care that went into the rearing and selecting of our table birds. Now a visit to the supermarket will buy you a fat bird, guaranteed tender and tasting of … nothing. In the 1920s, although Father did none of the work he had his finger on the pulse of the poultry yard, supervising the setting of the eggs, watching the young birds as they grew, then putting the roosters when almost mature into a small pen to be fattened. Eventually the two best would be chosen for our Sunday dinner. As children my brother and I were practically vegetarians so this meal was a great event and we watched fascinated as Father sharpened the knife and plunged the fork into the bird's crisp brown breast. Then we waited with almost holy awe as, with the knife, he gently prised the thigh away from the body. If it came away easily we all sighed with relief. The bird was tender.

The guaranteed tenderness of the battery chicken has come at the expense of flavour, flavour which must be compensated for in the kitchen. The following 1970s recipe is typical in its inclusion of tasty ingredients. It comes from *Good Cheap Cooking* by Jean Hatfield, a cookery editor and writer who belongs to a family of famous Scottish-Australian cooks which includes Margaret Fulton.

425 g can apricot halves	1 tablespoon lemon juice
1 tablespoon soy sauce	1¼ cups chicken stock
1 tablespoon honey	Salt and freshly ground black pepper
1 tablespoon tomato sauce	1.5 kg chicken pieces
¼ teaspoon rosemary	Olive oil

▪ Strain the apricots and place the fruit into a food processor or blender reserving 6 halves for a garnish. Purée the fruit and then heat gently in a saucepan over a low heat with the soy sauce, honey, tomato sauce and rosemary, until the honey is melted. Add the lemon juice.

▪ Place the chicken on a baking dish and brush with oil. Pour over the sauce and bake in a preheated oven at 220°C for 10 minutes. Lower the heat to 190°C and cook for a further 20 minutes or until the chicken is tender, basting occasionally.

▪ Remove the chicken to a warm serving dish. Add the stock to the pan, bring to the boil, reduce slightly and season to taste. Pour it over the chicken and garnish with apricot halves.

How to Cook a Galah

SERVES 1 NEW CHUM

THIS famous bush classic needs no introduction to Australians and I recommend it wholeheartedly to any unacquainted with the delights of our cuisine! With all such recipes one cannot stress enough the importance of employing only ingredients of the choicest quality.

1 galah, plucked and drawn	1 bouquet garni
1 stone, brick or axe head	A dash of very dry white wine
1 onion, stuck with 6 cloves	A good pinch salt

▪ Put all ingredients in a large pot and add enough water to cover well. Replace the lid and bring to the boil. Simmer very gently until the stone, brick or axe is soft when pierced by a fork. The galah will then be ready to serve.

6

From the market gardens

*Flavours are bought in books and bottles nowadays; then, they grew in the family
garden, and were collected in the family mind.*

*Besides the use of vine-leaves, in baking ... poultry and other meats, vine-leaves
were sometimes tied round cabbages that were boiled with peppercorns in vinegar and
water along with lard or bacon bones. Sometimes it was the spathes or swaddling-leaves
of young corn-cobs were used. I have known a cry for a leaf of the sweet brier ... and I
have been sent post-haste up to the orchards for a cherry-leaf, a fig-leaf, or the leaf of
some special peach-tree. Mint, parsley, cloves, sweet-basil, marjoram, common and
lemon-scented thyme, shallots, garlic, rosemary, all grew in the garden and all gave their
flavourings for the kitchen.*

DAME MARY GILMORE, *OLD DAYS: OLD WAYS*, 1934

*By the time Max Dupain took this photograph, Crow's Nest fruit market, in the
1950s, the influence of immigrant farmers and greengrocers was becoming apparent in
the cornucopia of fruit and vegetables available in local shops.*

The Gatherer's Harvest

VEGETABLES are very important in the traditional Aboriginal diet. In some regions vegetables, fruits, nuts and cereals make up about half of all food eaten; elsewhere they form the bulk of the diet with meat more of a special, luxury food. Only in fishing areas along the coast or rivers do plant foods contribute less than half of the nutritional requirements.

It has always been the women's job to harvest the various plants needed for health. Status and pride attach to women who are good providers. In a legend of the Gunwinggu people from western Arnhem Land a group of women went out with their digging sticks to crop long yams but only some of them were successful. Back at camp, while sharing the harvest, those who had returned empty-handed felt ashamed and prepared to leave and go and live in the sky. The remaining women decided to join them and all were changed into stars, those of the good breadwinners shining the brightest.

A wide variety of vegetables are available in different parts of the country. The leaves and stems of the native leek are wetted and steam-roasted on a fire until done. Hearts of palm are eaten cooked or raw. The fiddle-heads of bracken and tree ferns are cooked in hot ash to destroy any poisons; and the soft starchy pith of tree ferns and grass trees can be eaten either roasted or raw. Some bush tomatoes are skewered on twigs and lightly grilled. Bull kelp must be grilled, soaked and then grilled again to make it edible.

More important are root vegetables, such as yams, bracken fern and rhizomes, the roots of various wattles, nutgrass, wild arrowroot, the tap roots of maloga and coastal beans, tubers of bulrushes and club rushes, young water chestnuts, and water-ribbon and water-lily tubers. Most of these are roasted on hot coals or cooked in ground ovens. Lily tubers are usually steam-roasted. Myrnong, or yam daisy, was once a staple food in south-eastern Australia, and its bunches of white 'fingers' were roasted in fibre baskets or eaten raw. Orchid roots were also an important food in the south-east whereas in the desert the staples are bush potatoes, bush onions and the thick tap roots of convolvulus. Cheeky yams, taro, mangrove radicles and some water-lily tubers must be leached before they are edible.

From Garden Plot to Market Garden

Vegetables are the staple of the traditional Torres Strait Island diet, although unlike Aboriginal people, they grow these in garden plots. Rotation of crops is practised with yams, sweet potatoes, taro, pumpkins and other vegetables being grown for one or two years, followed by bananas and plantains. After the bananas have born fruit the plot is allowed to go back to bush for a time before burning off for a new planting. Most are starchy roots although long beans and taro leaves provide some greens in the diet. Most vegetables are boiled, either in coconut milk, or in water into which a little coconut milk may be squeezed at the end. In addition, they may be bundled up in banana leaves with coconut milk to be cooked in the ground oven. Grated cassava is made into pakalolo, flavoured with lemon, a little sugar, coconut milk and sometimes other vegetables. Green pawpaw may be treated as a vegetable, at times combined with minced meat. Fried yams are a common dish, as are vegetables cooked with rice.

Cultivation was the main source of vegetable supplies after 1788 even though the gathering of natives like pigweed, warrigal greens, wallaby bush, saltbush, parakeelya, sea celery, native parsley, samphire and certain seaweeds supplemented the diet in times of shortage. Despite experimentation by some with a wide variety of exotic vegetables, many people unfortunately lived from one day to the next on a very limited range. Dr Philip Muskett, writing in 1893, complained of the prevalence of potatoes and cabbage to the exclusion of other vegetables. Compared to some six hundred butchers' establishments in Sydney at the time there were less than half that number of greengrocers and these 'represented by dingy-looking places, and by a collection of faded vegetables which seem always to be apologising for being on view at all'. He also lamented the 'crude cookery' of such vegetables as were available and the 'endless recurrence of boiled potatoes, boiled cabbage, boiled this and boiled that'. Few cookbooks of the day devoted much space to the preparation of vegetables and even the cookery educators were not exempt from criticism: Fanny Fawcett Story gives less than three pages on vegetables in her cookbook, and Harriet Wicken instructs her readers to soak chokoes in salted water for an hour and then to boil them for the same length of time, excessive by today's standards.

In spite of the predominance of boiling and overcooking, there were some cooks, like Mina Rawson, who treated vegetables with more respect. Naturally, most of their recipes are for the common varieties such as potatoes, onions, cabbage, cauliflower and green as well as ripe tomatoes. Pumpkin along with other cucurbits, flourished in the Australian climate and quickly became a favourite with bush and city cooks alike. Sweet potatoes and chokoes were adopted from South America. The tender young shoots of pumpkin, sweet potatoes and choko vines were found to make excellent greens and pawpaw and bananas made good vegetables if cooked unripe.

Even some of the introduced weeds ended up in the pot. Frying and baking were popular and the most imaginative and tasty dishes usually involved stuffing or layering vegetables with other ingredients.

Expanding Harvests

Throughout the colonial period acclimatisation societies actively promoted new vegetables and fruits, and Chinese market gardeners provided high-grade produce to many households. The establishment of agricultural colleges at the end of the nineteenth century led to the development of cultivation practices suitable to Australian conditions, and the discovery of vitamins in the first decades of the twentieth century gave a big boost to vegetable cookery with many new recipes appearing in cookbooks and magazines by the 1930s. The variety and quality further increased after World War II as migrants from Mediterranean countries with a better appreciation of vegetables started to dominate the greengrocer trade, and Chinese and Vietnamese vegetables became increasingly available from the 1970s with more migration from Asia. Many country people had to wait until the 1980s for improved produce when supermarkets were established in their towns with greengrocery sections of a uniform national standard.

Despite the move towards supermarkets and even Internet ordering of vegetables, markets are flourishing everywhere in Australia. The single two outstanding food markets are the Queen Victoria in Melbourne and the smaller Central Markets in Adelaide. Elsewhere small farmers' markets have cropped up with specialist growers. Whether it is organic produce or free-range eggs and meats, rare tropical fruits and rare leaf vegetables, or tree-ripened nashi pears and vine-ripened tomatoes, quality predominates.

Yam Cakes

8 CAKES, SERVES 4

THERE are several species of Australian native yams, vines with heart-shaped leaves and underground tubers which form a significant carbohydrate food for many Aboriginal people.

There are three main types: the long yam up to a metre in length which grows along the northern beaches and throughout the eastern rainforests as far south as Sydney, the round yam of the northern forests, and the warrine of the south-west. Jennifer Isaacs, in her book *Bush Food*, details the harvesting technique:

The digging of a yam takes skill and determination, particularly if the leaves are no longer visible and the dead parts above ground are simply dried, twining tendrils. Patience is needed to track the plant, particularly in rocky areas as it winds through the rocks and goes underground. Often the tuber itself may not be found where the vine enters the ground but some distance away. Aborigines know exactly where to dig: usually at an angle to the tuber so that the hole, which may be a metre or more deep, meets the tuber at an acute angle. It is important that the tuber itself is not damaged and even a large yam must be dug out intact.

The yams are cleaned and some of the hairs rubbed off before being roasted on hot coals or placed in a small hole in the ground lined with coals, in which case more coals and then earth are placed on top and left for twenty minutes till cooking is complete. Alternatively, they are steam-baked alongside meat or fish in a large ground oven. Occasionally they are made into cakes which are easier for young children and old people to eat. Round yams are 'cheeky' and need to be leached in running water for a day or more to remove poisons once they have been roasted, grated and mashed to a pulp. The resulting cakes are 'hot' food which 'picks you up'. Dry leaching is an alternative for people living in the Kimberley: the yams are roasted, peeled and sliced about a centimetre thick, coated in wet ash and then roasted again for several hours. The ash gradually absorbs the poisons and is washed off before eating. Cultivated yams can be bought from markets in northern Australia or sometimes from Vietnamese grocers in the south, and they make a pleasant change from potatoes, easily baked or fashioned into small cakes.

---

50 g yams, scrubbed clean

▪ Place the yams in an ungreased baking dish then bake in a preheated oven at 180°C for about 1–1¼ hours until soft when pierced by a skewer. Let cool.
▪ When cold, peel the yams with a knife, removing the skin and hairy roots. Grate the flesh and press firmly into small cakes about 6 cm diameter. These cakes may be eaten cold, or fried in a little oil until lightly browned.

Sop-sop

SOP-SOPS are among the most characteristic dishes of Torres Strait Island cookery. Roland Raven-Hart, in *The Happy Isles*, describes a meal he enjoyed during his sojourn on the island of Mer in the 1940s:

And then we ate; and I met with 'sop-sop', and fell in deathless love with it.

One of the island-mothers who were waiting on us put a large green parcel in front of me: it was wrapped in banana-leaves, and when opened it gushed out a mouth-watering steam. 'We take yam, plenty yam, and pumpkin, and chicken, and fish, and—oh, everything. And we put all them in coconut milk and wrap them up like that. And then we find big stones, flat stones, and make fire on them stones, and make them stones hot … And then we pull fire away, quick, and some of them stones, and put all them parcels down on stones, and other stones on top, and cover up with palm-leaf and banana-leaf and then put sand, plenty sand, heap up sand like someone dead in there. And when them ready we open that oven, pull away sand, and eat them parcels. We call them 'sop-sop': you like them?'

All sop-sops are good: an excellent sop-sop is a thing to remember with reverence.

Sabee Sabee

SERVES 4

COCONUTS are the most important flavouring ingredient in Torres Strait cookery. To extract the milk the mature coconut is husked, then cracked open by sharply tapping it around the middle with a heavy knife or cleaver. The flesh is grated using a mardoo, a wooden plank on which the cook sits while pushing the inside of the nut against a toothed metal scraper attached to the end. The grated flesh is kneaded with some water until milky and then strained off. A yeast can be made from the milk for leavening cakes; and a thick extract called coconut cream is used for frying. Coconut milk flavours curries, seafood and vegetable dishes. Most of the common island vegetables can be simmered in coconut milk, either separately as sabee sabee sweet potatoes, sabee sabee pumpkin, or as a mixed dish of two or more vegetables. Potato, though not a traditional ingredient, is good, too.

---

1 kg vegetables (yams, sweet potato, pumpkin, taro, cassava)
1 onion, finely chopped

½ teaspoon salt
2½ cups coconut milk

▪ Peel the vegetables and cut into large chunks. Place in a saucepan with the onion and salt and cover with the coconut milk. Bring to the boil over a moderate heat then simmer gently, without a lid, until the vegetables are tender when pierced by a fine skewer and the milk is reduced to a creamy sauce, about 40 minutes. Stir occasionally while it is cooking.

Broome Style Vegetables

SERVES 6

BROOME represents one of those half-way points where Australia and Asia meet and mingle: the corrugated iron emporia of Chinatown, the headstones at the Japanese cemetery powdered with red dust, the pair of pearl luggers at Streeter's Jetty waiting the change of tides for their journey out through the mangroves of Roebuck Bay. In Broome's heyday before World War II the morning market was the place where this mixture was most apparent: produce from the market gardens alongside turtle steaks and turtle eggs, strips of dugong strung on bamboo with the rank smell of fried blatchan filling the air, huge chunks of beef slung on poles, hurried off to the foreshore camps of the pearling masters.

Oriental taste is still prominent in much of Broome's cuisine. The following dish of mixed vegetables flavoured with soy, ginger and garlic, is from the *Broome Shinju Matsuri Cook Book* contributed by Linda Fernihough.

---

1 tablespoon olive oil
2 teaspoons grated fresh ginger
2 teaspoons crushed garlic
¼ cup soy sauce
½–1 cup water
8 cups slow cooking vegetables like carrot,
eggplant, pumpkin, potato, onion, cut into bite-size pieces
4 cups softer vegetables like zucchini, cauliflower, cabbage, cut into bite-size pieces
2 tablespoons finely chopped fresh herbs

▪ Gently heat the oil over a medium heat in a large saucepan and sauté the ginger and garlic for 1 minute. Add the soy sauce and ½ cup of water. When bubbling, add the slow cooking vegetables. Simmer gently, covered, over a low heat until half cooked, about 15 minutes, stirring occasionally. It may be necessary to pour in extra water if the sauce looks like drying up.

▪ Add the softer vegetables and half the herbs. Continue to cook as before until just tender, about 10 minutes. Serve sprinkled with the remaining finely chopped herbs.

Bunya Bunya Feast

THE most famous historic gathering of Aboriginal people was the feast that took place in the Bunya Bunya Mountains in southern Queensland every three years from the end of January to March. The mountains, which form part of the Great Dividing Range, are noted for their rainforest dominated by the giant bunya bunya pine whose domed crown towers above the figs, red cedars and lesser acolytes surrounding it. They are amongst the most magnificent of all creation, the stalwart trunks like great pillars supporting the green roof of the forest and blue heaven above, the deep shade below resembling the meditative gloom of some gothic sanctuary.

Although they fruit each year it is only once in three years that the harvest of huge cones, larger than a human head, is really plentiful. Up until the last grand feast in 1875 hundreds of family groups from within a radius of 300 kilometres or more would join the resident Kabi and Wakka clans to consume their share of the nuts, engage in conferences, trade, sports and corroborees. The cones were collected from the forest floor or the young people would climb the trees with the help of a vine slung around the trunk and foot holds cut into the bark. Many of these foot holds are still visible in the older trees. The cones were smashed apart with a stone axe to reveal the large nuts which were eaten raw or roasted, ground into flour, or fermented by burial in moist earth. The people thrived on the diet of nutritious kernels, which in taste and texture are not totally dissimilar from chestnuts but with a suggestion of pine.

Mina Rawson's Stoved Potatoes

SERVES 6

POTATOES were introduced into Australia by the British in 1788. The general opinion amongst Irish immigrants was that the quality of the 'taties was inferior to those back home but that the quantity of meat more than made up for it. Certainly the early farmlands in and around Sydney were too warm for the potato varieties brought from a cold climate. Production moved in time to colder climates with Tasmania still yielding the premium varieties such as the superb pink-eyes. Many wonderful potatoes have since been bred for our warmer climates including Pink Fir Apples, Prince Edwards, Desirées and Kipfler.

Before World War II a large dinner plate heaped up with meat and spuds formed the dietary staple for many people and certainly bore a straight-forward masculine appeal. Potatoes could be bought by the stone (6.4 kg), the normal weekly consumption for a family of five, though compared to Britain and northern Europe, Australians have always been poor potato eaters. The cheapness of meat reduced the dependence on the potato which also had a rival in colonial times in flour-based foods like damper and an alternative vegetable like pumpkin. Since the war potato consumption at home has declined still further, replaced by salads and a wider variety of vegetables, although this trend has been more than offset by an increase in potato crisps and hot chips eaten outside the home.

A healthy way of preparing potatoes is the following colonial recipe from Mina Rawson in which the vegetable is stewed on top of the stove in milk, gradually reducing to a thick, creamy sauce.

1¼ kg potatoes

12 spring onions, sliced

2 cups milk

1½ teaspoons salt and freshly ground pepper

■ Peel the potatoes and slice 1 cm thick. Place in a large saucepan with the remaining ingredients. Boil gently over a low heat, uncovered, until the potatoes are cooked and the milk is reduced to a sauce, about 30 minutes. Stir occasionally while cooking.

The Husbandman

THE need for suitable farming land by the first colonists caused Governor Phillip to make frequent exploratory trips in the Sydney region which led in 1789 to his most important discovery, a large river, called Deerubin by the Kooris, flowing eastwards from the Blue Mountains. He renamed it after Baron Hawkesbury, a member of the British administration who had considerable influence over the young colony. In 1793 white settlement of the area was established and the rich alluvial flats fed by the river soon yielded abundant crops.

The most evocative description of the early Hawkesbury comes from *Settlers and Convicts* by Alexander Harris, who migrated in the 1820s:

… I felt at once that I was in the land of the husbandman. Whichever way I looked I could see fields of the tall green Indian corn (maize), with its tassel tops, bending and waving under the fresh breeze that was sweeping over it. Here again a square of orchard loaded with splendid peaches broke the uniformity of the surface; there a piece of ground new ploughed or with the teams at work upon it, and here a square of wheat stubble on which a boy tended a herd of pigs as they picked up the scattered grain, still further varied the prospect … There were excellent figs, gooseberries, currants, lemons, oranges, melons, peaches as large as a good sized breakfast cup and of the most exquisite flavour; potatoes, pumpkins as big as a large bucket, cabbages, radishes, onion, beans, pease; in short everything of the kind profusely produced and of the most superior quality.

Two proud vegetable gardeners survey the results of their toil at the gold-mining town of Hill End, near Mudgee in NSW, in the early 1870s.

Val Steed's Grabben Gullen Pie

SERVES 12

IN COLONIAL times one of the most interesting uses to which pumpkins were put was as Grabben Gullen pies, named after a hamlet near Goulburn in New South Wales. Initially filled with joints of possum, later they came to be made with rabbit or savoury minced beef instead. In *A Girl at Government House* Agnes Stokes describes such a dinner on the Darling Downs soon after her arrival in the colonies from her English village in 1887:

They cut a large Turk's head, a vegetable something like a pumpkin. The top was sliced off, all the pips scooped out; some rabbits were shot, skinned, cleaned, cut up and put inside with onions.

A hole was dug and a pile of wood shoved in. When it was well alight a lot of stones were thrown in, then more wood, next the Turk's head which was covered and left till cooked. Some rabbits they roasted and they made some dampers—bushmen's bread—just flour and water cooked in ashes, and jolly nice they were, eaten as soon as cooked. Altogether, it was great fun, and made me feel as if I'd really travelled far from the little round at home.

An alternative stuffing is this superb version from Yass contributed to Ruby Brown and Marion McCarthy's *'Explorer's' Country Kitchen* in 1986.

1 x 4–5 kg Queensland blue pumpkin, stalk intact
500 g bread
2 tomatoes, diced
3 spring onions, sliced
1 tablespoon finely chopped fresh parsley
1 tablespoon fresh herbs

1 teaspoon salt and freshly ground black pepper
2 teaspoons lemon juice
3 rashers bacon, diced
2 tablespoons butter, softened
1¼ cups (300 ml) sour cream

■ To prepare the pumpkin, find the point at which the sides of the pumpkin curve over to form the top. Insert a large sharp knife at this point at a 45° angle. Remove the knife and insert again, gradually working your way around the top and ease it off. With a metal spoon scoop out all the seeds and fibre from the middle and if the cavity is very small scrape away some of the flesh.

■ To make the stuffing, process the bread into fine crumbs in a food processor or blender. Mix the crumbs with the tomatoes, spring onions, parsley, mixed herbs, salt, pepper and lemon juice in a large bowl. Lightly fry the bacon in a pan over a medium heat then add to the stuffing with the butter. Mix well.

■ Fill the cavity of the pumpkin with the stuffing and replace the lid. Put in a greased oven-proof dish and bake in a preheated oven at 200°C for 30 minutes. Reduce the temperature to 150°C and cook for a further 2–2½ hours until the pumpkin is soft when pierced by a skewer and the stuffing is well heated.

■ Remove the lid and stir in the sour cream. Replace the lid and stand for 10 minutes before serving.

Choko Cheese

SERVES 4

A SIGNIFICANT factor in Australian eating habits has been the home vegetable garden. To isolated bush people it often meant the difference between living out of tins or having fresh vegetables. Jill Ker Conway, in her memoir of a childhood spent on the Western Plains of New South Wales in the 1930s and '40s *The Road from Coorain*, describes the miracle wrought in her life when a bore was sunk on the family property. Her mother would then race through the household chores to spend three or four hours in the garden after lunch, and her father built a high windbreak of cane grass to protect the seedlings:

To the south of the house was the vegetable garden, and to the north the citrus orchard. The northern side of the cane windbreak became a trellis for grapes, and a little to the northwest was the potato bed …

The fruits and vegetables were as marvellous to a child raised on canned vegetables and dried apples. The scent of orange and lemon trees, the taste of fat green grapes, and the discovery of salads were marking points of that first year of water.

The character of the Australian city with its miles of never ending suburbs, each house set squarely on its own block of land, has created great possibilities for the home gardener, providing at the least some parsley and mint, a few lemons or passionfruit, at best enough to feed a family and produce certain vegetables not easily obtainable from the shops. The choko is one inhabitant of the backyard which almost always results in an embarassing overabundance. A tasty way to serve it in winter is with a cheese sauce, baked to a crusty golden brown.

CHOKO CHEESE

500 g chokoes	*1 cup milk*
2 tablespoons butter	*125 g tasty cheese, grated*
1½ tablespoons plain flour	*¼ teaspoon dry mustard*
½ teaspoon salt	*1 tablespoon extra butter*
Freshly ground black pepper	*½ cup fresh breadcrumbs*

▪ Peel the chokoes if large. Cut in half lengthwise, then crosswise and slice about 5 mm thick. Place in a saucepan and cook in boiling water for about 4 minutes until just tender. Drain and reserve.

▪ To make the sauce, melt the butter in a saucepan over a medium heat and stir in the flour. Cook gently for a couple of minutes. Remove from the heat and blend in the milk. Return to the heat and cook, stirring constantly, until it thickens. Season with salt and pepper. Stir in the cheese and mustard and when blended remove from the heat.

▪ Place the chokoes in a greased oven-proof dish. Pour the sauce over, making sure all the chokoes are well covered. Melt the extra butter in a small saucepan over a medium heat and stir in the breadcrumbs. Drain and sprinkle over the top of the dish. Bake in a preheated oven at 180°C for about 30 minutes until bubbling and golden brown.

Early Flavourings

MANY people these days assume that the cookery of previous generations must have been very bland, but reading accounts of life in old Australia a picture emerges of seasonings being employed frequently and creatively. Aboriginal cooks depended heavily on native herbs as did the colonists, most famously in billy tea where a gum twig gave that essential hint of the bush. On Leichhardt's expedition of 1846 native marjoram was used for tea, and to season soup, boiled jerky and the black puddings, made by his German cook Henry Boecking on killing days. Chinese station cooks had their mysterious supply of oriental herbs to render corned beef more appetising. And William Howitt, writing home to Britain from the Victorian goldfields in 1852, described a savoury dish prepared at his camp:

We buy either the loin or a leg of lamb. If we use a leg we insert a sharpening steel down by the bone and stuff the cavity made with rosemary and three cloves of garlic. We rub the outside of the leg with crushed rosemary and butter, pepper and salt.

The joint was then wrapped in paper and cooked in a ground oven with a quick browning over the fire to finish.

The herbs utilised by many white settlers came from their gardens, as recalled by Dame Mary Gilmore in *Old Days: Old Ways*:

Flavours are bought in books and bottles nowadays; then, they grew in the family garden, and were collected in the family mind.

Besides the use of vine-leaves, in baking poultry and other meats, vine-leaves were sometimes tied round cabbages that were boiled with peppercorns in vinegar and water, along with lard or bacon bones. Sometimes it was the spathes or swaddling-leaves of young corn-cobs that were used. I have known a cry for a leaf of the sweet brier ... and I have been sent post-haste up to the orchards for a cherry-leaf, a fig-leaf, or the leaf of some special peach-tree. Mint, parsley, cloves, sweet-basil, marjoram, common and lemon-scented thyme, shallots, garlic, rosemary, all grew in the garden and all gave their flavourings for the kitchen.

Buttered Warrigal Greens

SERVES 4-6

WARRIGAL greens or cabbage was one of a number of Aboriginal vegetables that early colonists living near the coast experimented with in their diet. Known across the Tasman as New Zealand spinach, it has a pleasant acidulated flavour and makes a nutritious green vegetable. Typically it is steamed in the water which clings to its leaves and served with a little butter. It may be used in most dishes where spinach or silverbeet is called for. It is excellent as one of the leaves in a mixed green salad.

Warrigal was originally an Aboriginal term for the dingo but came to be used by white settlers to denote anything wild. It grows abundantly along the coast of eastern Australia.

500 g warrigal greens	*¼ teaspoon salt*
2 tablespoons butter	*Pinch nutmeg*

▪ Pick over the leaves and tender shoots of the warrigal greens. Wash them thoroughly and place in a saucepan without adding any water. Cover tightly and steam over a moderate heat for about 3–5 minutes until wilted and tender. Add the remaining ingredients and toss until the flavours combine.

Mina Rawson's Pigweed Cheese

SERVES 6

THIS recipe comes from Mina Rawson, the greatest of bush cookery writers. Born in Sydney in 1851 she moved with her family to a sheep station near Tamworth when she was twelve, and then as a bride to Queensland in 1872. It was in the Queensland bush, living firstly on a cattle station near Mackay, and subsequently on a Maryborough sugar plantation, and almost penniless at Boonooroo south of Hervey Bay that she learnt the skills of bush cookery and survival housekeeping. From 1878 onwards she published a total of five cookbooks 'written expressly to meet the wants and circumstances of those living in the far Bush, as well as those who dwell within reach of the amenities of civilised existence'. In addition she wrote books and articles on raising poultry, numerous bush tales and newspaper columns, and taught swimming in Rockhampton, Townsville and Brisbane. She died in Sydney in 1933.

Her books are whimsical, entertaining collections of recipes, household hints and anecdote, a lasting record of a woman's fortitude and good humour

Pardey's corner stores at Albury, New South Wales, about 1907. Country stores like this sold just about anything from rock salt to rabbit traps, good country butter to chaff for the horse, and local fruits and vegetables.

in the face of adversity, a mirror to the great warmth and humanity of her personality. The cookbooks were no doubt widely read since they contained much practical information derived directly from personal experience. They assume little in the way of kitchen staff, equipment or ingredients as in the bush 'servants come and go like angels' visits' and the cook must make do with what is available: 'One great art in cooking especially in the Bush consists in making the best of poor materials, and in utilising whatever we find ready to our hands, and in being able to use any oven or fireplace, even an open fire on the ground'.

As well as the usual dishes Mrs. Rawson gives many recipes for native game and for indigenous fruits and vegetables. She advises the bush housewife to try everything as 'the blacks or her own common sense will soon tell her what is edible and what is not.' She acknowledged her own indebtedness to Murri people for her understanding of native foods, in a few cases giving classic Aboriginal recipes and in others adapting expertise gained from them. Hers were, in fact, the first cookbooks to give any credit to Aboriginal cuisine and to suggest that the new settlers might learn from it. Pigweed, or purslane, was just one of many local foods she recommended and this tasty layered gratin dish comes from her *Antipodean Cookery Book* published in 1895.

750 g pigweed (purslane)	*40 g butter*
1 tablespoon vinegar	*1 teaspoon dry mustard*
125 g cheese, grated	

▪ Wash the pigweed thoroughly and discard any tough stalks. Bring a large saucepan of salted water to the boil over a medium heat and drop in the pigweed. Boil rapidly until the thickest stalks are tender, about 3 minutes. Drain well in a colander and let cool a little before chopping up roughly.

▪ Place half the pigweed in a greased gratin or oven-proof dish. Sprinkle with half the vinegar and half the cheese. In a small saucepan melt the butter and stir in the mustard until smooth. Spoon half of this over the cheese in the gratin dish. Repeat the layers finishing with the melted butter.

▪ Bake in a preheated oven at 200°C until cooked, about 20 minutes.

Mrs Maclurcan's Curried Bananas

SERVES 4–6

HANNAH Maclurcan was one of Australia's most esteemed colonial cooks and hoteliers. Born near Hill End in New South Wales into a family of hotel owners, by the age of seventeen she had moved to Queensland to manage the Club Hotel in Toowoomba for her father. Later she built up two hotels in Townsville, where she also published what came to be known as *Mrs Maclurcan's Cookery Book*. In 1901 she returned from Queensland to Sydney as managing director of the old Wentworth Hotel, one of the city's grandest and noted for its fine table, where she worked until her retirement in 1932.

She was famous for her restaurant meals, particularly the cold buffet luncheons served at the Wentworth's Palm Court, and renowned for her banquets, which must have been very elaborate affairs to judge by the menus given in her cookbook. Her speciality was delectable seafood, often prepared with a French accent, like bêche-de-mer and turtle soups, barramundi au gratin or à la Normandie, fish à la Victoria and homard en bellevue à la Wentworth. Most of the recipes though, in her cookbook are for plain home cookery and lack the flair and elaborate presentations for which she was known in her day. With her Queensland background Hannah Maclurcan was naturally interested in tropical fruits and gives recipes for grenadilla, pawpaw, pineapple, prickly pears, mangoes, rosellas and bananas. The latter when green are a good vegetable and can be fried, boiled or cooked in milk or coconut milk. Here they form quite a tasty vegetarian curry.

1¼ cups milk

½ cup desiccated coconut

2 tablespoons curry powder

¼ teaspoon salt

Pinch cayenne pepper

1 teaspoon Worcestershire sauce

1 teaspoon anchovy sauce or paste

1 kg green bananas

1 egg, beaten

▪ Pour the milk over the coconut in a bowl and let stand for 1 hour. Stir in the spices and sauces into the coconut milk. Peel the bananas and cut into slices about 1 cm thick.

▪ Place the bananas in a saucepan with the milk mixture. Simmer gently, covered, for 10–15 minutes until the bananas are cooked. If the mixture becomes very dry add a little more milk or water. Just before serving, add the egg and stir to combine. Remove from the heat as soon as the egg loses its raw look and the milk has thickened.

Ladies' Cabbage

SERVES 4

BEFORE Federation the residents of the various colonies received nicknames based on their gustatory and agricultural predilections. South Australians were given the appellation Croweaters, Tasmanians were naturally Apple Islanders, and Western Australians were called Sandgropers, a reference to the barrenness of much of that state. For Queenslanders, Bananalanders was an obvious choice although in modern times this has received a jocular twist in the term Banana Benders. The New South Welsh were named Cornstalks because they shot up tall and straight like the maize which flourished in the colony as opposed to their shorter and punier British cousins living on an inferior diet. Victorians were Cabbage Patchers after one of their most reliable crops and in allusion, too, to their state's small size.

The following cabbage recipe is not confined to Victoria but is widespread in bush and city alike throughout Australia. Another name for it is royalist cabbage, the implication being that cabbage baked like this with eggs makes for a rather fancy dish.

500 g cabbage, thick ribs removed

½ teaspoon salt

Freshly ground black pepper

2 tablespoons butter, softened

2 eggs, beaten

½ cup fresh breadcrumbs

▪ Cut the cabbage into wedges and cook in boiling water over a low heat until done, about 10–12 minutes. Drain well and then chop finely. Place in a greased oven-proof dish and toss with salt, pepper and butter. Pour the eggs over and sprinkle with the breadcrumbs.

∎ Bake in a preheated oven at 190°C until the egg is cooked, about 35 minutes.

Stewed Tomatoes

SERVES 2–4

WHEN I was a young child living in my grandfather's house at Mosman there were many magic things: kookaburras that came in the morning to breakfast on scraps from the chops, and families of possums that came in the evening for suppers of apple, or bread and jam. There was the 'jungle' out the back with its banana palm, and the giant mulberry tree near the house, beloved by us children as much as by the birds. There were also home-grown tomatoes with their big, bright red orbs held up by stakes.

Pop would tend these assiduously and we always seemed to have plenty of tasty tomatoes. His favourite cooking method was to stew them in a frying pan with onions and a little butter or dripping. This was a great breakfast treat, served with buttered toast, but it also makes an excellent accompaniment to chops or steak for dinner. It is an old Aussie standby and known to many people in the bush.

1 tablespoon butter or dripping
1 large onion, thinly sliced
500 g tomatoes, thickly sliced

½ teaspoon salt
White or black pepper

∎ Melt the fat in a frying pan over a moderate heat and fry the onion for a few minutes until soft and golden. Add the tomatoes, salt and pepper and stir occasionally. Stew for 10 minutes until cooked and some of the liquid from the tomatoes has evaporated, stirring occasionally to prevent them from catching.

7

Radish roses and celery curls

… attractively arranged salads inspired by American models were popularised by women's magazines and cookbooks with ingredients presented in lettuce cups, on nests of shredded lettuce or in hollowed out tomatoes. Radish roses, parsley sprigs, gherkin fans, celery and spring onions curls, stuffed eggs and salad balls of cheese all blossomed on the plate to tempt the appetite of those needing conversion to the idea of eating raw vegetables.

Enterprising farmers still set up roadside stalls to catch the passing trade, just as they did in the 1930s when Max Dupain took this photograph, On the Hume Highway—*only the currency has changed.*

From Truffles to Tomatoes

MOST native vegetables are cooked but some are eaten raw by Aboriginal people. Salad vegetables include the peeled flower stalks of the water lily as well as the immature flower itself. The shoots of the bulrush and common reed are edible raw, as are tubers of many water reeds; best of all, perhaps, are water chestnuts, related to those cultivated in Asia and, like them, crisp and sweet. The stems and leaves of pigweed (purslane) can be made into a salad as can the heart and growing shoot of several palms, including the cabbage-tree palm, well known to colonial Australians. Various edible fungi are part of the diet, amongst which are the truffles of the desert sandhills and the famous delicacy blackfellow's bread, a type of large truffle weighing up to 22 kg. Normally, these salad vegetables are consumed fairly simply at their absolute pinnacle of freshness without dressing or seasoning of any kind.

The Australian colonists occasionally used native vegetables, but generally salads depended on lettuce, tomato, celery, cucumber, onion, spring onion, radish, beetroot and potato. They were usually dressed with a boiled dressing made of milk and vinegar, thickened with flour and eggs, and seasoned with salt, pepper and mustard. Alternatively, the eggs would be hard-boiled first and the mashed yolks mixed with vinegar and cream or milk, and sometimes oil. This made a thinner dressing but was still quite good. Most salad recipes were fairly basic and colonial books tend to give very few. After all, meat was nearly always served hot and so it followed that the vegetables to accompany it would also be cooked and hot. Furthermore, there was a suspicion by some that raw vegetables caused indigestion. Dr Philip Muskett complained about the 'meagre list' of salad vegetables available and that salad herbs were 'literally unknown'. One would have to say that it is in the area of salads that white colonial cooking was at its very weakest.

Salad Days

Increased usage of salads only came when the universal adoption of firstly ice-chests and then refrigerators made it easier for housewives to serve cold meals; and also when the discovery of vitamins gave a scientific basis to the nutritionists' cause. Over the years both the variety and quantity of salads has increased, with a greater range of vegetables as well as a diversity of fruits, including apples, oranges, grapefruit, melons and tropical fruits, becoming a feature. Between the two world wars attractively arranged salads inspired by American models were popularised by women's magazines and cookbooks with ingredients presented in lettuce cups, on nests of shredded lettuce or in

A transparent setting: gelatine held everything together in this jellied prawn and olive salad promoted by food manufacturer Foster Clark in the 1940s.

hollowed out tomatoes. Radish roses, parsley sprigs, gherkin fans, celery and spring onion curls, stuffed eggs and salad balls of cheese all blossomed on the plate to tempt the appetite of those needing conversion to the idea of eating raw vegetables. Salads set in gelatine were launched at this time, also from the United States, but never took off in a big way, apart from jellied beetroot.

Some of these new salads were served undressed although a spoonful of thickened dressing, usually designated by the generic term 'mayonnaise', was commonly placed on the side of the plate or on top of the salad. Sometimes this was the old boiled dressing but more often than not, from the early twentieth century onwards, it was a dressing based on condensed milk. The sweetened condensed milk was mixed with powdered mustard, salt, white pepper and vinegar and, if desired, thinned to a pouring consistency with fresh milk. Though too sweet for many people's taste nowadays it did have the advantage of being high in calcium and low in cholesterol and fat.

In the 1960s and '70s the decorative salad of carefully composed ingredients was superseded by the tossed salad based on a French approach with French dressings such as vinaigrette and French mayonnaise. Shredded lettuce was surplanted by torn lettuce. The crisp iceberg lettuce shaped like a cannonball was joined by softer-leaved varieties such as butterhead and mignonette, and also by a variety of leafy greens including endives, spinach, lamb's lettuce, rocket and other small greens. Bean, rice and pasta salads, coleslaws and salads with mushrooms, corn and avocado became commonplace.

By the final decade of the twentieth century restaurateurs and market gardeners from Vietnam, China, Indonesia and Thailand had brought new flavours, textures and shapes to the Australian salad plate. Herbs like Vietnamese mint exploded on the taste buds, bean sprouts gave a crisp crunch, and green pawpaw (a Torres Strait favourite) made a comeback.

Munyeroo Salad Balls

MAKES ABOUT 12 BALLS

MANY of the early colonists found foods in their newly adopted land to which they were not accustomed. Some rejected these out of hand, perhaps from nostalgia for more familiar fare or perhaps because, not knowing how to cook them properly, their first experiences were not the most favourable. One such pioneer was Rachel Henning, who migrated to Australia in 1854. Her first encounters with pigweed, or purslane, for example, evoked its description as 'rather a nasty wild plant'. Yet, gradually, a shift in attitude occurred as she came to accept her new home and the wonderful foods which it yielded. Writing to her sister in England two years later there is quite a different tone:

But we have a wild plant which makes a capital salad and which we very seldom dine without. It rejoices in the name of pigweed, and is a small plant with thick green leaves like the ice-plant and tastes slightly acid and slightly hot, something like watercress.

Pigweed has been used as a vegetable since ancient times by the Greeks, Romans and Arabs and, long before them, by Aboriginal Australians, who sometimes call it munyeroo. Its sprawling, succulent form is found growing all over the continent in many backyards, public parks and even in the cracks of footpaths during the summer. For desert people the tiny black seeds are collected by upending the plants to dry on sheets of bark or animal skins, the grain shaken out then ground into flour for damper or wrapped in bark and stored away carefully for future use. Pigweed leaves may be eaten whole as a salad green but often the women mash them between stones to form a rough purée which is shaped into small balls, a refreshing addition to summer meals.

4 cups pigweed

▪ Discard any tough, old stalks and wash the pigweed well. Shake off excess water. Place the pigweed in a food processor and blend to form a rough paste. It should not be too smooth: small pieces of leaf and stalk will still be present in the green mass. Form into 12 balls of about 4 cm diameter.

Sow Thistle Salad

SERVES 6

WILD greens have been an important source of nutrition for many groups of Australians. Comedian Mary Coustas recalls in a radio broadcast the cookery of her mother:

She cooked a lot of food with a lot of garlic and a lot of oil. I mean it was olive oil. We didn't know olive oil was good for you back then, so it all appeared very heavy. My mother and most Greeks love anything grown from the earth, so weeds fell into that category. It's like a vegetable like any other in the way the Greeks think but my mother and her cousins and friends would go out to a local park and pick the weeds and cook the weeds and make salad out of the weeds, just like you would have rocket, lettuce or any sort of vegetable like that … And she'd pick up the bowl and she'd start putting vinegar and oil and salt on them and the table would be set and the weeds would be sitting in the middle.

One of the weeds beloved by Greeks is sow thistle said to have been eaten by Theseus to give him strength to slay the Minotaur. Sow thistle (*Sonchus oleraceus*) is a tall slender green plant with small yellow flowers. It has a similar nutritive value to spinach with a slightly bitter taste like endive. Mary Coustas reports the horror of some of her school friends at her mother's weed salads but, as a lover of weeds myself, I pass on this recipe from Mina Rawson, suitable for tender, young plants.

4 cups young sow thistles, picked over, flowers retained	*1 teaspoon olive oil*
	½ teaspoon Worcestershire sauce
1 hard-boiled egg	*1 tablespoon vinegar*
½ teaspoon dry mustard	*¼ cup cream*
Pinch salt and freshly ground black pepper	

▪ The sow thistles should be picked over and any tough leaves, wiry stems, and seed heads discarded. Wash well in 2–3 changes of water if very gritty. Place on a chopping board and shred finely as you do for lettuce. Place in a

bowl with plenty of water to cover and soak for 1–2 hours to remove some
of the bitterness. Drain well and shake dry.

∎ To make the dressing, mash the yolk of the egg in a bowl with the
mustard, salt and pepper. Beat in the oil with a whisk, then the Worcestershire
sauce, vinegar and finally the cream. Just before serving pour the dressing over
the greens and toss. Decorate with finely chopped egg white, and a few of
the thistle's yellow flowers if available.

Richard Beckett's Mixed Salad

SERVES 1

GOOD health through diet is a concept inherent in the traditional Aboriginal
lifestyle. Native meats are low in saturated fats and native fruits, vegetables and
grains are often higher in protein, vitamins, minerals and dietary fibre than
their cultivated equivalents. The consumption of many fruits, vegetables and
raw insects immediately after harvest and the rarity of boiling maintains the
vitamins intact. Nuts, grains and tubers have a high proportion of complex
carbohydrates which render food more slowly digestible and ward off diseases
such as diabetes, cardiovascular problems and obesity. Most Aboriginal people
lived on a wide variety of foods and hence received a good balance of
different nutrients.

Health food writing began in the decade before Federation with books
by Dr Phillip Muskett and Harriet Wicken, as well as temperance authors
Anna Colcord and Olive A. Lucas. Cookbooks on health themes proliferated
in the twentieth century, spurred on by scientific discoveries about food
values, but government intervened only in the 1940s. In New South Wales
free milk was dispensed to all primary children every school day from 1941
to 1973, a practice doomed to unpopularity because of the habit of leaving
the bottles to warm and sour in the sun. After World War II, canteens were
established in many government schools, and encouraged to sell wholesome
foods such as the Oslo lunch, invented in Norway by Professor Schiotz. It
came to Australia in 1940, initially tested on disadvantaged children, and
consisted of three slices of buttered wholemeal bread with 30 g of cheese, a
cup of milk plus a piece of fruit or serving of salad vegetables.

The following tasty, highly decorative and nutritionally superior meat
salad is another post-war approach to the health issue, from Richard Beckett's
history of Australian cookery *Convicted Tastes*.

1 slice each of leg ham, corned beef, and
  chicken or turkey breast
3 cup-shaped lettuce leaves
3 slices beetroot
A good scoop of potato salad
1 tomato, halved
Mayonnaise or boiled dressing (optional)

2 fresh parsley sprigs
1 wedge Australian cheddar
3 radish roses
1 hard-boiled egg, halved
1 or 2 small cocktail gherkins
1 slice cut from a large orange, halved

▮ Overlap the slices of meat on a dinner plate. Place the lettuce cups around
the edge of the plate. Fill one with beetroot slices, one with potato salad and
one with the tomato halves. Dab a little mayonnaise on the tomato halves if
you like and decorate with a sprig of parsley. Arrange the cheese, radishes and
egg between the cups. Fan-cut the gherkins and place on top of the egg. Snip
the rind of the halved orange slice, twist and use for decoration.

Australian Housewife's Salad

SERVES 8

MANY colonial households depended on the Chinese for their supply of fresh
vegetables and fruits. Chinese people first came to Australia in 1838 as coolies
indentured to squatters for domestic and kitchen work, and then in the
1850s, with the cessation of convict transportation to the eastern states, as
labourers. With the discovery of gold in the 1850s mass migration began,
peaking in 1858. As alluvial gold mining declined many Chinese began to
service the diggers as restaurant cooks, storekeepers, merchants, laundrymen,
herbalists and market gardeners.

On the outskirts of many towns their market gardens sprang up, well
maintained and weed-free because of the diligence of their owners. The
vegetables flourished under a regimen of liquid manuring from nightsoil and
irrigation using windwheels and pumps adapted from alluvial mining. Four or
five men would often work in partnership, sharing the labour-intensive
chores and hawking their produce to the kitchen doors of their customers,
carrying it in a horse-drawn cart or else in two baskets suspended from a
pole balanced across their shoulders. In Melbourne in the 1880s one in every
three Chinese men of working age was employed in market gardening.

Author and historian Patsy Adam-Smith, in her book *Hear the Train Blow*,
remembers the Chinese greengrocer Charlie who supplied her family during
the Depression:

He was a small yellow man wearing in winter a black skull-cap and in summer a battered grey felt. He spoke as we expected Chinese to speak—as many English-speaking people still expect them to do.

'Velly nice lipe melon. You tly?' He'd slice off a piece and we'd 'tly'.

'You likey lettucey? You likey clisp radish? Fluit?'

One Christmas, when the family had fallen on hard times, Charlie came all the same even though there was no money to pay him:

'Melly Clissmus, missus,' he beamed, handing Mum the traditional jar of ginger in syrup. Then he turned to us girls. 'Melly Clissmus, missee,' he wished each of us, and pushed a large parcel in our arms ...

Our vegetables were in the parcel he had given Mick, and there was fruit in the parcel I held. There was everything we could have wished for, lettuces, new carrots, new potatoes, spring onions, parsley, mint, green peas, marrow, asparagus and tomatoes, apples, bananas and a big red watermelon.

'Holy Father in heaven bless that little yellow man,' Mum prayed that night, and we all said 'Amen', and Dad who didn't pray said, 'Too right!'

The Chinese provided the sorts of vegetables which the Australian cook demanded, including the ingredients necessary for the following excellent mixed salad published in 1896 from the *Housewife's Cookery Book*.

AUSTRALIAN HOUSEWIFE'S SALAD

1 lettuce	HOUSEWIFE'S DRESSING
8 radishes, thinly sliced	1 hard-boiled egg yolk
6 spring onions, thinly sliced	150 g boiled potato, peeled and mashed
2 tomatoes, peeled, halved and sliced	¼ cup desiccated coconut
⅓ cup watercress, finely chopped	1½ teaspoons ground almonds, optional
1 sprig fresh parsley, finely chopped	½ teaspoon dry mustard
1 sprig lemon thyme, finely chopped	½ teaspoon curry powder
1 hard-boiled egg white, finely chopped	¾ teaspoon salt and pinch white pepper
	¼ cup white wine vinegar
	½ cup milk

∎ Wash and dry the lettuce and tear into pieces. Toss with the other ingredients in a large bowl.

∎ To make the dressing, place the yolk of the hard-boiled egg in a mixing bowl with the potato. Beat with an electric mixer or whisk until smooth. Add the coconut, almonds, spices and vinegar and beat until combined. Beat in the milk. When ready, pour the dressing over the vegetables and toss.

Asparagus Salad

SERVES 5 – 6

FRESH vegetables and fruits were not always available to white people living in the outback. Myrtle Rose White, in her account of life on a cattle station in the South Australian desert from 1915 to 1921 *No Roads Go By*, describes the pitiless months of summer heat-waves when, too hot and dry for cultivation, the longing for cold, fresh food became almost unbearable:

The morning's milk was sour by night. Butter was a hope of the future and a thing of the past. There was the terrible unappeasable craving for cool fresh green salads, tomatoes, fresh fruit, and the like. An endless wringing out of clothes from blue water, and from soda water, to wrap round foods in order to tempt jaded appetites; and round jellies that would not jell, and which, even if they did, would melt before they could travel from plate to mouth, and for cold puddings that were cold in name only. There is fresh beef for one day, and salt beef for twenty-nine …

There were times in the latter years, at Noonameena, when I would have considered a lamb chop above rubies, cabbage food for the gods, and a beautiful scented rose a fair exchange for my soul. Live on a diet of beef for seven years only relieved by goat about four times in twelve months, and see how you feel. Live on dried vegetables for two unbroken years on end and you will know how alluring can be the thought of fresh vegetables.

Many country cooks depended heavily on tinned vegetables and, even for city folk until the 1970s, the only form of asparagus came in a tin. The following recipe is from the *WMU Cookery Book*.

DRESSING
1 tablespoon butter
1 tablespoon plain flour
½ teaspoon salt
½ teaspoon dry mustard
½ teaspoon sugar
Pinch white pepper
½ cup milk

½ cup water
2 egg yolks
1½ tablespoons white wine vinegar

1 green cucumber
440 g tin asparagus spears, drained
125 g lettuce
2 tablespoons finely chopped gherkins

▮ To make the dressing, melt the butter in a small saucepan and stir in the flour until smooth. Cook for a minute or two over a moderate heat. Remove from the heat, stir in the spices and gradually blend in the milk and water. Return to the stove and cook, stirring constantly, until it comes to the boil and thickens. Lightly beat the yolks with the vinegar, add to the saucepan and cook for a minute more but make sure it does not boil. Let cool, covered.

▮ Peel the cucumber and cut into 2.5 cm lengths. Scrape out the seeds to form rings. Push about 3 spears of asparagus through each ring and arrange on small nests of lettuce, shredded with a knife or torn into little pieces. Spoon some dressing over the asparagus and sprinkle with chopped gherkin.

Broccoli and Capsicum Salad

SERVES 6

MOST early Italian arrivals worked in primary industries such as fishing and farming although a few were involved in manufacturing foods such as macaroni. The first Italians to enter Australia in any number (we are talking here of hundreds rather than thousands) came in the last three decades of the nineteenth century, mainly as agricultural labourers on sugar-cane farms in the tropical heat of Queensland. Mass migration began in 1920, and following the World War II they represented the biggest non-English speaking migrant group.

Because of their numbers, the richness of their culinary heritage and its adaptability to manufacturing, Italians have had an enormous effect on the way we eat, greater indeed than any other migrant group of the post-war period. During the 1960s and '70s many Italian food products became widely available, including cheeses like parmesan, pecorino, provolone, mozzarella and ricotta, Italian salamis and prosciutto, a great range of pasta shapes, olive oil, black olives, tomato paste, tinned tomatoes, giardiniera pickles, gelato, cappuccino and espresso coffee. In the 1980s these were joined by fresh pasta, virgin olive oil, balsamic vinegar, sundried tomatoes, focaccia and mascarpone.

A significant impact has been in the fruit and vegetable trade with Italian greengrocers setting a standard of quality and freshness as well as introducing previously little known varieties such as zucchini, broccoli, globe artichokes, fennel, eggplant, radicchio, different types of lettuces and capsicums, chillies, fresh chestnuts and flat-leaved parsley. One of the most famous greengrocers was Giuseppe De Luca, who arrived from Boston in 1886 and opened a shop in King Street Sydney which specialised in fruit, wines and confectionery. In 1916 the business was taken over by the Donato brothers who brought in presentation fruit baskets and a fruit salad renowned with lunchtime office workers. They pioneered the sale of broccoli in the early 1940s when the Edgell company, canning for American troops in the Pacific, had an excess they could not use. In 1987 De Luca's closed its doors for the last time.

Broccoli and red capsicums have now achieved wide acceptance in Australia and they marry well in this colourful salad.

---

500 g broccoli florets
1 red capsicum, halved, seeded and cut in
strips
½ cup currants

¾ teaspoon salt and frsehly ground black
pepper
⅓ cup olive oil
1 tablespoon cider or wine vinegar

▪ Steam the broccoli florets in a steamer basket over boiling water until barely cooked but still crisp, about 4–5 minutes. Drain and combine in a large bowl with the capsicum, currants, salt and pepper. Pour over the oil and toss well to coat. Add the vinegar and toss.

Tropical Tabouleh

THE first Middle Eastern people to arrive in Australia were the 'Ghans', brought in as camel drivers. Only some of these men actually came from Afghanistan, others originating in Pakistan, Egypt, Iran and Turkey. They often planted date palms along their camel routes but, as they were not involved in the food industry, had negligible impact on Australian cooking.

Lebanese people started arriving in significant numbers after World War II and particularly from 1967. During this period they opened restaurants, take-aways, milk bars and coffee shops. For the first time Middle Eastern foodstuffs such as burghul, pita bread, chick peas, sesame seeds and yoghurt appeared in the diet of ordinary Australians who also developed a liking for hummus, falafel, doner kebabs, shish kebabs and baklava. Tabouleh has perhaps been the single most widely accepted Arabic dish, and so it is not surprising to find local adaptations of this salad, including this excellent one with finely chopped fresh pineapple.

TROPICAL TABOULEH

1 cup burghul (crushed wheat)	2 tablespoons finely chopped fresh mint leaves
1½ cups finely chopped pineapple (or pineapple and tomato)	1 teaspoon salt
	Freshly ground black pepper
6 spring onions, finely sliced	2 tablespoons olive oil
1 cup finely chopped fresh flat-leaf parsley	1½ tablespoons lemon juice

▪ Place the burghul in a large bowl and cover with water. Leave to soak for 1 hour. Drain well in a fine colander or sieve for at least a couple of hours and press out as much of the excess water as possible. Transfer to a salad bowl and stir in the pineapple, spring onions, parsley and mint. Season with the remaining ingredients and mix well.

8

Pavlova to jump-up

A whole array of Aussie desserts were created in the refrigerator era and fruit, particularly tropical fruit, featured in many of them including Australia's national dessert the pavlova, with its passionfruit and cream topping.

The Edwardian kitchen—captured by Alfred Chambers in The Kitchen *(circa 1910)—before gas and electric stoves, built-in cupboards and bench tops, and the appliances that grace them changed the way we cook forever.*

The Grand Finale

APART from meat dishes, the strongest suit in the Australian cook's repertoire is surely in the area of desserts, cakes and other sweet things. Antipodeans are notorious for having a sweet tooth and most would not consider a good dinner complete without a dessert to finish off. Dessert is the grand finale to a meal, the bribe for munching one's way through nutritious but at times reluctant helpings of vegetables.

This addiction to sweets is of long-standing. Aboriginal people have a marked fondness for sweet things, a tradition confirmed in time by British migrants in whose cuisine puddings and desserts feature prominently. Added to this, conditions in colonial Australia meant that for many bush people, their diet was rather monotonous. Whatever the ingenuity of the cook, nothing could disguise the unfailing appearance on the dinner table of mutton and salt beef, potatoes and pumpkin. However, when it came to the end of the meal, the housewife or bushman could vary the bill of fare with a relatively small number of foods: flour, sugar, a few dried fruits and some spice could be made into a whole range of different puddings. By adding more or less of an ingredient or by varying the method from boiling to steaming, baking or frying, the cook could produce a welcome variety to the meal.

For the cook living in the cities and coastal areas the making of puddings and invention of new recipes also flourished. An important factor here was the abundance of fruit, cheap enough to be within the reach of all. Tropical fruits in particular, lend themselves to dessert cookery since most require some preparation in the kitchen, such as peeling, seeding and cutting into manageable portions before they are ready to eat. Passionfruit alone has been responsible for hundreds of new desserts.

Mostly, these dishes are the inventions of ordinary cooks since preparation of desserts and cakes are part of the regular cooking repertoire in Australia, not a separate branch executed by specialist pastry cooks as it so often is in continental Europe. For the most part, these are the creations of women because dessert and cake making is 'the peculiarly and appropriately feminine department of the noble art of Cookery'. In the words of the anonymous author of the *First Australian Continental Cookery Book,* published in Melbourne in 1937, it is here 'the eternal feminine is wont to revel in results that mere man, unless a culinary genius, can only contemplate and enjoy with respectful admiration'. It is here especially that generations of Australian women, confined by society to the home, have sought to express their creativity by inventing new recipes and presenting them in an attractive way.

Bush Sweets

The types of desserts created over the years have varied tremendously. For Aboriginal Australians, dessert traditionally forms no fixed course and may be taken at any time. Notable among sweet foods are sugarbag—the honeycomb of our little native stingless bees—and, in the central deserts, the swollen bodies of honey ants. Fruit provides the most important sweet food gathered by the women and children. Many of our native fruits make excellent eating and present a far greater and more interesting range of flavours than is available from the greengrocer's shelves, tasting sometimes pleasantly acidulous, sweet or fruity, but occasionally spicy, salty, salt-sweet, aromatic, piney, bland or tangy, according to the particular fruit. They include the famous lilli pillies and quandong, midyim berries and aspens, finger limes and wild tamarinds, native raspberries and currants, the fruits of the dodder laurel and pig-face, the ooray or Davidson's plum, the bolwarra or native guava, salt-bush berries, bush bananas, emu berries, cocky apples, cherry ballarts and Illawarra plums. Figs are a common fruit, occurring in all mainland states: probably the best are the desert fig, which grows in rocky crevices throughout the arid regions, and the sand fig of Arnhem Land. Some figs are eaten as they are but others are pounded to a smooth paste, sometimes mixed with water and honey. The boab trees of the Top End produce a fruit which may be roasted when immature or let ripen, when the pith dries to a pleasant-tasting powder. Geebungs are edible once peeled and the milky plum, a northern species, can be pounded to a paste with other fruits to make a fruit leather, which may be eaten straight away or stored for weeks. The green plum is the richest natural source of vitamin C in the world and its tart fruits, tasting something like a gooseberry, make a refreshing pick-me-up. The nonda plum is an important fresh fruit in the far north during September and October and the dried fruits and kernels can be pounded and soaked to produce a nut milk for infants being weaned. For Torres Strait people, too, fruit are significant, served with the main course and traditionally eaten without cooking.

The All-conquering Pudding

During the colonial period the eating of sweets was transformed and their making reached a high art. When households were large and diets non-existent, the meal ended with a large, hot, filling pudding or pie. The English novelist Anthony Trollope, writing of his visit to a Victorian country gentleman's residence in the 1870s, noted the presence of no more than two puddings at lunch but an unlimited number at dinner. For humbler households, one pudding would have been enough, but still served with an appropriate hot sauce, such as boiled custard, sweet, foamy or jam sauce. Even the bushman, eating his meal by some lonely campfire at the back of beyond, would have finished his repast with a pudding wrapped in calico and boiled in the billy or camp oven, or a simple dish of sweetened rice or, at the very least, bachelor's tart, that is a slice of damper and jam.

For grander occasions or for variety cooks would exert themselves in the preparation of a cold dessert: elegantly moulded jellies, frothy creams, and, most difficult of all without refrigeration, ices and ice creams. The ordinary housewife, lacking the resources of the larger establishments with their kitchen staff, freezing vases and cooling houses, would have limited herself mainly to those which did not require chilling, such as moulded blancmange and sago, tapioca, custards, stewed fruit and trifles.

Refrigerators and Flummery

With the introduction of ice chests in the late nineteenth century and refrigerators from the 1920s a major revolution in dessert cookery occurred. Hot puddings were relegated to the short Australian winter and refrigerated desserts took over for the major part of the year. For the first time, it was quick and easy for the housewife to make jellies, whips, flummeries and fruit mousses in her new refrigerator, with shallow trays of delicious home-made ice cream in the small freezer compartment at the top. Convenience foods such as powdered gelatine, packaged jellies and tinned milk and fruit, which had appeared on the market in the 1880s, formed the basis of many of the new cool dishes packed with vitamins. A whole array of Australian desserts were created in the refrigerator era and fruit, particularly tropical fruit, featured in many of them including Australia's national dessert the pavlova.

Hopetoun Lemon Pudding

SERVES 6

STEAMED puddings belong very much to a pre-refrigeration age but also to the age of wood-fueled cookery when, having lighted the fire in the morning, it was easier left alight the whole day while soups and stews bubbled slowly along and puddings bathed indefinitely in a constant sweat until dinner was ready. Even the three hours usually recommended for a suet pudding were no problem, requiring no extra expenditure of fuel and little extra generation of heat in the already hot kitchen.

In the colonial period many new steamed and boiled puddings were invented. Dates and figs, apples and berries, pineapple and passionfruit, left-over damper, spices, jam and golden syrup all found their way into a variety of puddings. To judge by the recipes that remain, best loved were plum puddings, including the banana plum pudding of dried fruit and breadcrumbs bound together with mashed banana. On a more sinister note, the poison plum pudding, laced with strychnine or arsenic, formed a Christmas 'treat' for unsuspecting Aborigines, whose removal from grazing land ensured vacant possession for pastoralists.

The following golden, lemon-flavoured pudding, rich with butter and eggs, is a tribute to Lord and Lady Hopetoun from Fanny Fawcett Story. John Hope, born at Hopetoun in Scotland in 1860, became Australia's first Governor-General when the colonies federated in 1901, although he and his wife had already established their popularity while he served as Governor of Victoria some years before.

---

125 g butter, softened
½ cup castor sugar
1 teaspoon finely grated lemon rind

3 eggs, beaten
1 cup self-raising flour, sifted
⅓ cup mixed peel

▪ Place the butter, sugar and lemon rind in a bowl and cream with an electric beater, that is, beat until they are light, pale and fluffy. Gradually add about ⅔ of the eggs, beating very well to incorporate. Beat in about ⅓ of the flour and then gradually beat in the remaining egg. Fold in the rest of the flour with the beaters at low speed and stir in the peel. Place in a greased pudding basin, ⅔ full. Cover with 2 layers of foil, folding the foil down the middle to form a pleat to allow for expansion. Secure with string.

▪ Place in a large saucepan and pour boiling water ½ of the way up the basin. Cover and steam at a simmer for 1½ hours. Check the water level and replace if necessary. Serve in slices with custard or cream.

Mittagong Dumpling

SERVES 6–8

PROBABLY because of its relative scarcity fat was much prized originally in Australia, not only for its gustatory value but also as a skin and hair moisturizer and conditioner. Chief sources were the goanna and emu but animals like the kangaroo have a certain amount of kidney fat.

With the introduction of domesticated animals during the colonial era fat became an everyday article of diet, seen by nutritionists of the time as a necessary source of energy without which the body could not function. Most men and women led far more physically active lives then and could afford to eat more fat while remaining healthy. Fat took various forms either as an integral part of meat and dairy foods or in its pure form as butter or dripping, the latter collected from baked joints. Dripping is an excellent frying medium and a butter substitute in outback cakes, biscuits and pastry. In *Bread and Dripping Days* Kathleen McArthur describes a treat enjoyed by many during the Depression:

After the long walk home from school there was bread and dripping for afternoon tea, liberally sprinkled with pepper and salt. In sheep districts it was mutton dripping and those children swore it was the best, but the cattle families plumbed for beef dripping as the tastiest.

Suet is another fat that, like dripping, has fallen from grace in modern times. Taken from around the kidneys of sheep or cattle it was an essential ingredient in many colonial puddings giving a slightly heavier texture than butter but lending them a rich and delicious unctuousness. This suet pudding recipe was collected by Harriet Wicken from the little town of Mittagong, south-west of Sydney whose Koori name means 'place where the dingoes play'. One of my favourites, it encloses a pocket filled with a lemon–honey sauce which pours out as you cut into it. If your butcher has no suet, offcut lamb or beef fat will do well.

MITTAGONG DUMPLING

Juice and finely grated rind of 1 lemon	*175 g suet (or any hard lamb or beef fat)*
1 cup honey	*¾ cup (4 oz) currants*
1¼ cups plain flour	*⅓ cup mixed peel*
1¼ cups self-raising flour	*1 cup water*

▪ Mix the lemon juice and honey in a bowl until smoothly combined. Set aside.

▪ Put the flours in a mixing bowl and stir in the lemon rind. Dice the suet and blend in the food processor with the flours until reduced to tiny pieces. Remove to the mixing bowl and stir in the currants and peel. Pour in the water and mix with your hand to make a dough.

▪ Flour a pastry board and press out about ⅔ of the dough with your hands to form a circle large enough to cover the bottom and sides of a 6-cup pudding basin. Line the greased basin, leaving a cavity sufficient to hold the lemon-honey sauce. Pour in the sauce.

▎ Pat out the remaining dough into a circle. Put the circle in, pressing down around the edges so that it seals with the first layer. Cover the basin with 2 layers of foil, pleated down the middle and secure with string. Place in a large saucepan and pour boiling water half way up the basin. Cover and steam at a simmer for 2½ –3 hours.

▎ When cooked, select a serving dish deep enough to contain the pudding and its sauce. Turn out and serve with whipped cream.

Hot Hobart Mulberry Cake

SERVES 8

AUSTRALIA has many native berry fruits enjoyed by Aboriginal people but also cooked up by early white settlers into preserves, pies and summer drinks. Most of these fell out of general favour during the twentieth century and, even with respect to exotic species, there have been distinct changes in fashion over the years. Kiwi fruit and blueberries were popularized only in the 1970s and '80s whereas the Cape gooseberry was probably introduced on the First Fleet. It was widely propagated during colonial times as was the blackberry, which soon became a noxious pest.

Mulberries are one of those old-fashioned fruits, growing singly in home gardens, their spring harvest welcomed by birds, possums and children alike as well as by cooks who can turn them into delicious jams, pies and crumbles. Like strawberries they flourish in all states but grow exceptionally well in Tasmania which, with its cool climate, established itself in the early nineteenth century as a major berry producer. In his book *Australia and New Zealand* Anthony Trollope describes his visit to the island during the 1870s:

She is full of English fruits, which grow certainly more plentifully and, as regards some, with greater excellence than they do in England. Tasmanian cherries beat those of Kent … Strawberries, raspberries, gooseberries, plums, and apples are in almost equal abundance … And then the mulberries! There was a lady in Hobart Town who sent us mulberries every day such as I had never eaten before, and as—I feel sure—I shall never eat again.

450 g mulberries

Juice of 1 lemon

1¼ cups (300 ml) sour cream

2 eggs

1 cup sugar

1½ cups self-raising flour

1 tablespoon extra sugar

▪ Nip the stalks from the mulberries and gently mix the fruit with the lemon juice. Beat the sour cream and eggs together in a mixing bowl with a whisk. Beat in the sugar, then the flour. Pour the mixture into a buttered oven-proof dish. Spoon the mulberries evenly over the top and sprinkle the fruit with the extra sugar.

▪ Bake in a preheated oven at 180°C for 40–45 minutes until done. Serve hot with whipped or thick cream if liked.

Golden Apple Crumble

SERVES 4–6

FRUIT crumbles, particularly those made from apple, are very popular winter desserts in Australia and the following recipe is especially good, flavoured with ginger, coconut and golden syrup, or cocky's joy.

The word cocky was originally an expression of contempt for the small farmer who at times led a wretched existence and had a habit of seizing on the best pieces of land and then abandoning them when the ground was exhausted. Cocky's joy was cheap and therefore preferred by the poor farmer. It has been beloved by most Australians since the 1880s and is particularly handy for the bushy, as journalist and historian C.E.W. Bean explained in 1910 in *On the Wool Track*:

Cocky's joy was golden syrup in 2-lb. tins, then costing sevenpence—four times as cheap as jam and six times as portable. Every boundary rider's camp was littered with half-empty tins of it. They were witty at its expense, and yet they cherished it, too.

The climax of misery for a man, according to Bean, was for his tent to blow down, his fire to go out, his dog to curl up in his blanket wet, a crow to steal his soap—and ants to get into his cocky's joy.

3 large cooking apples	CRUMBLE TOPPING
2 tablespoons golden syrup	½ cup self-raising flour
2 tablespoons chopped preserved ginger	½ cup desiccated coconut
1 teaspoon lemon juice	½ cup brown sugar, firmly packed
¼ teaspoon ground cinnamon	60 g butter

▪ Peel, core and slice the apples and place in a saucepan with the golden syrup. Simmer over a moderate heat for 10 minutes, covered, and then a further 10 minutes, uncovered, until the apples are cooked and most of their juice has evaporated. Remove from the stove and stir in the ginger, lemon juice and cinnamon. Turn into a buttered 20 cm oven-proof dish.

▪ To make the crumble topping, mix together the flour, coconut and sugar in a bowl. Melt the butter in a small saucepan over a low heat. Stir into the dry ingredients. Spoon lightly over the apples. Bake in a preheated oven at 190°C, for about 20 minutes until golden brown on top.

Bundaberg Bananas

SERVES 4

RUM was the most important alcoholic beverage in early colonial times and an important article of commerce. Under Governor Phillip it was denied to convicts, who would, however, band together and barter some of their rations with an officer or civil servant for a bottle of rum or arrack. With Lieutenant-Governor Grose liquor became plentiful and convicts were paid in spirits by the merchants, large land owners and officers of the NSW Corps (nicknamed the 'Rum Corps') who held a monopoly. The Rum Rebellion resulted when Governor Bligh tried in vain to stop this illegal trade. Governor Macquarie was more successful, reducing the number of liquor licences, imposing import duties, and establishing a bank and silver coinage to supplant rum as currency.

Since 1888 rum has been distilled in Bundaberg, a by-product of the cane-sugar industry. Here it combines with citrus in a dish of banana fritters.

4 bananas	2 tablespoons sugar
¼ cup Bundaberg rum	¾ cup plain flour
¼ cup orange juice	1 egg white
2 teaspoons lemon juice	½ cup water
½ teaspoon finely grated orange rind	Oil for frying

▪ Peel the bananas, slice in half lengthwise and put in a shallow dish. In a jug combine the rum with the citrus juices, rind and sugar. Pour over the bananas and allow to marinate for an hour or two, turning them carefully half-way through.

■ Remove the bananas and dust with ¼ cup of flour. Put the citrus marinade in a small saucepan and heat gently over a low heat.

■ Meanwhile, make the batter. Beat the egg white until stiff with an electric beater or whisk. Put the remaining flour in a separate bowl and gradually beat in the water until smooth. Fold in the egg white with a spoon. Pour the batter into a shallow dish and dip the bananas in to coat.

■ Heat some oil in a frying pan over a high heat. Fry the bananas in batches until golden, turning half-way through, about 3 minutes each side. Drain on paper towels and keep warm while you continue cooking. Serve with the marinade as a sauce and with ice cream or whipped cream.

Baking, Old Ways

PIES were an important area of dessert cookery in colonial times, baked in the camp oven, the solid-fuel stove or in an oven built into the kitchen.

In *Old Days: Old Ways* Dame Mary Gilmore, the great humanitarian and poet, describes her grandmother's cooking arrangements in her house on the Hawkesbury River:

It is Easter. I am a child again in the big old kitchen at Brooklyn. My grandmother sits in her rocking-chair at the side of the deep-spaced fire-place; behind her is the cavern in the wall that is the brick baking-oven. There a whole sheep could be roasted, three sucking-pigs, and half a barrow load of potatoes and pumpkins; while wild fowl, ducks, and chickens disappeared into its vastness, and were lost in the far corners at the back where the heat was less. The bread that was baked in it made a mountain, and the pies, cakes, and buns were hills.

Amongst the 'hills' of colonial pies were many distinctive types. They could easily be filled from the store of golden syrup, treacle, jam, coconut, ginger or dried fruits if fresh fruit supplies were unreliable. Vegetables were sweetened to taste, so that there are numerous references to 'apple' pies of pumpkin, sweet potatoes and chokoes, as well as green tomato pies resembling gooseberry. Naturally, the common European fruits such as apple, rhubarb, stone fruits and berries formed fillings, as did the quandong and many tropical fruits.

Mango Pie

SERVES 6

THE Queensland mango industry started as the result of trade with India in the mid 1800s. Ships landing at Bowen brought mangoes as part of their cargo and some of these were planted on the local farms. By the 1880s one such farmer had developed a new strain, known after his property as the Kensington Pride or Bowen Special. It has since become our most famous mango, distinguished by its attractive red blush and on the inside by its rich orange flesh, free of fibre. These, as well as the common stringy mangoes, are now found all up and down the Queensland coast growing eventually into immense and handsome trees.

December and January are the great mango-eating months. Mangoes have a flavour and perfume which evoke images of palm-fringed beaches and mythic tropic paradise like no other fruit. English sojourner Thomas Wood, in *Cobbbers* saw them as 'all that you have *imagined* beforehand a tropical fruit should taste like':

You must slash the thick hard skin with your knife, criss-cross right round: peel it off in quarters, and take four bites, two on one side, two on the other, and throw the stone away. Then close your eyes in gratitude and let the fruit melt into you lusciously; cheering your senses with the flavour and aroma of orange and jasmine, mellowed into a poem by golden sunlight.

Mangoes make a wonderful pie, nestling under flakes of crispy and delicate puff pastry.

1 kg mangoes
2 tablespoons lemon juice
¼ cup sugar

1½ tablespoons plain flour
225 g puff pastry
1 egg yolk, beaten (eggwash)

∎ Cut the 2 cheeks from the mango. Score the flesh into slices or cubes without cutting through the skin. A little pressure on the underside of the skin and the flesh opens up ready for slicing off. Cut off any other flesh remaining and discard the skin and stones. Toss the mango slices in a bowl with the lemon juice. Combine the sugar and flour and mix thoroughly with the fruit. Put into a 20 cm pie or flan dish and pile up towards the centre.
∎ On a lightly floured board roll out the pastry thinly to fit the dish. Brush the rim of the dish with a little eggwash. Place the pastry over the dish and

trim the edges. Press firmly onto the rim crimping the edges by pinching the pastry between the thumb and forefinger. Cut a small hole in the centre as a steam vent and decorate with shapes cut from the scraps if liked. Secure them on the pastry with eggwash. Mix the remaining eggwash with 1 teaspoon of water and brush over the pie to give a glazed finish.

▪ Bake in a preheated oven at 230°C for 15–20 minutes. Reduce the temperature to 190°C and cook for a further 15 minutes until golden brown. Serve hot with whipped cream or ice cream.

Pavlova

SERVES 8

THE famous Russian ballerina Anna Pavlova toured Australia twice, the second time in 1929 including Perth in her itinerary. While there she stayed at the Esplanade Hotel, one of the leading establishments in the city. Six years later in 1935 Elizabeth Paxton, owner of the hotel, requested her chef create some delicacies to attract the ladies of Perth to the Esplanade for afternoon tea. So it was that Herbert Sachse, born on the goldfields of Western Australia, failed wheat farmer turned cook, came to invent the meringue cake which is now recognised as Australia's national dessert. When the cake was presented, the hotel manager Harry Nairn declared that it was 'as light as Pavlova', and the name stuck.

The greatness of the pavlova, that which sets it above all other meringue cakes, derives from its symphony of contrasting textures. By lowering the sugar content and introducing small quantities of cornflour and vinegar, Bert Sachse created a soft marshmallow-like meringue, encased within a thin crunchy shell. Cooking it as one big round ensured the dominance of the soft centre. Combined with whipped cream and passionfruit it achieved a sublimity which quickly addicted the nation.

6 egg whites	1½ teaspoons white wine vinegar
Pinch cream of tartar	½ teaspoon vanilla essence
1/¼ cups castor sugar	1 cup cream
2 tablespoons cornflour plus extra	4 passionfruit

▪ If new to meringue-making see the tips following. Whisk the egg whites with electric beaters or a whisk until frothy. Add the cream of tartar and beat until stiff. Add 1 cup of castor sugar, a tablespoon at a time, beating well between additions until the sugar has dissolved. Mix the remaining sugar with the cornflour and fold gently into the meringue with a spoon. Fold in the vinegar and vanilla.

▮ Line a flat baking tray with baking paper and dust lightly with extra cornflour. Spoon the meringue onto the baking paper making a mound 20 cm in diameter. Make a slight depression on top for the filling and swirl the meringue to create an attractive effect. Bake in a preheated oven at 130°C for 1 hour. Turn off the heat and leave in the oven for another 2 hours without opening the door then remove and let cool completely.

▮ Transfer the pavlova to a serving plate, discarding the baking paper. Whip the cream and spread on top. Spoon the pulp of the passionfruit over the cream. Sliced strawberries and kiwi fruit are also acid enough to offset the sweetness of the meringue, but passionfruit is traditional.

Making Meringue

Make sure the bowl and beaters or whisk are completely clean and dry. Avoid plastic bowls. Carefully separate the whites from the yolks while the eggs are cold. Even a skerrick of yolk or fat in the whites will prevent them beating up properly. Place the whites in the mixing bowl and let them come to room temperature. Beat until they hold stiff peaks when the beaters are withdrawn. Gradually add castor sugar, sprinkling it lightly over the whites and beating thoroughly so that the sugar dissolves before adding more. The finished meringue should be smooth and glossy, not grainy.

Federation Pudding

SERVES 8

ON 1ST January 1901 the six independent colonies were united into a single nation, the Commonwealth of Australia. This had implications for many areas of Australian life but in the culinary field it meant the free movement of foodstuffs around the country due to the elimination of all trade barriers between the states, especially the restrictive tariffs which had operated in the colonial period. There was no doubt a uniting of the national consciousness and a progression towards a national cuisine although local influences obviously still persist.

To celebrate Federation, Fanny Fawcett Story invented this lovely cold pudding consisting of a sponge cake filled with apple, masked with whipped cream and decorated with tiny meringues. The hot-water sponge recipe on page 181–2 makes a suitable size cake for filling or simply buy one.

MERINGUES

1 egg white

Pinch cream of tartar

Pinch of salt

¼ cup castor sugar

¼ teaspoon vanilla essence

FILLING

1 kg Granny Smith apples, peeled, cored and
   sliced

⅓ cup sugar

½ cup raisins

¼ cup chopped almonds

2 tablespoons butter

⅓ cup water

TO FINISH

1 x 20 cm sponge cake

1 cup cream, whipped

6 glacé cherries

30 g angelica, if available

▪ Whisk the egg white with the cream of tartar and salt with electric beaters or a whisk until stiff. Gradually beat in the sugar until the meringue is thick and glossy and all the sugar is dissolved. Beat in the vanilla. Line a baking tray with baking paper and onto it pipe or spoon 12 small meringues about 2.5 cm in diameter. Bake in a preheated oven at 140°C for 30 minutes. Remove from the oven and peel off the paper immediately. Cool on a rack.

▪ For the filling, place all the ingredients in a saucepan and bring to the boil over a moderate heat. Simmer, covered, for a few minutes until the apples start to soften and release their juices. Uncover the saucepan and cook until any excess juice has evaporated. Stir occasionally and break up the apples roughly with a wooden spoon. When done, taste and add more sugar if necessary. Allow to cool, uncovered.

▪ To assemble the pudding, cut a circle in the top of the sponge about 1 cm within the outside edge. Cut or spoon out the centre of the cake to create a container for the filling. You will need a cavity about half the depth of the sponge. Spoon in the apple filling. Spread the whipped cream over the top and sides. Decorate with the meringues. Place a half glacé cherry in the middle of each meringue (and triangular or diamond-shaped leaves of angelica around the meringues if liked).

Tropical Trifle

SERVES 10

A CONSTANT factor in Australia has been the quality and abundance of fruit. As early as 1819 statesman William Charles Wentworth summarised the situation in New South Wales, where only the apple, currant and gooseberry failed to thrive (instead doing well in Tasmania):

The colony is justly famed for the goodness and variety of its fruits: Peaches, apricots, nectarines, oranges, grapes, pears, plums, figs, pomegranates, raspberries, strawberries, and melons of all sorts attain the highest degree of maturity in the open air; and even the pineapple may be produced merely by the aid of the common forcing glass.

Fruits find their way into a host of desserts including trifles, which are usually somewhat fruitier than their British cousins, with fruit or jelly often replacing the sponge or custard layers. The following delicious trifle from the 1930s features both passionfruit and jelly.

1 cup water	280–350 g sponge cake
1 tablespoon gelatine	1¼ cups (300 ml) cream
½ cup sugar	⅔ cup passionfruit pulp
1 cup pineapple juice	2 tablespoons chopped almonds, walnuts or
2 tablespoons lemon juice	pecans

▪ To make the jelly, pour the water into a small saucepan and sprinkle over the gelatine. Heat gently over a low heat until dissolved. Remove from the heat and stir in the sugar and then the juices. Refrigerate until the jelly is nearly set, about 1 hour.

▪ Place half the cake in the bottom of a large crystal or glass bowl. Whip the cream not too stiffly with a whisk or electric beaters. Spread about ⅔ over the cake. Put the other round of sponge cake on top and spread with passion-fruit. Remove the almost-set jelly from the refrigerator, stir in the nuts and spoon over the trifle. Cover and chill until completely set, about 30 minutes. Whip the remaining cream stiff and spread it on top of the trifle.

Colonial Custards

OVER the last two centuries custards have been a favourite dessert with many people, including baked custards flavoured with sliced banana or thickened with rice, tapioca, sago, macaroni or vermicelli, and boiled custards, the usual accompaniment to puddings and pies. Evelyn Maunsell, in *S'pose I Die*, recalls the sweets one Christmas at Mount Mulgrave Station:

I made a fruit salad from tinned fruit, and a custard. I cooled half the custard for the fruit salad by pouring it into a five-pound treacle tin, clamping the lid on tight, and putting it in a hole in the ground with ashes on top of it and filling the hole with water.

Custard was one of a number of delicacies that Ruby Langford Ginibi, writing in *Real Deadly*, remembers her mother cooking for her as a young child: 'When she made custard she always put young crinkly peach tree leaves in and the flavour of peaches went right through it.'

Jump-up
SERVES 4

THE introduction of European foods into Australia generally meant a decline in nutritional standards for Aboriginal people who, deprived as they often were of lands for hunting and gathering by grazing and agriculture, came to depend increasingly on rations earned for work on the stations or handed out by government or by missions. Many learned to survive on white flour, sugar, tea, cheap cuts of meat, sometimes an allowance of fat, rarely a few potatoes or onions. Marnie Kennedy, in *Born a Half-Caste*, recalls the diet of children abducted by the authorities to Palm Island off the Queensland coast:

For breakfast we would have porridge or bread with jam, syrup or fat. Same for lunch. For supper we had stew … During the Depression years we were always hungry. We ate green fruit, any roots, and once we tried eating frogs. About four of us kids hunting for something to eat decided to have a go at some frogs. We made a fire and two went off to hunt frogs. We heated a piece of iron and threw the frogs on the hot iron. Poor creatures. Their legs started to stretch out and we got a big fright and ran away. Hunger brought us back so we had a go. God, how much you can get off a frog when you are hungry. That was a washout and we never tried it again. So we tried the slops buckets from the guest house and found lots of goodies to eat. We would just brush off the tea leaves and eat, but God couldn't help us if we were caught. After that the slops buckets were an everyday thing.

Despite the low quality of the foods, Aboriginal Australians used their inventiveness to create new dishes, proving themselves to be not a dying race, as many colonists had thought but a people capable of evolving to new circumstances, with a culture full of potential for the present and the future.

One new dish is this dessert from the mid-nineteenth century, its name deriving from the bubbles of air which 'jump' to the surface during cooking. It is basically a sweetened flour and water paste, a good cheap filler food to be eaten straight from the billy or from tin plates. I like to serve it in small mousse pots with whipped cream.

½ cup plain flour	½ cup powdered milk, optional
½ cup sugar	¼ cup golden syrup or honey

▪ Place the ingredients in a food processor or blender and add 1 cup of water. Blend together until thoroughly combined. Pour into a small saucepan and add another ¾ cup of water.

▪ Cook over a moderate heat, stirring constantly, until it boils. Cook for a couple of minutes more until thick. Spoon into mousse pots, cover and allow to cool to room temperature.

Macadamia and Chocolate Mousse

SERVES 6

THE name 'macadamia' has come into common usage only since the 1960s but originated in 1858 when botanists formally classified the tree in honour of Dr John Macadam, President of the Philosophical Society of Victoria. Previously they were sold as Queensland nuts, while in Queensland Murri people called them kindal kindal and white settlers referred to them as bush or bauple nuts after Mount Bauple where they grew.

This white chocolate mousse studded with chocolate macadamias is the result of my own musing on the mountain.

CHOCOLATE MACADAMIAS	WHITE CHOCOLATE MOUSSE
50 g dark chocolate	2 eggs, separated
18 whole unsalted macadamias	¼ cup castor sugar
	150 g white chocolate
	80 g unsalted butter, softened

▪ To make the chocolate macadamias, melt the dark chocolate in the top of a double saucepan over simmering water or in a bowl sitting in a simmering saucepan of water. As soon as it is melted remove from the heat and stir in the nuts. Spoon them individually onto an oiled flat baking tray, making sure that each is completely covered in chocolate. Refrigerate until firm.

▪ To make the white chocolate mousse, whip the egg whites with a whisk or electric beater in a large mixing bowl until stiff. Gradually add the sugar, beating well until completely dissolved. In a clean bowl sitting in a saucepan of simmering water melt the white chocolate. Remove from the heat and beat in the butter with an electric mixer or whisk. Add the egg yolks and beat well for a minute or two until smooth and golden. Fold 1 tablespoon of the whites into the white chocolate mixture. Gently fold in the rest with large sweeping movements while keeping the mixture light.

▪ Remove the macadamias from the tray, reserving six. Spoon some mousse into 6 small ramekins or mousse pots, add a nut to each, cover with more mousse, add another nut and top with the remaining mousse. Cover with cling film and refrigerate until firm, about 2 hours. Serve decorated with the reserved nuts.

Quandong Cream

SERVES 4

THE quandong is one of our most typical outback fruits, growing from Perth in the west and all through the Red Centre to the drier areas of the eastern states. About the size of an apricot with a decorative stone, the round red fruits form a staple food for the Pitjantjatjara, Pintubi and other desert peoples who eat them fresh or dry them for future use. Some plants have edible kernels which can be eaten raw or pounded to a cosmetic oil.

European explorers also liked the quandong, which they named the native or emu peach since it is a favourite food of that bird. White settlers stewed the fruit or cooked them into richly flavoured jams and pies but were never very successful with cultivation owing to two factors: firstly the difficulty of germinating the seed unless passed through the gut of an emu, and secondly the partial parasitism of the plant. Recently, farms like Shoalmara at Tumby Bay in South Australia, have at last succeeded in growing this truly excellent fruit.

50 g dried seeded quandongs
1½ cups boiling water
⅓ cup sugar
2 teaspoons rum

1 egg white
2 tablespoons castor sugar
⅔ cup cream

▪ Place the quandongs in a small saucepan and pour over the boiling water. Let soak for 1 hour. Bring to the boil and simmer, uncovered, for 5 minutes until soft. Remove from the stove and stir in the sugar and rum. Purée in a blender or food processor till smooth and chill in the refrigerator.

▪ Whisk the egg white until stiff with electric beaters or a whisk. Gradually beat in the sugar until it has dissolved. In a separate bowl whip the cream and fold gently into the quandong purée with a spoon. Gently fold in 1 tablespoon of the egg whites into the quandong cream then fold in the rest keeping the mixture airy. Spoon into glass dessert dishes and refrigerate.

Passionfruit Velvet

SERVES 4

IT IS difficult to praise the passionfruit too highly. It is one of Australia's favourite fruits, easily grown in the smallest backyard and prolific until the woody or bullet virus sets in after two or three years and replacement of the vine becomes necessary. The purple variety is the most familiar but yellow-skinned types are often preferred for their disease resistance in Queensland and the Northern Territory, where the giant grenadilla also grows.

Passionfruit are rarely eaten as they are, the pulp is spooned over ice cream or blended with fruit salad and is suitable for a host of recipes from desserts and jams to cakes and biscuits, embuing these with a warm golden hue and the exquisite flavour and perfume of tropic paradise. There are at least hundreds, more likely thousands, of recipes for passionfruit scattered throughout Australian cookbooks, magazines and the culinary pages of newspapers over the last two centuries. For both immigrant and Aboriginal cooks this South American fruit was an exotic ingredient, one for which they had no established recipes and were therefore forced to adapt and invent.

Passionfruit velvet is an adaptation of that simplest of all British desserts, syllabub. Thomas Wood highly recommended its 'mellowed fragrance' during his visit to Australia in the 1930s: 'passion fruit, squeezed into a wineglass, mixed with cream and sugar and a spoonful of sherry, has a rich smoothness which holds you silent in thankfulness that such perfection can be'.

½ cup passionfuit pulp
¼ cup sherry

⅓ cup castor sugar
1¼ cups (300 ml) cream

▪ Place the passionfruit, sherry and sugar in a mixing bowl and stir to combine. Pour in the cream, stirring all the time, and then whip with a whisk until thick. Spoon into wine glasses or dessert dishes, cover and chill.

Colonial Jellies

IN COLONIAL times jellies involved a long and drawn-out preparation. Isinglass was the preferred setting agent but, since it derived from the air bladder of sturgeon, was relatively expensive. A popular alternative was gelatine extracted by boiling up calves' feet, straining the resulting liquor, and clarifying it with beaten egg white. After a final straining, a clear liquid was obtained which had a certain flavour of its own even before sugar, fruit juices or fruit were added. Some cooks complained about the tastelessness of manufactured gelatine when it appeared around the 1870s and recipes for calves' feet jelly persisted into the first decade of the twentieth century.

The main difficulty with jellies before refrigeration was setting them in the Australian climate, although from the 1850s discoveries about the cooling properties of ammonia were utilised by some. Mary Gilmore, in *Old Days: Old Ways*, describes how the ladies of Wagga Wagga prepared for the annual Gold Cup Ball in the face of almost insurmountable odds:

Anyone who knows the Riverina and the heat of its half-the-year summer will realise at what a cost of trouble the original cooking for the ball was done, and the food kept sweet and firm. Jellies had to be made by main force, that is, with as much isinglass and as little water as possible. There was no ice to be had, and no ice-chests then! The sweets, brought twenty or thirty miles by buggy, would be wrapped in wet clothes and carried in the moulds in which they were made. Then they were ranged along the walls of the supper-room, down on the floor, to keep as cool as possible; and even then they fell. But one year my father brought out coarse salt and ammonia for Mrs John Stinson, and that year her jellies were a triumph. They stood when everyone else's ran. It was talked about for the rest of the year.

The golden age of the jelly began in the 1920s, by which time most Australian homes had an ice-chest, some even a refrigerator, and ended in the late 1960s when ice creams took over in popularity.

Watermelon Cream

SERVES 4–6

MELON and cucurbits of all types flourish in Australia and watermelons especially have been popular since early colonial times, as noted by Alexander Harris in *Settlers and Convicts*:

The chief vegetable was the pumpkin, which I preferred to any vegetable we use in

England; and the chief fruit was water-melons, the size, colour, and delicious refreshing coolness of which, eaten during the three hours of mid-day heat when most farming people pause for a time from their field labour, it would be impossible for me to describe by mere words.

Townspeople also enjoyed them, since in season they were to be seen piled up like huge green cannon balls at every greengrocer's door. Water-melons are the most thirst-quenching fruit and therefore the conclusion to many family picnics throughout the hot summer months. In Queensland, in particular, they have integrated into local culture with the Watermelon Festival at Coominya featuring a melon marathon and seed-spitting competition; and large quantities are traditionally disposed of by Queensland school children at their end-of-year break-ups. Zara Baar Aronson, a journalist for the *Sydney Mail* and author of three cookbooks, the first published in 1900, obviously had a penchant for watermelon and gives several methods for its use, amongst them this delicately flavoured, romantically pink, moulded dessert.

500 g peeled watermelon
1 tablespoon gelatine

⅓ cup sugar
⅔ cup cream

▪ Remove all the seeds from the watermelon and purée in a food processor or blender. Place about ⅓ of the purée in a saucepan and sprinkle over the gelatine. Add the sugar and heat gently over a low heat until dissolved. Remove from the heat and stir in the remaining purée. Refrigerate until half set, about 1–2 hours.

▪ Whip the watermelon jelly lightly with a whisk. Whip the cream in a separate bowl and fold into the jelly with a spoon until combined. Spoon into a decorative mould and chill until set.

▪ Dip the mould into hot water and turn out on to a serving plate. Decorate with piped whipped cream if desired.

Passionfruit Flummery

SERVES 10

SUMMER is a season of many delights. Adelaide printmaker and novelist Barbara Hanrahan describes the summers of her 1940s childhood in *The Scent of Eucalyptus*:

The summer drifts on, and Nan outwits it with cucumber peel stuck to her forehead, home-made lemon-cordial, heart-shaped Fiji fan; with lettuce like mermaid's hair, condensed milk mayonnaise, Narcissus Blancmange, Dainty Chocolate Mould, Delicious Hawaiian Cake.

The iceman becomes important.

I wait for him to come round the corner with his cabbage-leaf hat, nose hung with an icicle, sad-eared horse. I cry 'Ice-o!' with the others, and dance after his cart and the wet trail of drips it leaves behind; watch him juggle the blocks from house to house; crow when he smashes one to shivers and gives us each a piece.

The iceman frequented the rear lane—a friendly lane of broken palings, nettles and manure—to service the ice chests of kitchens where housewives worked with packaged gelatine and electric mixmasters to produce a whole range of dainty summer desserts. Passionfruit flummery was one of these: dating from the 1920s, its frothy fruitiness made it popular with children and adults alike, so much so that it became one of the classics of twentieth century Australian cookery, usually served in a large crystal bowl at family get-togethers.

2 tablespoons plain flour	2½ cups boiling water
2 tablespoons gelatine	1 cup passionfruit pulp
1 cup sugar	1 cup orange juice

▪ Mix the flour, gelatine and sugar together in a saucepan. Slowly stir in the boiling water until smoothly combined. Place over low heat and bring to the boil, stirring constantly. Add the passionfruit and orange juice and bring to the boil again. Boil for 1 minute. Remove from the heat and, if you wish, strain through a sieve to remove the seeds. Pour into a large mixing bowl and refrigerate until partly set.

▪ Whip the flummery until thick and frothy and doubled in bulk, for about 5–10 minutes with an electric mixer, placing the bowl on a bed of ice if it is a hot day. Pour into a crystal bowl or individual dishes and refrigerate until set.

Mock Pears

SERVES 4–6

I DON'T know exactly when chokoes were introduced from Central America to Australia but in the 1880s they were still regarded as a new vegetable. They rapidly became a feature of many suburban backyards, paling fences often sagging under the weight of their rampant foliage and the harvest of pale green fruit perhaps too prolific for some over-satiated appetites. They yield their main crop every autumn and, unlike other cucurbits, are a perennial although suffering winter die-back in colder regions. Chokoes are most often simply boiled or steamed and served with a little butter or white sauce but they can also make scrumptious desserts such as mock apple pie and mock pears. A great favourite with many Australians.

1.25 chokoes

1 lemon

1¼ cups sugar

8 cloves

Cochineal

▪ Peel the chokoes and cut lengthwise into eighths. Place in a saucepan with water to cover and boil for about 10 minutes over a moderate heat until tender. Drain.

▪ With a vegetable peeler, remove the thin yellow rind from the lemon and juice it. Put the rind, juice, sugar, cloves and 1¼ cups of water in a saucepan and bring to the boil. Add enough cochineal to colour the liquid pink. Add the chokoes and cook, uncovered, over a moderate heat until the liquid reduces and becomes syrupy, about 30–40 minutes. Long cooking is essential here to draw out all the wateriness from the choko flesh and prevent the dessert from being insipid. Let cool to room temperature and serve with pouring cream.

Peach Melba

SERVES 4

DAME Nellie Melba, Australia's first internationally acclaimed opera singer, made her debut in *Lohengrin* at Convent Garden in 1892. To celebrate her triumph the Duke of Orleans hosted a dinner at the Savoy Hotel where Auguste Escoffier presented her with a huge ice swan filled with peaches and ice cream. Later, in 1900, he added raspberry purée to create what we know today as peach Melba.

Simple versions of peach Melba, using tinned peaches, factory-made ice cream and bottled raspberry sauce, frequently make an appearance on the menus of old-fashioned Australian cafes.

At home, a far superior dessert can be obtained using fresh fruit and a good creamy ice cream.

4 ripe free-stone peaches	200 g raspberries, fresh or frozen
¾ cup sugar	Castor sugar
1 vanilla bean	About 2 cups vanilla ice cream

▪ To make the peaches easy to peel, plunge them into boiling water to cover for about 20 seconds. Drain and immerse in cold water. Peel and cut in half, discarding the stones. Combine 1½ cups water with the sugar and vanilla bean in a saucepan and bring to the boil over a moderate heat. Simmer, covered, for 5 minutes. Add the peach halves and simmer for about 8–10 minutes until only just tender and still in shape. Let cool in the syrup and refrigerate.

▪ To make the raspberry sauce, purée the raspberries in a food processor or blender. Strain through muslin to remove the seeds, squeezing out as much of the juice as possible. Stir in enough castor sugar to sweeten, about 1½ table-spoons for fresh raspberries or less for frozen. The sauce is best fairly tart. Chill in the refrigerator.

▪ When you are ready to serve, spread some ice cream in the base of 4 dessert dishes. Lift the peaches out of their syrup with a slotted spoon and place two halves in each dish. Spoon over some raspberry sauce.

Tutti-frutti Ice Cream

MAKES ABOUT 5 CUPS

SINCE the 1960s ice cream has taken over as the most popular summer dessert, yet in the past it was a much rarer treat. Peters, with their famous motto 'Health Food of a Nation', started manufacture in 1907, and the Streets company in 1920. For many decades ice cream was consumed mainly outside the home, scooped into cones at the milk bar or eaten outdoors between wafers like a slippery ice-cream sandwich. At the theatre it was pecked at daintily with a flat wooden spoon from little buckets, brought to the patron's seat by the lolly boy with his tray of cordials, peanuts and confectionery strung over the neck.

When ice cream was purchased for the home it was relatively expensive. It came in a stream-lined form to fit the slim freezing compartment of the old-fashioned fridge. No tubs of ice cream then, instead rectangular bricks enclosed in cardboard with a cardboard 'zipper' which was pulled undone to reveal the contents of vanilla, strawberry or chocolate, or all three together under the name of Neapolitan. It was usually served in slices rather than scoops because of its shape.

Colonial cookbooks included a few recipes for ices and ice creams but home production only became practicable when the ice-chest was replaced by the refrigerator. Mothers saw ice cream as a palatable source of calcium, vitamins and protein and in order to serve it to their children on a regularly affordable basis they made their own. Most recipes were founded on American models and were fairly nutritious, economical affairs, with less cream and fewer egg yolks than their French counterparts. Milk, fresh, powdered or tinned, formed the base, cooked into a custard with flavours like vanilla, chocolate, coffee, golden syrup, nuts, ginger, fruit salad and my own favourite, Mum's special cassata. Although many recipes were stirred or beaten during the freezing process, many were of the no-stir type, deriving their lightness from whipped cream or egg white folded in just prior to freezing in shallow aluminium trays. Tutti-frutti was one flavour which appeared in cookbooks around the 1940s, and this recipe reminds me very much of the cassata of my childhood.

2 egg yolks	*¼ cup finely chopped dates*
1 cup sugar	*¼ cup finely chopped glacé cherries*
1½ tablespoons cornflour	*¼ cup finely chopped walnuts or pecans*
1¼ cups milk	*2 tablespoons sherry*
¼ cup finely chopped raisins	*1¼ cups (300 ml) cream*

▪ In a mixing bowl beat the egg yolks and sugar with electric beaters until pale and the sugar is dissolved. Beat in the cornflour. Scald the milk in a saucepan by bringing it almost to the boil over a low heat. Gradually beat the milk into the egg yolks. Return this mixture to the saucepan and cook over a low heat, stirring constantly, until it thickens and boils. Remove from the heat and stir in the fruit, nuts and sherry. Cover with cling film and chill.
▪ Whip the cream lightly with electric beaters or a whisk and fold into the fruit custard. Pour into an ice cream tray, cover and freeze without stirring.

The First Refrigerators

THE refrigerator was a particular boon to the bush cook. In *Childhood Memories of Life on a Sheep Station* Frank Waterhouse remembers the coming of the 'flame that freezes' to his Flinders Ranges home back in the 1930s:

Then one day Dad arrived back from his annual trip to Adelaide with a large wooden crate on the back of the utility.

What a wondrous sight when the crate was unloaded and opened. There, in all its glory, stood a gleaming white Electrolux kerosene operated refrigerator. This was quickly installed in a corner of the dining room, the flame lit and wonders upon wonders, the interior soon became very cold.

From then on we always had fresh meat, home made ice cream, iced drinks. Really, a bigger impact on our life style than ever before, or since.

It was our first introduction to ice and ice-cream.

Henriette Pearce, in *Two at Daly Waters*, recalls her first experiment in ice cream production:

It was a landmark in our house-planning when the electric light and a refrigerator were installed. I made my first ice-cream, and although it was a little too hard, it was wonderful all the same, as only those who have lived in the Territory in the days of isolation and scant supplies can fully understand. We gave all the natives some, but Micky voiced the general feeling when, after transferring it from one cheek to another, with an anguished expression, he carefully took it out altogether.

'Him cold fellow; more better you cook him Boss,' he advised.

Many of the early home-made ice creams were firmer and icier than modern taste would allow but compensated in their healthful goodness and the almost unlimited range of flavours.

Macadamia Ice Cream

MAKES ABOUT 2 LITRES

MACADAMIA nuts were introduced into Hawaii from Australia in 1892 by two brothers R.A. and E. W. Jordan, the former securing the seeds in Queensland and the later growing them at his home in Honolulu. However it was not until the 1930s and '40s that the industry became firmly established there following a long period of selection of suitable trees, the development of propagation techniques a well as machinery to process the nut's hard shell. Similar difficulties were encountered in Australia to which were added serious insect and pest problems, not to mention the general lack of interest in native foods. It was only in the 1960s that large scale plantings of macadamias in their homeland began.

Most Australian recipes for the nut are therefore of fairly recent origin. Macadamia ice cream dates from the 1980s. Like many new ice creams it is made in the French way, cooked with lots of cream and egg yolks and then

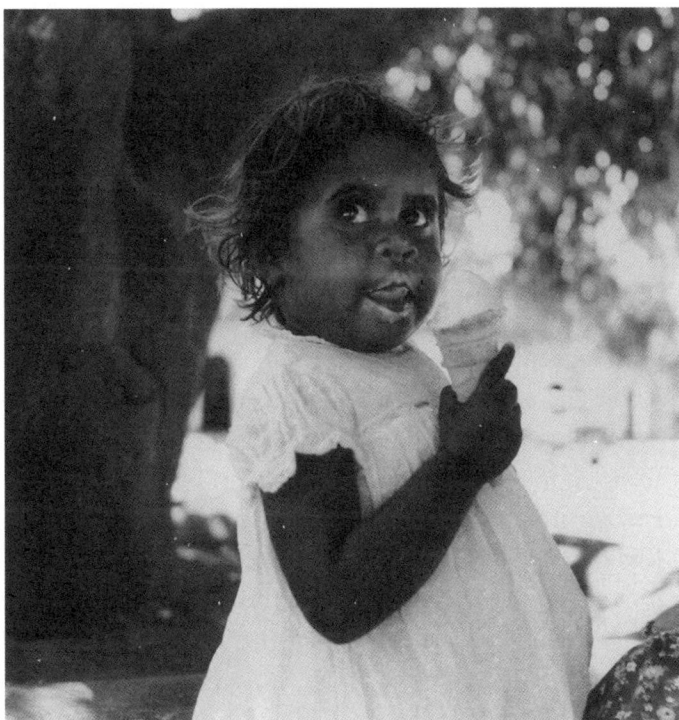

The little Cairns girl photographed by Max Dupain clearly shares the national taste for ice cream—Australia's favourite dessert.

beaten. This particular one is based on a recipe in Maureen Simpson's *Australian Cuisine.*

1½ cups milk	*1 tablespoon honey*
2½ cups cream	*2 teaspoons vanilla essence*
6 egg yolks	*2 tablespoons sugar*
1 cup raw sugar	*60 g macadamias, chopped*

▪ Scald the milk and cream, that is, bring almost to the boil, in the top of a double saucepan or in a bowl set in a saucepan of simmering water. In a large bowl beat the egg yolks with the raw sugar and honey with a wooden spoon. Gradually stir the hot milk mixture into the egg mixture. Return it to the saucepan or bowl and cook over boiling water, stirring constantly, until the custard thickens but does not boil. Remove from the heat, cover and cool. Stir in the vanilla and pour into a container and freeze until solid.

▪ To prepare the macadamias, heat the sugar in a heavy saucepan over a medium heat, shaking until the sugar melts into a clear golden liquid. Add the macadamias, stir to coat and then scrape them onto a buttered baking tray to set. Chop finely in the food processor.

▮ Break up the frozen ice cream and beat with an electric mixer for a few minutes until smooth. Stir in the nuts and refreeze.

Fruit Salad Ice Cream

MAKES ABOUT 1 LITRE

JEWISH people arrived in Australia on the First Fleet and have formed a visible and well respected minority ever since, with the largest communities in Melbourne and Sydney. Nearly all Australian Jews in the early years were British born, joined later by immigrants from Central Europe and elsewhere. Few involved themselves in primary production, although there were some Jewish pastoralists, and at the beginning of the twentieth century a group of fruit growers at Shepparton in Victoria of Russian origin. Some set up as merchants and shopkeepers supplying the characteristic food needs of their communities. Melbourne became known for its shopping neighbourhoods, especially Carlisle and Acland Streets, St Kilda, with their wealth of kosher butchers, grocers, bakers, confectioners and restaurants. The best-known cooks to make their home in Australia were food writer Zara Baar Aronson and restaurateur Oliver Schaul, with Jewish housewives sharing their recipes with other Australians in a number of fundraising cookbooks since the 1960s.

Jewish-Australian cookery reflects the diaspora and the diverse countries from which our Jewish citizens have come. Traditional dishes figure prominently on religious days and other important occasions. For example, an English visitor to Perth in 1920 Israel Cohen noted amongst the 'tempting viands and delicacies' laid out at the annual Jewish ball the prominence of the challah: 'In the middle of the head table there was a gargantuan plaited load adorned with the "Shield of David", and there was a brave array of iced cakes with similar symbols.'

In addition, there has been a ready adaptation to local ingredients within the dietary laws laid down by the Torah. The following creamy ice, flavoured with typical Antipodean fruits, is a 'pareve' or neutral food, suitable for either a meat or dairy meal. It comes from *Secrets from Our Kitchens* published in 1993 for Moriah College in Sydney.

Juice of 1 orange
Juice of 1½–2 lemons
Pulp of 2 passionfruit

1 banana, mashed
2 eggs, separated
1 cup castor sugar

▪ Place all the fruit in a mixing bowl with the egg yolks and ¾ cup of the castor sugar. Beat with electric beaters until thoroughly combined. Cover and freeze overnight.

▪ The next day whip the egg whites until they hold soft peaks. Break up the frozen mixture with a spoon, add the remaining sugar and beat with an electric mixer until smooth. Gently fold 1 tablespoon of egg white into the fruit mixture. When incorporated, gently fold in the rest of the egg whites. Refreeze, either in an ice-cream tray or in a serving dish. Delicious served on its own or with fresh fruit or a slightly tart compote.

Tropical Plum Pudding

SERVES ABOUT 12

FOR the sake of tradition many colonials tried to transpose the inappropriately heavy English Christmas dinner to the sultry Australian summer, but inevitably adaptations crept in. Rachel Henning, writing from Exmoor Station in Queensland a few days before Christmas 1863, describes the preparations:

Annie has been concocting mincemeat. She and Mr Hedgeland held a great chopping in the veranda yesterday while I was settling the week's accounts inside, and when I went out I beheld a black-looking mass like a huge dirt-pie. It was made of dried apples and currants, raisins, spice, brandy, etc., and I dare say will prove very nice, though it looks queer. Of course it would be bad in a day if you put meat or suet with it.

We have doubts about the plum pudding, as we have no eggs at present, and the fowls refuse to lay.

The resulting dinner represented a mixture of traditional and Australian elements: in addition to the pudding and mince-pies adapted from British recipes they ate rather well with that old English favourite roast beef, two brace of wild Australian duck, Australian summer vegetables in the form of pumpkin and okra, apple tart (presumably done bush-style with dried apples) and, for a good Queensland finale to the meal, watermelons.

By the beginning of the twentieth century some cooks had developed the concept of the 'frozen' plum pudding, initially jellied desserts set in a basin and chilled in the ice chest. Truly frozen puddings came only later with refrigerators and the expansion in the size of the freezer from the 1960s. From that decade comes the following ice-cream plum pudding like a rich chocolate bombe, from Lady Patricia Harris' *Accept with Pleasure*.

TROPICAL PLUM PUDDING

1 cup milk

200 g dark chocolate, broken into squares

4 cups chopped fruit and nuts (such as 450 g
   can crushed pineapple, drained; ¾ cup
   raisins; ¾ cup dried figs; ½ cup glacé apricots
   and cherries; ⅓ cup pecans)

2 eggs, separated

2 tablespoons castor sugar

1¼ cups cream (300 ml), lightly whipped

MERINGUE, OPTIONAL

3 egg whites

¾ cup castor sugar

▪ Place the milk in the top of a double saucepan or a bowl set in a saucepan of simmering water. Add the chocolate and cook over simmering water until melted. Stir in the fruit and nuts and cook for 10 minutes until softened. Mix in the egg yolks, beaten lightly, and remove from the heat straight away and chill completely in the refrigerator.

▪ Beat the 2 egg whites and the castor sugar in a mixing bowl with a whisk or an electric beater until soft peaks form. Gently fold this mixture into the chilled fruit mixture with a wooden spoon. Then fold in the cream, and if you wish stir in some sterilised silver coins or charms. Pour into a pudding basin, cover with 2 layers of foil and secure with string. Freeze until firm.

▪ To serve, loosen the pudding from the sides of the basin with a knife and dip the bowl into hot water. Unmould onto a plate or, if presenting it with meringue, onto a wooden board.

▪ The top may be decorated with meringue, if wished. To make the meringue, whisk the 3 egg whites with the castor sugar with electric beaters until stiff. Swirl over the pudding, covering it completely. Place in a preheated oven at 230°C for about 4 minutes until the meringue is just tipped with light brown. Decorate with a sprig of Christmas bush.

9

'... a cup of tea and a chat'

CAKES

I could not keep track of all that went into that cake, but I know that as well as flour and sugar there were about five pounds of butter, four large dippers of mixed fruit, two cups of treacle and quite a lot of rum.

EVELYN MAUNSELL, *S'POSE I DIE*, 1973

The kitchen table, here being 'set' by the subject of Woman in Kitchen *by Charles Kerry (circa 1895–1910), was the centre of food preparation as well as a dining table for family meals before twentieth-century ideas on efficiency transformed the kitchen.*

CAKE baking, like the preparation of desserts, is one of the most important areas in the Australian cuisine. During the colonial era afternoon tea became an established institution, ladies calling at each other's homes for cups of tea and a chat. On these occasions, as well as for family celebrations and reunions, an often lavish spread of home-baked cakes, scones, biscuits, tarts and sandwiches would be laid out. The housewife took pride in doing the thing properly and a reputation earned for having the lightest sponges, the fluffiest scones or the richest fruit cake would be reinforced at the cake stall of the annual school fête or church bazaar.

In the country, particularly, cake baking achieved a high standard. When the nearest neighbour lived many miles away, a visit from anyone was a big occasion, to be celebrated by an impressive display of cookery skills. The Country Women's Association from its inception has promoted feminine accomplishments, including cake baking, both through its publications and also through the meeting of local groups which provide an opportunity for the exchange of recipes and advice. Agricultural shows have fostered a competitive spirit amongst women and the cookery section of the Royal Agricultural Shows is well patronised with its cakes, dampers, scones, biscuits and preserves proudly swathed in their blue, red, white and marroon ribbons and prize certificates. The decorating section is the most sought after with everyone lining up in the crush to view the loveliest wedding, christening, birthday and novelty cakes enshrined in glories of sugar embroideries and filigree lace, showers of bush and garden blossoms, cradles, keys, figures and fans mounted on ever ascending tiers of fruit cake. These works of art epitomise feminine grace and daintiness and it has been said that Australia leads the world in fine cake decorating.

The archetypal Australian cake is the bush brownie, derived from the damper, the archetypal Australian bread, just as early European cakes developed from yeast breads. Always prominent among Antipodean cakes have been sponges filled with jam, fruit or whipped cream, and tea cakes dusted with sugar and eaten in thin buttered slices. The lamington, our national cake for the last hundred years, cannot be passed over, omnipresent at fundraising stalls, children's parties and afternoon teas, equally favoured by girl guides and elderly matrons, a perfect combination of flavours with its chocolate and coconut coating. Fruit cakes have held pride of place, especially with country cooks, since dried fruit might at times be the only fruit available in the bush diet. Actually, many Aussie cakes are not merely a pleasant addition to the diet but also make a valuable contribution to nutrition: a surprising number include fruit, either fresh or dried, in addition to milk, eggs, nuts and other wholesome ingredients.

Passionfruit Sponge

SERVES 8

CAKES have always held centre stage at children's festivities. Margaret Ford, a Cape York missionary, describes in her book *End of a Beginning* a 1950s birthday party at Wilandspey Station for young Ralph Martel:

… in front of our eyes was spread a most wonderful children's party—fancy biscuits, bread and butter spread with 'hundreds and thousands', lamingtons, 'fairy bread', cakes gaily iced in different colours, fruit cup, an enormous rainbow cake, every possible item which goes to make the sort of birthday party every child dreams of, even to party caps and balloons … For days that young mother had cooked and decorated.

Apart from rainbow cakes and lamingtons, the most popular birthday cakes are surely sponges. Passionfruit sponges are one of Australia's great classics, a perfect combination of light-as-air cake, whipped cream and passionfruit filling, topped off with passionfruit icing.

PASSIONFRUIT SPONGE

HOT WATER SPONGE	FILLING
3 eggs, separated	1 cup cream
¾ cup castor sugar	¼ cup icing sugar, sifted
1 cup self-raising flour	2 passionfruit
Pinch salt	
1 teaspoon butter, melted	PASSIONFRUIT ICING
3 tablespoons hot water	1 cup icing sugar, sifted
	1 passionfruit
	30 g butter, softened

▪ Grease a 20 cm cake tin and dust lightly with flour. In a bowl whisk the egg whites with electric beaters until stiff. Beat in the sugar, a tablespoon at a time, until thick and the sugar has dissolved. Beat in the yolks all at once. Sift the flour with the salt. Sift it again over the egg-sugar mixture and fold in lightly but evenly with a wooden spoon. Fold in the butter and hot water quickly. Pour into the prepared tin and bake in a preheated oven at 180°C for about 35 minutes until cooked. Test for doneness with a fine skewer in the centre of the cake—when it comes out clean it is ready. Turn out onto a wire rack to cool after resting in the tin for 4 minutes.

▪ When the cake is completely cool, cut in half horizontally with a bread knife. Whip the cream until nearly stiff with electric beaters. Add the icing sugar and beat until stiff. Lightly fold in the pulp of the passionfruit. Spread this mixture over one half of the cake and place the other half on top (or alternatively fill with unsweetened whipped cream and passionfruit cheese).

▪ To make the icing, put the remaining ingredients in a bowl and beat until smooth with a wooden spoon. Place the bowl in a saucepan of simmering water and stir for a couple of minutes until it is a spreadable consistency. Pour on the cake and with a spatula quickly spread smoothly over the top.

Mrs Seccombe's Chocolate Walnut Cake

SERVES 8

HEAT, flies and ants are the three enemies of the Australian housekeeper. Aboriginal cooks have ways of holding flies and the diseases they carry at bay: food is usually eaten immediately after it is cooked, or kept sealed in the ground oven or covered until ready to eat. Smoke is a good deterrent and flies can also be distracted by placing scraps at a distance from the main food.

Northern Territorian Henriette Pearce, writing in *Two at Daly Waters,* found fly spray and sticky fly papers apparently of little use:

Flies worsted me then and always did. Wire screens we had, but flies rode in on every newcomer's back. At meal times we just held our own by hiring a six-year-old little native boy, Jackie, with damper and jam and other things dear to his soul. He sat on the doorstep and worked a punkah. Sometimes he jerked it violently so that it startled us as much as the flies; sometimes he lost interest in it and went to sleep. But we were always glad to have him.

For Australians consuming meals in the open air flies are a constant nuisance. The workmen building a church on Tamrookum Station in Queensland in 1913 christened their dining quarters 'Café de Blowfly'. Henriette's husband Bill managed to find an efficient flytrap only once, when he was sharing Christmas dinner with some bushmen. One man, Afghan Charlie, had gone to sleep under the table and the others dribbled condensed milk over his face and boots which immediately drew in all the flies: the sleeper remained oblivious to what was happening and the men had their dinner in unwonted peace.

For the home baker a throw-over of gauze to cover a batch of biscuits or cake while it cools is often a necessity. The following cake comes from the CWA *Calender of Cake and Afternoon Tea Delicacies*.

250 g butter, softened

1 cup castor sugar

2 cups self-raising flour

2 tablespoons cocoa powder

2 teaspoons mixed spice

1 teaspoon vanilla essence

3 eggs

½ cup milk

2 cups chopped walnuts

CHOCOLATE GLACÉ ICING

100 g dark chocolate

¼ cup water

1¾ cups icing sugar, sifted

½ teaspoon oil

Walnut halves to decorate

▮ In a bowl, cream the butter with the sugar with electric beaters until light and fluffy. Sift the flour with the cocoa and spice, and beat into the butter-sugar mixture. Beat in the vanilla and the eggs, one at a time. Stir in the milk and then the walnuts. Turn into a greased 23 cm tin and bake in a preheated oven at 180°C for about 1 hour until cooked. Test for doneness with a fine skewer in the centre of the cake—when it comes out clean it is ready. Turn out onto a wire rack to cool after resting in the tin for 4 minutes.

▮ Ice with your favourite chocolate icing or the one given here. Break the chocolate into squares and place with the water in a bowl sitting in a saucepan of simmering water. As soon as the chocolate has melted remove the bowl from the saucepan and beat in the sugar a spoonful at a time with electric beaters. Beat in the oil. Quickly spread the icing over the top and sides of the cake with a spatula before it sets. Decorate with walnut halves.

Warbreccan Cake

SERVES 8

WITH ants as with flies Australia has a peculiar abundance which creates no end of problems in the kitchen, although Henriette Pearce had her ways of dealing with them:

Against ants I had my small successes. All safes and kitchen tables have to be kept with the legs standing in little tins of water with kerosene added. There are more ants in the Territory than Solomon dreamed of when he gave his kindly testimony to these little creatures. As soon as you begin to make a cake all the ants smell it and in they come—sugar ants, bull ants, meat ants and the very tiny ones that march in thousands.

Some outback housewives doused the whole floor with kerosene but this was only a temporary discouragement and had to be reapplied daily. Presumably similar problems were suffered at Warbreccan, a sheep station southwest of Longreach in outback Queensland from which comes this excellent lemony cake, first published in Brisbane in the *Twentieth Century Cookery Book*, 1899.

WARBRECCAN CAKE

250 g butter, softened
1 cup castor sugar
1 teaspoon vanilla essence
2 egg yolks
2 eggs
2 cups plain flour
1 teaspoon baking powder
½ cup milk

LEMON CHEESE
1 egg
½ cup sugar
¼ cup lemon juice
1½ tablespoons butter

LEMON ICING
2 cups icing sugar, sifted
2 tablespoons lemon juice
3 tablespoons desiccated coconut

∎ In a bowl cream the butter with the sugar and vanilla with electric beaters until light and fluffy. Add the egg yolks and whole eggs, one at a time, beating well after each addition. Sift the flour with the baking powder and fold into the butter-egg mixture alternately with the milk with the beater on low speed. Spoon into a greased 23 cm cake tin and bake in a preheated oven at 180°C for about 1 hour until cooked. Test for doneness with a fine skewer in the centre of the cake—when it comes out clean it is ready. Turn out onto a wire rack to cool after resting in the tin for 4 minutes.

∎ While the cake is cooking, make the lemon cheese. Beat the egg and sugar together in a bowl. Add the lemon juice and butter. Place the bowl in a saucepan of simmering water and cook, stirring constantly with a wooden spoon, until it thickens and coats the back of a spoon, about 10 minutes. Make sure that it does not boil. Remove from the heat and cool, covered.

∎ Cut the cake in half. Spread the lemon cheese over one half then sandwich together. Spread the top and sides with a simple icing. Beat the icing sugar with the lemon juice in a bowl until smooth. Spread over the surface with a spatula and sprinkle with coconut.

German Cake

SERVES 8–10

SINCE the 1840s German immigrants have formed a substantial minority in Australia. A self-portrait of the industrious German farmer was given by Jacob Stern to Caroline Chisholm in January 1846:

… 10 lbs. meat, 20 lbs. flour, milk of one cow, pint of wine a day, with a garden; have plenty of potatoes, fruit, vegetables, corn, everything; pumpkins, melons; well furnished house,—see how the grapes grow in the verandah,—have five rooms, with brick floor, rent free. Have two pigs; fowls, ducks, run about plenty,—sell three or four dozen a week of eggs. Like this country very well; Oh! very well … Plenty more grapes in this country, better crops,—good crops every year, double so much as at home. I have two cows, two calves; make 8 lbs. butter a week from one cow, sell it at a 1s. the lb.

Many families had a cellar where sausages, hams and wines could be stored and cheeses and dairy foods made. In addition, projecting out of the house or at a small distance from it, there was a brick baking oven with smoking chambers connected by vaulted flues to a central chimney for curing the products of the family pigs over gum leaves or almond husks. Bread was baked in the oven along with yeast cakes topped with streusel and Berliner pfannkuchen, renamed Kitchener buns during World War I when many Teutonic customs were repressed. In South Australia, where the German influence is still felt, mock yeast cakes are very much a part of today's baking repertoire.

1 cup milk
1 tablespoon vinegar
40 g butter, melted
1 cup sugar
1 egg
2 teaspoons lemon essence or finely grated rind
2 cups self-raising flour, sifted
½ teaspoon grated nutmeg

¾ cup currants or sultanas

STREUSEL
⅓ cup plain flour
¼ cup sugar
¼ teaspoon ground cinnamon or nutmeg
40 g butter, melted

▪ Combine the milk and vinegar in a cup to make the 'yeast' and set aside. (Alternatively, use buttermilk.)
▪ In a bowl pour the butter over the sugar and beat with electric beaters until combined. Add the egg and lemon and beat well. With the beaters on low

fold in the flour and nutmeg alternately with the milk. Lastly stir in the dried fruit. Spoon into a greased 20–25 cm springform tin.

▮ To make the streusel, combine the flour, sugar and spice in a mixing bowl and stir in the butter. Sprinkle over the top of the cake batter. Bake in a preheated oven at 180°C for 50–60 minutes until cooked. Test with a fine skewer in the centre of the cake—when it comes out clean it is ready. Remove the sides from the tin after resting for 4 minutes and let cool on a rack.

Gidleigh Cake

SERVES 8

GIDLEIGH Station, situated at Bungendore near Goulburn in New South Wales, was the home of Jean Rutledge, author of *The Goulburn Cookery Book*. Published in 1899 it was reprinted almost every year until 1945 and was probably the most successful of all colonial cookbooks, benefiting the Anglican Church to which Mrs Rutledge had generously donated all proceeds. The book was directed towards the women of the bush and included many excellent local recipes such as Quong Tart scones, Garroorigang biscuits, Barrier goose, salmon à la Hopetoun, drought plum pudding, passionfruit sago shape, dried fruit tart, brownie, Johnny cakes, kangaroo steamer and melon jam.

Jean Rutledge was obviously a practical cook dealing constantly with many of the day-to-day problems of the colonial kitchen such as how to consume left-over meat, how to cook sheeps' heads, rabbits and old fowls, how to remove the bristles from a pig, to cure bacon and hams, to make brawn and sausages. She gives methods for preserving butter and eggs, for making soap and furniture polish, for cleaning copper pans and marble. In later life she became increasingly concerned with health issues, writing a supplement of health recipes for the 1930 edition, two years before her death. For nutritional reasons, but also as an anti-waste measure, she was strongly opposed to peeling vegetables, especially potatoes. Like many country cooks she was a fine baker as exemplified by this cake, good plain or buttered.

125 g butter, softened
½ cup brown sugar, firmly packed
1½ tablespoons treacle
3 eggs, beaten
1½ cups self-raising flour, sifted

½ teaspoon grated nutmeg
1 cup raisins or chopped dates
⅓ cup mixed peel
¼ cup roughly chopped almonds

▮ With electric beaters, cream the butter with the sugar until light and fluffy. Beat in the treacle. Gradually add half of the beaten eggs, beating in well. Fold the flour and nutmeg into the butter-egg mixture. Gently mix in the rest of the eggs with the beaters at low speed. Stir in the fruit and peel.

▮ Pour into a greased 20 cm cake tin and sprinkle the almonds on top. Bake the cake in a preheated oven at 180°C for about 40 minutes until cooked. Test for doneness with a fine skewer in the centre of the cake—when it comes out clean it is ready. Turn out onto a rack to cool after resting in the tin for 4 minutes.

Bush Pumpkin Cake

SERVES 8

MANY bush cooks, particularly in the past, depended heavily on the contents of their store cupboard. On the large stations the store contained a huge stock, sometimes larger than carried by a country grocer's. Evelyn Maunsell, in *S'pose I Die*, describes the six-month order for Mount Mulgrave Station:

There were four tons of flour in fifty-pound bags, one ton of coarse salt, one bag of fine salt, twelve seventy-pound bags of sugar, one bag of brown sugar (for spiced beef), one large case of tea, two twenty-eight-pound cases each of dried raisins, currants, and sultanas (I was later able to add to our ration by making our own candied peel), twenty pounds each of cream of tartar and carbonate of soda, two cases of mixed jams, one case (two hundred two-pound tins) each of treacle and golden syrup … , six bags of Japanese polished rice, three bags of Chinese unpolished rice (packed in matting), one large cask of curry powder, two ten-pound cases each of dried apricots, peaches, prunes, and apples, one fifty-pound sack of dried peas, one sack of potatoes, one sack of brown onions, one case each of Holbrooks and tomato sauce, one small case of lemon and vanilla essence, twelve pounds of hops, and two cases of one-ounce packets of Epsom-salt.

The Christmas order had a few special foods like tins of fruit, crab and asparagus, nuts and olives, hams, and some bottles of 'Christmas cheer'.

The arrival of the loading was a big occasion and it took several days for everything to be stowed away. The potatoes and onions had to be laid out on wire netting to keep them fresh and anything in damaged containers repacked lest it spoil. If the flour was full of weevils, a frequent occurrence, it all had to be spread out on galvanised iron in the sun to bring out the vermin and then twice sieved before rebagging.

Most of the flour went into bread and damper, some into puddings and the rest into a variety of cakes. Pumpkin cake is well-known in the bush, depending on the most reliable bush vegetable as well as many ingredients from the store.

BUSH PUMPKIN CAKE

1 cup warm mashed pumpkin	2 cups self-raising flour, sifted
125 g butter, softened	¾ cup mixed dried fruit
1 cup brown sugar	½ cup chopped walnuts or pecans
1 tablespoon golden syrup	1 dozen walnut or pecan halves
2 eggs	

▪ Put the warm pumpkin in a mixing bowl with the butter and beat with electric beaters until thoroughly combined and the butter has melted. Beat in the sugar and golden syrup. Add the eggs one at a time, beating well. Fold in the flour with the beaters on low speed. Stir in the fruit and chopped nuts.

▪ Pour the batter into a buttered 20 cm cake tin. Decorate with walnut or pecan halves. Bake in a preheated oven at 160°C for about 1¼ hours until cooked. Test for doneness with a fine skewer in the centre of the cake—when it comes out clean it is ready. Turn out onto a wire rack to cool after resting in the tin for 4 minutes.

Tully Banana Cake

SERVES 6–8

BANANAS were first grown in large quantities by Chinese workers in the 1890s along the Barron, Johnstone and Tully rivers in Queensland. Commercial farming began in the Northern Rivers district of New South Wales after a cyclone devastated Fiji, our main supplier, in 1909. During the Great Depression bananas attracted poor farmers, requiring only physical strength, four or five hectares of land and little capital. Though started by the Chinese, the development of the industry depended largely on the hard work and skill of Indians, particularly Fijian-born Sikhs, who established plantations from Woolgoolga near Coffs Harbour north into Queensland.

Banana palms are greedy feeders and grow on rich volcanic soil, usually on hill slopes near the sea. They spring from suckers planted three metres apart, fruiting after two years. Rosa Caroline Praed describes banana cultivation in *My Australian Girlhood*:

One could write a whole essay about the delights of a banana field—the succulent stems, running with innocent sap … Then the lovely sheaths of royal purple, unfolding and revealing the creamy blossoms and baby fruit: and lastly, the long-drawn joy of watching the green fingers swell and take a tinge of yellow—and maybe a surreptitious filching, wrongfully charged to flying foxes, before the bunch is gathered and hung under the verandah eaves, when the lawful authorities take jurisdiction thereof.

For safe transport to the markets they are always cut and packed green, ripened at their destination with ethylene, a gas produced when bananas mature naturally. They are one of the best eating fruits and make a particularly moist cake.

---

140 g butter, softened
¾ cup castor sugar
2 eggs, beaten
1⅔ cups self-raising flour, sifted
Pinch of salt
¼ cup milk

2 passionfruit
2 bananas (about 400 g), mashed
1 cup water
2 cups icing sugar, sifted
2 tablespoons extra butter, softened

▪ With electric beaters cream the butter with the sugar until light and fluffy. Gradually add the eggs, beating well. With the beaters on low speed fold in the flour and salt alternately with the milk. Stir in the pulp of the passionfruit (reserving the skins) and the bananas. Turn the batter into a greased 18 cm cake tin and bake in a preheated oven at 180°C for about 55 minutes until cooked. Test with a fine skewer in the centre of the cake—when it comes out clean it is ready. Turn out onto a rack to cool after resting for 4 minutes.
▪ While the cake is cooking, prepare the icing. Place the skins of the passionfruit in a small saucepan with the water. Bring to the boil and simmer, uncovered, for about 20 minutes until the water is well coloured and reduced to a couple of tablespoons. Let cool.
▪ With electric beaters combine the icing sugar with 2 tablespoons of the passionfruit-skin water and the extra butter. Beat well until smooth. Spread over the cooled cake with a spatula.

Lilli Pilli Upside-down Cake

Serves 6

LILLI PILLIES are the most important berry fruits native to Australia. Popular with Aboriginal people, they were quickly taken up by white settlers, who appreciated their refreshing flavours and their nutritive value in the diet. There are over thirty species of these rainforest trees, some rather floury and tasteless but many with a delectable fruity taste and crisp texture.

For this cake I have used the small-leaved lilli pilli *Syzygium luehmannii*, which has red, pear-shaped berries with a pleasant flavour spiced with clove and soft, edible seeds. The cloves used in cooking are a species of *Syzygium* from the Moluccas.

LILLI PILLI UPSIDE-DOWN CAKE

2 cups lilli pillies
½ cup raw or white sugar
60 g butter, softened
1 teaspoon finely grated orange rind

CAKE BATTER
60 g butter, softened
¾ cup castor sugar
1 egg, beaten
1½ cups self-raising flour
½ teaspoon salt
½ cup milk

▪ Discard any stalks from the lilli pillies, wash them and drain in a colander. Mix with half of the sugar and set aside. With electric beaters cream the butter with the orange rind and the remaining sugar until light and fluffy. Spread this over the base and sides of a 20 cm square cake tin. Spread the lilli pillies evenly over the bottom of the tin.

▪ To make the cake, cream the butter with the castor sugar with electric beaters until light and fluffy. Add the egg in thirds, beating well after each addition. Sift the flour with the salt and stir into the creamed mixture alternately with the milk. Spoon the batter carefully over the fruit. Bake in a preheated oven at 180°C for about 50 minutes until cooked. Test for doneness with a fine skewer in the centre of the cake—when it comes out clean it is ready.

▪ When cooked, loosen the cake from the sides of the tin with a knife and invert onto a cooling rack or, if you intend serving it hot, straight onto a serving plate. Serve plain or with whipped cream for afternoon tea or dessert.

Bush Brownie

SERVES 8–10

THE Aboriginal kitchen centres around the campfire and the expert manipulation of flame, hot coals, hot ash and heated stones. Campfire cookery is still a reality for many Aboriginal people in the bush today, as described by Ruby Langford Ginibi in *Don't Take Your Love to Town*:

In the afternoon I decided to make a chocolate cake. We were burning off, so there were plenty of ashes. I lined a Christmas cake tin with brown paper and made up the mixture and poured it in, put the lid on. Sat the tin on hot earth and scooped ashes all over it. Waited. Done. When the cake was cool I made icing and spread that over—'Come and get it!'

When I made damper I rolled it in flour and put it straight into the ashes. So when you took it out, it was covered in ash and dust. You flick this off with a tea towel or a switch off a pine tree. Then to keep it fresh you wrap it in a damp tea towel. There was no need to try and keep the chocolate cake fresh—blink and it's gone.

The bush brownie is the quintessential campfire cake. Delicately spiced and dotted with dried fruits, it was initially identical to the fruit damper and therefore derives from Aboriginal breadmaking traditions. It may be put directly in the campfire ashes, or in the camp oven, or nowadays many bush housewives cook it in a baking dish. This recipe is best eaten hot, straight from the oven.

3 cups self-raising flour
1½ cups sugar
2 teaspoons cinnamon
80 g dripping or butter, chilled and diced

1 cup dried fruit, such as raisins, sultanas or currants
1 cup milk

∎ Sift the flour with the sugar and cinnamon into a large mixing bowl. Rub in the fat with fingertips until the mixture resembles breadcrumbs. Stir in the fruit with a spoon so that the pieces are evenly coated with flour. Stir in the milk until thoroughly combined.

∎ Grease a rectangular baking dish and line the bottom with a sheet of baking paper. Turn the batter into the dish and smooth over the surface with a spatula. Bake in a preheated oven at 180°C for 1 hour until the cake is a good, crusty brown on top. Carefully turn out the cake onto a plate and discard the paper.

Maitland Cakes

MAKES ABOUT 20 TO 25

DURING the colonial period outdoor cooking was the norm not only for Aboriginal people but also for many white selectors settling on the land. In *Souvenirs d'une Parisienne aux Antipodes* Marie Rousselet Niau, a Daintree farmer in far north Queensland in the 1880s, describes her own simple arrangements:

As a kitchen, you'd look near the house for a tree trunk which needed clearing, and set the fire-dogs and grate right up against it. As for wood, there was an over-abundance, the only difficulty being that you could never burn enough.

This establishment was very primitive, but you were too busy clearing the forest, burning and planting, firstly maize, then sugar cane, not forgetting of course potatoes and vegetables, to be fastidious about one's abode ...

Before the kitchen was built, I very often cooked my bread by moonlight, to avoid the great heat of day.

Her kitchen, when finally erected, typically occupied a separate building, connected to her cottage by a covered walkway. Separation of living and cooking quarters prevented the house from overheating in the summer months and from burning down should the wooden kitchen happen to go up in flames.

The colonial kitchen had an earthen floor or paving of brick or stone. Furnishings included a scrubbed deal table, a couple of chairs, a dresser for crockery and cutlery, a few shelves to hold canisters, a bread crock, a safe to keep insects from food, a separate meat safe, perhaps a saucepan stand and water filter. The focus of the kitchen in the early days was the fireplace with its fire jack from which pots and kettles could be suspended and its camp oven set in the coals. Often there was a 'colonial' oven, specifically designed to burn wood, the usual fuel in Australia, normally with two fire boxes, one above, the other below the oven. Sometimes instead there was a brick or clay baking oven in which whole batches of bread, cakes and pies as well as large joints of meat could be cooked. From the 1850s onwards these cooking appliances were gradually, over a period of decades, replaced by the 'American' or solid-fuel stove, made of cast iron with only one fire box and, unlike earlier ovens, transportable rather than built-in.

Along with the ovens came a range of cake tins, biscuit trays and baking dishes. The shape of the cake changed from the natural curves of the sweetened damper to a more mechanical form regulated by the tin in which it was baked. The following colonial cakes from the town of Maitland in the Hunter Valley north of Sydney can be cooked in any small tins, either decorative or plain. They are rich and moist with plenty of sour cream, a typical pre-refrigeration ingredient.

2⅓ cups (600 ml) sour cream
3 eggs
1¼ cups sugar
1 teaspoon vanilla essence

1¾ cups self-raising flour
¾ cup sultanas
¾ cup mixed peel

▪ In a large mixing bowl beat the sour cream with the eggs with electric beaters. Beat in the sugar and vanilla. Sift the flour and fold into the cream-egg mixture with beaters on low speed. Stir in the sultanas and peel.

▪ Grease some small cake moulds, patty pans or muffin tins. Fill the moulds about three-quarters full and bake in a preheated oven at 180°C for 20–25 minutes. Test for doneness with a fine skewer in the centre of the cake—when it comes out clean it is ready. Cool on a wire rack.

Cooking with Gas

GAS cookery was introduced to Australia in the 1870s but only became popular after World War I. The change-over to gas happened more quickly in the cities whereas country cooks, with better access to wood for fuel, held onto the older stoves much longer. Eleanor Alliston, living on a remote island off the coast of Tasmania, only received gas appliances in 1961 when her wood stove suddenly broke down on the eve of a visit from an old friend. In *Escape to an Island* she recounts how he bought her a new stove, hot water service, copper and heater, all run on gas, and how she burst into tears in the middle of the showroom, moved by his kindness. But tears quickly gave way to joy, a joy which many women back in the 1920s must have shared:

And nobody could be sad for long with the thought of so much comfort, so much more free time to spend in the open air. I felt that I was freed, by a miracle …

Now we had all those white enamel servants, how very much better than black ones, we felt!

Despite the new stoves the look of the 1920s and 1930s kitchen did not change a great deal: there was still the old-fashioned wooden furniture, the dresser, wooden table and chairs, and a few shelves. Even the ice-chest was often enclosed in a wooden cabinet. The smaller items were much the same as before: canisters, a bread bin, long-handled iron or enamel saucepans stacked vertically on a tripod pot-stand. However, the wooden floor was now covered in linoleum and the draining board was made of terrazzo. Restrained colours such as cream and brown dominated.

In this kitchen environment the ice-chest and the gas stove had the biggest impact on cookery. Gas was clean and efficient giving instantaneous heat at a reasonable cost, factors which maintain its popularity in many Australian homes today. In the 1920s gas ovens came fitted for the first time with a thermostatic control called the 'Regulo'. Baking was simplified and results could be repeated with reliability from day to day. Cake baking certainly became a lot easier, especially for the inexperienced.

Pawpaw Tea Cake

SERVES 6

ELECTRICITY first became available in Sydney in 1904 and electric stoves in the 1920s. By the mid 1920s less than half of Sydney homes had power and so the all-electric kitchen only turned into a reality for many after World War II. With electricity came the modern kitchen as we know it today with an emphasis on efficiency: the kitchen of the 1940s and '50s was well-lit with an easy-to-clean stainless steel sink and easy-to-clean, practical surfaces like linoleum and laminex. It was arranged so that, theoretically at least, there was a uni-directional movement of foods around the room towards the dining room or buffet servery. Also in the name of efficiency, bench tops were introduced at which the cook worked standing, rather than seated at the table as before. The kitchen table, now of laminex with tubular metal legs and surrounded by tubular, vinyl-covered chairs, was reserved for family meals.

The dresser was eliminated in favour of built-in cupboards which provided neat storage for the increasing number of consumer goods. Built-ins saved room and created an uninterrupted line and sense of spaciousness. The streamlined cupboards, fitted with tubular metal handles, were now in gay, feminine colours as were the laminex benches and lino floors, which came covered in marble, linen or mother-of-pearl patterns. Multicolour schemes were all the rage with sometimes a different tint on every cupboard door and perhaps a feature wall of a contrasting shade to the rest of the room.

In this kitchen electricity was 'the obedient servant that can be summoned and dismissed at the turn of a switch.' The electric range, like its forerunner in gas, had a completely thermoregulated oven but gave a more even heat, ideal for baking cakes. With the electric kitchen came a number of small electrical appliances: a toaster, mixer, electric jug or kettle, frypan, wall clock and steam-and-dry iron. Of these the mixmaster had the biggest impact on cookery, turning out a whole array of whipped desserts, biscuits and cakes relatively effortlessly.

Mothers, often forced to relinquish wartime occupations, welcomed their children home from school with a glass of milk or cordial and freshly made cake. Tea cakes were amongst the most easy and economical. For me they are evocative of fond childhood memories, of days spent at my Aunty Jitz's home eating slices of her own golden, buttery tea cake, sprinkled with sugar and cinnamon. The following Queensland recipe will make a similarly golden cake, but with pawpaw providing the warmth of colour and flavour.

1 tablespoon butter, softened
⅓ cup sugar
2 eggs, beaten

2½ cups self-raising flour, sifted
1 cup grated pawpaw

- With electric beaters cream the butter with the sugar until light and fluffy. Add the eggs all at once and beat well. Beat in the flour alternately with the pawpaw.
- Spoon the dough into a buttered 20 cm tin. Smooth the top flat. Bake in a preheated oven at 200°C for about 30 minutes until cooked. Test for doneness with a fine skewer in the centre of the cake—when it comes out clean it is ready. Turn out onto a wire rack after resting in the tin for 4 minutes. Eat hot or cold in buttered slices.

Boiled Fruit Cake

SERVES 12

FRUIT cakes are an extremely important part of home baking in Australia climaxing in the elaborate ritual of the Christmas cake, usually prepared months ahead and soaked with successive doses of rum or brandy. Evelyn Maunsell, in *S'pose I Die*, describes how the cook Bridget prepared a three-tiered cake for their last Christmas at Mount Mulgrave Station in 1916:

She began by breaking sixty [guinea fowl] eggs into a huge bowl and setting the gins to work beating them while I looked round for three big baking tins. The only thing I could find big enough for the bottom tier was an old prospector's dish. For the next tier we used a big tin I salvaged from the dump, and for the third the biggest of our cake tins.

 I could not keep track of all that went into that cake, but I know that as well as flour and sugar there were about five pounds of butter, four large dippers of mixed fruit, two cups of treacle and quite a lot of rum.

 The kitchen range had two big ovens, so there was no difficulty with the baking,

The Christmas cake, with its tempting decoration of nuts, cherries or pineapple and its rich fruit filling, is the crowning glory of Australian fruit-cake baking.

and all three tiers turned out beautifully. When Bridget put it all together she had to turn the bottom tier upside down because of the sloping sides of the prospector's dish. Then she iced it and the whole thing looked wonderful. The gins and boys all came to stare at it pop-eyed, and next day when it was cut each received a large slice on a plate.

Simpler fruit cakes are served at morning and afternoon tea. Favourite amongst these are boiled fruit cakes, always moist and practically foolproof, a great standby, their place in Australia's culinary culture firmly attested by their constant appearance at agricultural shows as well as in many homes.

BOILED FRUIT CAKE

450 g mixed dried fruit
125 g butter
1 cup sugar
½ cup brown sugar
1 cup milk
2 eggs, beaten
1 cup self-raising flour
1 cup wholemeal plain flour

1 teaspoon ground cinnamon
½ teaspoon grated nutmeg
¼ teaspoon ground ginger
½ cup chopped nuts
1 tablespoon sherry
1 teaspoon bicarbonate of soda
1 tablespoon extra milk

∎ Place the fruit, butter, sugars and milk in a saucepan. Bring to the boil over a low heat and simmer, stirring occasionally, for 5 minutes. Remove from the heat and let cool completely. When cool, stir in the eggs.

∎ In a mixing bowl, combine the flours and spices with a spoon. Stir in the nuts, reserving 2 tablespoons to decorate the cake. Pour in the fruit-egg mixture and the sherry and mix thoroughly. Dissolve the soda bicarbonate in the extra milk and stir into the batter.

∎ Turn the batter into a greased 20 cm square cake tin and scatter the reserved nuts over the top. Bake in a preheated oven at 180°C until cooked, about 1¼ hours. Test for doneness with a fine skewer in the centre of the cake—when it comes out clean it is ready. Turn out onto a wire rack to cool after resting in the tin for 4 minutes.

Lamingtons

MAKES ABOUT 3 DOZEN

AUSTRALIA'S most famous cake is said to have been named in honour of May, Baroness Lamington, wife of the Queensland governor from 1896 to 1901. There are two theories regarding its invention: one, that it originated in the Government House kitchens as a way of using up stale cake; or, the explanation favoured by the majority of commentators, that it was created by Brisbane cook Amy Schauer.

Amy Schauer was born in Sydney in 1871 and trained at the Sydney Technical College before taking up appointment at Brisbane's Central Technical College in 1895, where she continued to teach until 1937. She wrote three cookbooks with her sister Minnie, also a cookery lecturer at the College, their most popular, *The Schauer Cookery Book,* first published in 1909. In addition, she developed cookery courses for school and technical colleges throughout Queensland, delivered classes in war and invalid cookery, arranged displays and judged competitions. In particular, she was famous for her talent in the area of confectionery, cake decorating and cake baking. Miss Schauer was undoubtedly the most influential figure in Queensland cookery during the first half of the twentieth century. She died in 1956.

There are several variations on the lamington theme, the classic being small squares of butter cake covered in chocolate icing and coconut but strawberry icing, cream fillings and larger cakes are also well liked. Often they are made with sponge cake but really the lamington butter cake makes the most flavourful ones. Prepare the cake at least one day before icing so that it will be easier to handle.

LAMINGTON BUTTER CAKE
190 g butter, softened
1 cup castor sugar
½ teaspoon vanilla essence
3 eggs, beaten
1¾ cups self-raising flour
⅔ cup milk

ICING
60 g butter
½ cup boiling water
⅓ cup cocoa powder
4½ cups icing sugar, sifted
About 2½ cups desiccated coconut

■ Grease a deep rectangular tin about 23 x 30 cm and line with a sheet of baking paper.

■ With electric beaters cream the butter with the sugar and vanilla until light and fluffy. Gradually add the eggs, beating well after each addition. Sift the flour and fold in alternately with the milk with the; beaters on a low speed. Pour the batter into the prepared tin and bake in a preheated oven at 180°C for 30–35 minutes until cooked. Test for doneness with a fine skewer in the centre of the cake—when it comes out clean it is ready. Let cool in the tin. Leave for 1 or 2 days, then turn out and discard the baking paper. Cut into 3.5 cm squares.

■ To make the icing, place the butter in a bowl and pour over the boiling water. Beat in the cocoa and gradually beat in the icing sugar with a wooden spoon. Place the bowl in a saucepan of simmering water and cook for 5 minutes, stirring constantly. Leave over the hot water while you assemble the cakes.

■ To assemble, spread the coconut in a flat dish. Using a long-pronged fork to skewer each square of cake, dip into the hot icing one at a time to cover. Roll immediately in coconut and place on a cake rack to set.

10

Campfire baking and other refinements

B R E A D S   A N D   B I S C U I T S

The chief thing a shearers' cook had to be good at was baking bread. The next thing he had to be good at was fighting. Every shearer admitted that it was an advantage to a cook if he could use his hands. 'You know, there's always some in the mess that's ready to grumble however well he cooks. And it just makes the difference if they know he's game to call 'em out and tan 'em.'

C . E . W .   B E A N ,   *O N   T H E   W O O L   T R A C K ,   1 9 8 5*

By the twentieth century, Australian cooks had started to adopt self-raising flour for their breads, cakes and scones.

Bread—an Old Tradition

Australian bread-making traditions are firmly rooted in Aboriginal culture, in the flattish loaves of unleavened bread cooked in the hot coals of the campfire and known as damper. For tens of thousands of years Australian women have been making dampers from native-grain flours. Cereals, seed pods of water lilies, spores of the nardoo fern, pigweed and wattle seed, wild rice, native millet, prepared cycad kernels and many others are all used to make wholesome flours. The importance of damper varies greatly across the continent, increasing in significance in the western plains and deserts where cereals are abundant, and declining where alternative foods such as fruits, vegetables and seafood are to be found.

A large bundle of grass is gathered and the grain stripped from the ears by beating with a stick for twenty minutes. The husks are rubbed off, then winnowed by tossing in the wind. Seeds, like pigweed, which may have some grit or impurities, are yandied in a coolamon: a deft, rhythmic toss repeated over and over again quickly separates the seed from the sand. Hard seeds like wattle are dry milled after roasting in the ashes. Cereals are wet milled on a large flat millstone using some water and a small, round, smooth stone for grinding. Because of their weight and lack of portability millstones are often placed at strategic locations for use when needed. The semi-liquid paste is collected in a coolamon at the side of the millstone, then poured onto hot, fine ash, covered with more ash to prevent burning and heaped with hot coals to bake for about thirty minutes.

These dampers are satisfyingly solid and tasty and of course highly nutritious, something like the heavy, whole-grain black breads of central and northern Europe. Sometimes, instead of baking the dough as one round or oval loaf, it is made into smaller cakes of varying sizes and cooked on the embers or on hot, flat stones by the side of the fire. The Torres Strait Islanders, too, make dampers, often flavoured with coconut milk or wrapped in banana or coconut-palm leaves.

When Europeans arrived in this country, the refined flour they brought with them was quickly turned to damper making by both whites and Aborigines. Since unleavened white bread does not have the virtues of unleavened whole-grain breads, leavening agents were soon included, ranging from Eno's fruit salts to bicarbonate of soda combined with an acid ingredient such as sour milk or cream of tartar. From the middle of the nineteenth century onwards this was superseded by baking powder, and during the twentieth century self-raising flour took over as the most popular ingredient. Because white flour has little flavour, before long, colonial cooks included other additives, such as salt, sugar, milk, a little dripping or butter, even an egg. Sweet versions, in which sugar and dried fruit were added to the basic dough, also became favourites.

It is curious to speculate on why the newcomers so eagerly took up Aboriginal bread-making techniques. Probably necessity was the main reason: yeast cookery would have been near impossible for the bushman making his meal by the campfire; and for the colonial housewife, preparing meals for large families with limited domestic help, damper would have been a welcome time-saver. In addition, many of the new settlers, the Irish with their soda breads and the Scots with their bannocks, would have been pre-disposed to breads made without yeast. The British tradition of scones, adopted with great enthusiasm by Australian cooks, also had many similarities to the damper technique. Whatever the reasons, the colonists were well paid for their foray into Aboriginal cookery and Eneas MacKenzie, describing dampers to prospective immigrants in 1852, testified to 'their delightful sweetness ... when hot and well buttered, most delicious, more especially when seasoned by labour or hunger'.

This is not to say that all bread in Australia is baked without yeast or made into flat round loaves. Many colonial households went to the trouble of making their own yeast bread and nearly all commercial production has always been based on yeast. And yet Mina Rawson, writing in 1894, bemoaned the fact that few young women could make a good loaf, and most original Australian bread recipes are either of the damper type or based on some other baking-powder or soda approach. Likewise, buns, crumpets and pikelets, leavened with yeast in Britain, were adapted to the quicker chemical leavening agents when they migrated to the Antipodean home kitchen.

Anzacs to Saos

While bread in the past was the staple of the dinner table biscuits have become the necessary accompaniment to today's cup of tea. Though part of the Australian baking repertoire for two centuries colonial cookbooks give comparatively few biscuit recipes. Apart from rounds of shortbread, easily adapted from the griddle of the Scots to the Australian camp oven, many of the biscuits we know today would have been difficult to cook over the campfire. The increased availability of domestic stoves in the second half of the nineteenth century and the regulation of the oven by a thermostat from the 1920s made biscuits much easier to bake at home.

Factory biscuits were initially expensive relative to income but refinements in manufacturing gradually lowered their price and made them cheap enough to eat with every cup of tea and with every child's glass of milk. The largest biscuit company was founded by William Arnott who was born in Scotland in 1827, apprenticed to a baker, and migrated to Australia at the age of twenty. In 1870 he expanded his Newcastle biscuit shop into a factory with twelve rotary coke-fired ovens turned by a steam engine.

The manufacturers modelled some of their lines on established recipes like the ginger nut, but also invented new ones such as the sao whose name, according to folklore, is an acronym for Salvation Army Officer. In turn, dedicated home bakers sometimes imitated popular bought biscuits like the iced vo-vo. Plain, thinly rolled biscuits were prevalent in the late nineteenth and early twentieth centuries, but nowadays drop biscuits and quick slices are more familiar, including the most famous Australasian biscuit, the Anzac. For special morning or afternoon teas fancier biscuits come to the fore, sandwiched together with jam or delicately iced. Savoury biscuits flavoured with cheese are baked in many households although dry biscuits for serving with cheese are normally bought.

Rolled oats, desiccated coconut, chopped nuts and dried fruit are all frequent ingredients. Macadamias and pecans have increasingly found their way into biscuits since the 1970s. Butter is the preferred shortening, giving a wonderful flavour, but in the country clarified dripping from the Sunday joint was sometimes specified in the past as a cheaper and readily obtainable fat with better keeping qualities.

Damper

SERVES 6

Many newcomers to Australia have marvelled at the damper and its emergence from the ashes of the fire like a phoenix immaculate and unsullied. Jack Davis in *A Boy's Life* describes a campfire meal back in the 1920s presided over by his father while Jack, his brothers and an English workmate by the name of Geordie looked on:

Father put flour in a dish and adding baking powder and water, mixed it into a firm dough, while Geordie watched fascinated. Father scraped a depression in the hot ashes and he laid the flattened dough carefully in the makeshift oven. Geordie squatted on his heels and said, 'You mean we're going to eat that Bill?' Father laughed and replied, 'Well if you don't you're going to go hungry.'

After about twenty minutes father broke a bush and removing the now cooked damper from the ashes, dusted it rigorously, and there it lay cooked to a beautiful crisp white and brown. 'Well,' said Geordie, 'that really is something.' Tommy ladled out the stew broke the damper, handing a piece to Geordie and to each of us. Geordie bit into his piece tentatively. Father and us boys watched him with amusement. 'Well,' said father with a grin, 'what's the verdict?' Geordie gave a yell and replied, 'It's even better than bread.'

Apart from preparing the fire properly the main difficulty with damper is knowing the amount of liquid to add to avoid a 'mud spring', that is a doughy damper. Technique also requires a light touch for perfect results, with minimal handling. The resulting loaf should have a satisfyingly compact but not soggy crumb and a dense, crunchy crust.

---

3 cups self-raising flour (white or wholemeal) plus extra

1 teaspoon salt

2 teaspoons sugar

2 tablespoons butter or dripping, chilled and diced

1 cup milk plus extra

■ Sift the 3 cups of flour with the salt into a bowl and stir in the sugar. Rub the butter into the flour with your fingertips until it resembles breadcrumbs. Pour 1 cup of milk into the centre of the flour, stirring with a knife until roughly combined. If using wholemeal flour add an extra 2 tablespoons of milk.

■ Turn out the dough and any flour left in the bowl onto a lightly floured board and knead (page 205) until all the flour is smoothly incorporated. The damper should be handled as lightly as possible and the kneading kept to a minimum. Shape the dough into a round or oval loaf, about 4–5 cm high. Dust with flour. Cut a cross in the top about 1 cm deep to stop it bursting open as it swells in the oven.

■ Place the damper on an ungreased flat baking tray and cook in a preheated oven at 200°C for about 35–45 minutes until golden brown and it sounds hollow when tapped, or until a fine skewer inserted in the centre comes out clean. Serve hot, warm or cold.

FRUIT DAMPER (BROWNIE) Add 1 cup sugar and 1 cup dried fruit to the basic dough before stirring in the milk.

JOHNNY CAKES Flour your hands and pat out balls of dough between your palms to make cakes about 6 mm thick and the same size as the palms of

At the end of a day droving sheep or cattle the most important man in camp was the cook, shown here in Charles Kerry's Breakfast in a Drover's Camp. *This cook is removing the lid of the camp oven with a set of irons while large billies simmer over a big log fire. His staples would have been tea, damper, corned meat, stews, and a variety of ingenious camp-fire puddings.*

your hand. Dust with flour and cook in an ungreased frying pan over a moderately low heat for a few minutes, turning half-way through.

FAT CAKES Heat some dripping in a frying pan over a moderate heat and fry the Johnny cakes in this.

Damper Days

DAMPER is the universal bread of the bush and obviously there are plenty of variations on the basic recipe, perhaps as many as there are cooks. In 1918, when Wrotham Park Station played host to sixty guests down for the local picnic races, there was a bread crisis caused by the sudden departure of the Chinese cook. Evelyn Maunsell remembers the event in *S'pose I Die*:

In the meantime all the men stepped in and made dampers. It was interesting to see, because each of them had his own way of doing it. Jack Hamill made a very good damper, but he mixed it so wet that it went into the oven looking more like batter than anything else. Peter Cameron tended to work his dough too much and his dampers were always on the dry side. Jack Gliddon, who had come up from Southedge with Tom Kilpatrick, was an expert damper maker. Getting them all cooked was no problem because the Wrotham Park range had big double ovens, one on either side of the firebox, with room for dampers above and below.

As well as the various approaches to plain dampers there are fruit and savoury versions. Savoury dampers, as far as I can tell, are a child of the latter half of the twentieth century since there are no references to them in earlier literature. Herbs, cheese and bacon are common additions.

Coconut-milk Damper

SERVES 6

THE most decorative dampers are made by Torres Strait Island cooks for feasts: coconut-palm fronds are plaited around the dough which, when cooked in the ground oven, is deeply patterned by the leaves. Banana fronds are used for a less decorative wrapping.

Everyday dampers are cooked directly in the hot coals of the fire and the best of these are made with coconut milk. The Murri women of northern Queensland also prepare dampers like this. The coconut milk gives the damper a fine texture and subtle flavour resulting in one of the best white-flour dampers you are ever likely to eat.

---

3 cups self-raising flour, sifted plus extra
1 teaspoon salt, optional

1¼ cups coconut milk

▪ Combine the flour and salt in a mixing bowl. Pour the coconut milk into the centre of the flour, stirring it with a knife until roughly combined. Turn out the dough and any flour left in the bowl onto a lightly floured board. Knead a little until all the flour is smoothly incorporated into the dough.
▪ To knead, press down into the dough with the heels of your hands, then push away. Fold the dough in half, give a quarter turn and repeat the folding and pressing process.
▪ Shape into an oval loaf about 4 cm high and dust with flour. Place the loaf on a flat baking tray and cook in a preheated oven at 200°C for about 35 minutes until golden brown and a fine skewer inserted comes out clean.

The Billy

THE billy came into vogue in about 1850 and has remained the favoured cooking utensil of the camper ever since. It is basically a large can with a wire handle and lid. There is much dispute concerning the origins of the name, some suggesting it was called after King William, others that it derives from an Aboriginal word for water, or from the 'bully' beef tins which it resembles.

The billy has become intricately woven into Australian folklore, the prettiest story that I have heard being the Legend of Three Moon Creek. This creek runs near the little town of Monto in Queensland and in the course of millions of years has carved out the Cania Gorge whose coloured cliffs now overshadow it. Clothing the hillsides are magnificent gums, their skins orange like the rocks out of which they grow, and a tangle of rainforest covers the lower slopes, thick with brush cherries and tree ferns, orchids and wild hoya vines. Along the creek itself droop scarlet bottlebrush, and wallabies browse the grass much the same now as they must have done over a century ago when a swagman—some say a stockman—camped there and began his evening meal. That night a full moon shone over Castle Mountain, its wheel of light reflected in the still waters of the creek. The swaggie knelt down to fill his billy and, setting it on the fire to boil, suddenly realised that he had miraculously captured a third moon.

On a more prosaic level, the billy is ideally suited to campfire cookery: it is light to carry and good for nearly everything except baked dinners. Billy tea, soups, stews, meat loaves, fritters, vegetable dishes, puddings, dumplings, simple cakes and breads all can be made in the billy.

Shearers' Brownie

MAKES 2 LOAVES

SHEARERS' cookery is somewhat different from most bushmen's fare. Whereas the swaggie, for example, did his own cooking out on the road, the shearers have their meals cooked for them either by the lady of the homestead if their numbers are small or more often by a full-time cook, helped by an offsider in the really big sheds. The shearers pay the cook and the price of provisions out of their own wages. They expect plenty of well-cooked, hot food to keep them going at their long, hard hours of labour. In the past, at the beginning of the shearing season, the shearers would elect the cook from the various hopefuls who frequented the wool districts in search of this remunerative work. These cooks were generally male, some were professionally trained, others had picked up the art along the way, some were excellent cooks, some were not.

C.E.W. Bean, in *On the Wool Track*, defines the cook's necessary qualities:

The chief thing a shearers' cook had to be good at was baking bread. The next thing he had to be good at was fighting. Every shearer admitted that it was an advantage to a cook if he could use his hands. 'You know, there's always some in the mess that's ready to grumble however well he cooks. And it just makes the difference if they know he's game to call 'em out and tan 'em.' They told of one very brawny cook who determined to put things on a proper footing from the start. At the first dinner he marched into the hut with his sleeves rolled up and the knots on his arms well displayed, and planted the dinner decisively on the table.

'There's your tucker, gentlemen,' he said. 'You can have a piece of that or you can have a piece of the cook.'

He folded his arms and waited. It was the tucker they chose.

The cook's skill at bread baking is exemplified by the shearers' brownie which, unlike the usual bushman's brownie, is a proper yeast bread, rather like a raisin loaf. Good buttered, excellent toasted.

---

170 g butter or dripping, chilled and diced
6 cups plain flour
1 cup sugar
½ teaspoons salt
½ teaspoon grated nutmeg

2 cups currants or raisins
1 cup milk
1 cup water
40 g compressed yeast

▪ Cut or rub the fat into the flour with your fingers until it resembles fine breadcrumbs. Stir in the sugar, salt, nutmeg and dried fruit. Scald the milk, that is, bring it almost to the boil, and add the water, letting it cool to lukewarm. Mix the yeast with ¼ cup of the lukewarm liquid and then stir in the rest of the liquid. Stir into the flour mixture.

▪ Turn the dough out onto a floured board and knead (page 205) until smooth and elastic. Add a little extra flour, if necessary until the dough will not stick to the board. Place the dough in a large greased bowl and turn over so that the greased side of the dough is on top. Cover the bowl with a tea towel and let rise in a warm place until doubled in bulk, about 1 hour. Divide the dough in half and shape into 2 loaves, placing them in greased 500 g bread tins. Brush the tops with water, cover with the tea towel and let rise again until doubled in bulk.

▪ Bake in a preheated oven at 200°C for 10 minutes. Reduce the temperature to 190°C; bake about 35 minutes longer until the crust is a rich dark brown and the loaf sounds hollow when tapped. Turn onto a wire rack to cool.

Trials of Yeast Cooking

DESPITE the predominance of damper in the bush many country women tried to master the art of yeast bread, often initially with less than perfect results. Myrtle Rose White coaxed and pampered her first batches of dough with blankets, hot bricks and hot bottles but nothing would persuade them to rise until, having given up and buried them in the ground, the heat of the day's sun produced volcanic upheavals, proclaiming her failures abroad. Henriette Pearce relied on the kindly ministrations of a neighbour to set her on the right path:

I mixed the dough and wrapped it well to keep it warm by the stove, but the next morning it had not moved at all. Remembering that it must be kept warm, I put it out in the sun, but that dough never did move. I had made it too hot and killed the yeast plant. Finally I made a honeymoon loaf out of the solid stuff and baked it ...

Mrs Cranston, who was an old hand at Territory housekeeping and an excellent cook ... picked up my meagre little loaf and laughed. Then she set to work to make a batch of bread for me, showing me just how warm the dough was to be kept. Out of the same quantity of flour as I had used she made two lovely loaves.

I profited by her good teaching and never had a failure again. Many a time the smell of home-made bread in the wilderness made friends for me.

Drought Buns

MAKES ABOUT 16

WHITE Australians living in the bush often suffered great deprivation when their food supplies ran out. Marie Rousselet Niau, in *Souvenirs d'une Parisienne aux Antipodes*, describes how, returning to her Daintree farm from Port Douglas hospital with a sick husband, young child and baby, she found the house ransacked and all the food stolen. Fortunately, they had bought a bag of rice and coffee:

The dear child was so reasonable, conforming valiantly to this new way of life. During an entire month, morning, noon and night, we lived on rice cooked in water, without sugar, and black coffee, also without sugar. It was hard for my husband, too, recovering from illness and in need of fortifying nourishment. When, at the end of a month, our new order arrived, it was touching to see our poor little girl improvise a dance of joy around a sack of flour, singing with all her heart ... Later, we had bananas, pawpaws, grenadillas, rosellas, pineapples, tomatoes, but these fruits didn't grow in a day.

More often it was natural disaster, especially drought, flood and bushfire, which led to food shortages and so one finds various recipes like drought cake, drought pudding and drought buns to cope with the hard times when there was no milk, no eggs and very little else in the pantry. These buns from Jean Rutledge are good served hot with butter and jam for breakfast or supper.

3½ cups self-raising flour, sifted
¾ cup sugar
80 g dripping or butter, chilled and diced

1 cup water
2 tablespoons currants

▪ Mix the flour with the sugar. Rub the dripping or butter into the flour with fingers until the mixture resembles breadcrumbs. Gradually add the water, stirring until smooth. Stir in the currants.

▪ Place large heaped spoonfuls 5 cm apart on greased flat baking trays. Bake in a preheated oven at 180°C, until tinged with brown and cooked through, about 20 minutes.

Federation Scones

MAKES ABOUT 12

SCONES originated in Scotland many centuries ago: arriving in Australia with our British forebears, they have remained popular ever since. This recipe comes from cookery teacher and writer, Fanny Fawcett Story. Her mother Mrs Annie Fawcett Story had been educated at the National Training School for Cookery in London and migrated to Australia in 1884 to head the Department of Domestic Economy at Sydney Technical College before taking charge of cookery instruction in the public school system two years later and then, in 1898, becoming Directress of Cookery in Victoria. Fanny Fawcett Story received her training at the college while her mother was still teaching there, in turn taking over the headship of the department herself in 1896 after serving at various schools and technical colleges in the state. Between the two of them they did much to further the teaching of cookery in this country.

In 1900 Miss Story published the *Australian Economic Cookery Book* which embraced a number of recipes for native game and local fish as well as some fascinating Boer War puddings. In addition she gave several recipes to celebrate Federation, including this one which produces a light, moist scone, good buttered or served with whipped cream and jam.

1¾ cups self-raising flour plus extra

½ teaspoon salt

30 g butter, chilled and diced

¾ cup milk

1 tablespoon extra milk for glazing

▪ Sift the 1¾ cups flour with the salt into a mixing bowl. Rub the butter into the flour with fingers until it resembles breadcrumbs. Gradually pour the milk into the middle, stirring with a knife to make a very moist dough.

▪ Turn out onto a well-floured board, sprinkle with flour and pat out by hand 2 cm thick. Cut into 5 cm rounds with a floured glass or cutter.

▪ Place the scones on a greased flat baking tray and brush the tops with a little extra milk. Bake on the top shelf of a preheated oven at 215°C for about 12 minutes until cooked. Serve hot or else place on a rack to cool, covering with a tea towel to stop the crust becoming too hard if you wish.

Outback Hospitality

THERE is one particular trait of the outback Australian which many writers have observed, that of hospitality. It derives from the Aboriginal practice of common ownership and sharing and has been reinforced by the vastness and underpopulation of the interior. Where there are no close neighbours every traveller becomes a neighbour in the Scriptural sense, to be welcomed, then helped along the way.

West Australian Nancy Polishuk discovered this when she took up residence in the Northern Territory in the 1950s. In *Life on the Daly River* she describes the generosity of those living along the river, of Indamarra and Frog, of Joe and Ole Man Mickey, of Charlie Dargie and his daughter Mabel:

The Daly is the kind of place where neighbourliness comes next to godliness ... It was typical of bush hospitality that whatever Charlie Dargie had he would share with us. He didn't even have to be asked. Mabel knew that, and so did I. Whether it was flour and water, or rice and water, or rum and water, what belonged to Charlie also belonged to his friends. 'Help yourself.' That's the motto of the Territorians ... Neighbourliness is a habit and a state of mind in the bush. Nobody thinks of talking about it. Like I said, it's next to godliness.

The code of bush hospitality is often expressed in the sharing of food, of a dish of kangaroo or corned beef, damper or brownie, or perhaps some home-made buns or scones, quickly rustled up.

Quong Tart Scones

MAKES ABOUT 20

OF THE many thousands of Chinese migrants in the colonial period the best known was probably Mei Quong Tart, born in Canton in 1850. At the age of nine he came to make his fortune on the goldfields and fifteen years later was selling tea in Sydney. He opened a succession of popular tea rooms, lavishly furnished with Chinese wood-carvings, oriental fans, cool ferneries and goldfish ponds, noted, too, for their excellent service. He treated his staff well, operating his business on the Christian principles of his adopted religion. Amongst the delicacies that Sydneysiders flocked to partake of were tea and buns, oysters and chicken. He maintained the quality of the raw ingredients by managing his own oyster leases and poultry farm.

Another item on the menu were the justifiably famous Quong Tart scones, perhaps inspired by his great love of Scottish culture. These are made from a firmer dough than an ordinary scone with a sugary base, good flavour and texture. Like all scones they are best the day they are made, excellent simply buttered, or with jam or honey.

---

3 cups plain flour plus extra
4 teaspoons baking powder
1 teaspoon salt
60 g butter, chilled and diced

1 egg
¾ cup milk
Sugar

■ Sift the 3 cups of flour with the baking powder and salt into a large bowl. Rub in the butter with your finger tips until the mixture resembles breadcrumbs. In a separate bowl beat the egg with the milk and 1 tablespoon of sugar, beating until the latter dissolves. Pour the liquid over the flour and mix in thoroughly with your hand until you have a smooth, firm dough.
■ Sprinkle a board with a tablespoon or two of sugar but no flour. Using a lightly floured rolling pin roll out the dough 2 cm thick. Cut into 5 cm rounds. Place on greased flat baking trays and bake in the top half of a preheated oven at 215°C for about 12 minutes until cooked through and a crusty golden brown, top and bottom. Serve hot or place on a rack to cool.

From Annabella Boswell's Journal

MANY colonists, like Aboriginal cooks, lived close to the land, involved with all stages of food production and consuming the fruits of their own industry. In her journal Annabella Boswell describes the happy subsistence of her childhood home at Glen Alice near Bathurst New South Wales in the 1840s:

We grew our own wheat, and the sowing, reaping, and grinding in steel handmills interested us, and I may say that we watched the rise and progress of our bread from the time our seed was sown till it came out of the oven. The making of potato flour was another great joy. We watched also the manufacture of our candles, dips and moulds, from the melting and hardening of the fat to the lighting of the wicks, and were proud to assist in such a share of the work as was permitted to us.

The dairy was another great interest, and we often rose early to go with our little cousins to the milking yard for mugs of new milk, warm and frothy, from our favourite cows. Butter and cheese were made for home use, and occasionally for the Sydney market. We had a variety of jams and jellies, dried apples and peaches, and preserved grapes for use till late in the season by covering them with paper bags while still on the vines, which bags we had, of course, to make. We had a great variety of poultry, and more eggs that we could possibly use. Delicious cakes were of every day use, sugar being the only thing we had to buy.

Our Highland maid was a famous baker of bread, and made also delightful rolls and scones. Sometimes we children made a cake and had it baked in primitive fashion on the hot hearth under an inverted pot with hot coals placed on the top. Sometimes we had a damper, which is always best when made from steel-mill flour, and must be baked on the hot hearth and covered with wood ashes.

Damper and scones are still part of the modern Australian diet although few cooks would harvest and mill their own flour.

Gem Scones

MAKES ABOUT 36 LARGE OR 48 SMALL GEMS

GEM scones, or Australian gems as they are sometimes called, are reputedly an Antipodean invention. They consist of a light dough baked into dainty balls in the special cast-aluminium gem irons. This recipe comes from Flora Pell, who became the Supervisor of Domestic Arts of the Victorian Education Department in 1909 as well as publishing a popular cookbook. They are a pretty addition to the afternoon tea table, served with butter or cream and jam, but are good with soup and casseroles, too.

---

1 tablespoon butter, softened

2 tablespoons sugar

1 egg

¾ cup milk

1½ cups self-raising flour

■ Grease gem irons and place in a preheated oven at 215°C while you prepare the batter. In a mixing bowl cream the butter with the sugar using electric beaters until light and fluffy. Beat in the egg, then the milk. Sift all the flour into the bowl and beat well until smooth.

■ Fill the hot gem irons two-thirds full with batter. Bake in the hot oven 8–10 minutes for large gem irons, 6-8 minutes for small gems. Remove from the irons with a spoon or tip out and serve hot, or cool on a wire rack. To re-grease the irons between batches, simply put a piece of butter the size of a small pea into the bottom of each iron cup.

Pikelets

MAKES ABOUT 18

AUSTRALIAN pikelets are modelled on the Scottish drop scone, that is always made without yeast, unlike their namesake the English pikelet which is a yeast griddle bread. They are popular tea-time treats, served buttered, sometimes with jam, golden syrup or honey. Variants include wholemeal, orange, spice, muesli, cheese, gherkin and wattle blossom but plain ones are still the favourites by a long shot.

1 cup self-raising flour

¼ teaspoon bicarbonate of soda

2 tablespoons sugar

1 egg

¾ cup buttermilk, or ¾ cup milk plus

   1 teaspoon vinegar

2 teaspoons melted butter

■ Sift the flour and bicarbonate of soda into a mixing bowl then add the sugar. In a separate bowl beat the egg with the milk and butter with electric beaters. Gradually beat the liquid into the flour until the batter is smooth.

■ Grease a frying pan or griddle with a little butter. Place over a moderate heat. Drop tablespoonfuls of the batter onto the hot surface and cook until golden brown on the bottom and bubbles appear on top. Turn with an egg slice and cook the other side until done. Grease the surface again before cooking another batch. Serve hot or cold.

Wattle Seed Blinis

MAKES ABOUT 10

WATTLE seeds are a staple for many Aboriginal people, usually containing high levels of protein and carbohydrate. The green, immature seeds of some species are eaten raw or cooked whole but more often they are collected when dry and fully ripe, threshed and winnowed from the pods, then roasted and ground into coarse flour for damper. Some wattle meal can be mixed with water to make a porridge after roasting.

Ground wattle seed is now produced by Vic Cherikoff's Bush Tucker Supply company in Sydney. It has a coffee-like taste with an undertone of hazelnut and gives an interesting texture to any cakes, biscuits or desserts in which it is included. This recipe is from Stephanie Alexander.

WATTLE-SEED BLINIS

1 cup bread-making or plain flour	¾ cup milk
1 tablespoon ground wattle seed	⅓ cup sour cream
7 g dried yeast	2 eggs, separated
½ teaspoon salt	Butter for frying

▪ Scald the milk, that is bring it almost to the boil. Mix the flour, wattle seed, yeast and salt together in a bowl. Beat in the sour cream and the egg yolks into the milk with electric beaters. Check that the liquid is lukewarm then beat into the dry ingredients. Cover the batter with a tea towel and let stand until doubled in bulk, about 1 hour.

▪ Whisk the egg whites stiffly in a bowl. Fold gently into the batter and let recover for about 30 minutes before using.

▪ Put a frying pan over a moderate heat. Add a knob of butter to grease it and spoon in enough batter to make small, thick pancakes about 12 cm diameter. Cook 1–2 minutes each side, turning with an egg slice. Keep warm in a cloth-covered dish until all are ready. Serve with sour cream and smoked salmon, trout or eel, caviar or taramasalata, or smoked Australian game meats for an entrée, luncheon or brunch.

Vegemite and Walnut Sandwiches

MAKES 1 SANDWICH

IN 1923 a young chemist, Cyril P. Callister, was employed in Melbourne on the problem of converting spent yeast from a brewery into a marketable product. What he came up with was Vegemite, a savoury spread rich in thiamin, riboflavin and niacin which has by now helped nourish several generations of 'happy little Vegemites'. Vegemite toast or sandwiches are the usual methods of consumption. Here grated walnuts give a pleasant crunch.

| Softened butter | ¾ teaspoon vegemite |
| 2 slices of bread | 3 walnut halves, finely chopped |

■ Butter the bread. Spread one of the slices with vegemite and sprinkle with walnuts. Sandwich together the two slices and cut into ribbons or triangles. Remove the crusts for a dainty version.

Anzac Biscuits

MAKES ABOUT 50

THESE biscuits are named in honour of the Australian and New Zealand Army Corps who first fought in the unsuccessful Gallipoli campaign against the Turks in 1915. Anzac Day celebrations began on 25th April 1916 and continue to be the annual focus of the lofty ideals and virtues of our soldiers.

Anzac biscuits are probably the most common home-baked biscuits in Australia. They are tasty, cheap and easy to make, the little mounds of mixture melting into thin, crisp biscuits.

125 g butter	¾ cup desiccated coconut
1 cup sugar	1 tablespoon golden syrup
1 cup plain flour	2 tablespoons boiling water
1 cup rolled oats	2 teaspoons bicarbonate of soda

■ Melt the butter over a moderate heat in a saucepan large enough to hold all the ingredients. Remove from the heat and stir in the sugar, flour, oats and coconut. In a small bowl dissolve the golden syrup in the boiling water and stir in the soda so that it fizzes. Combine thoroughly with the oat mixture.
■ Place heaped teaspoonfuls of the mixture on greased flat baking trays, leaving room for spreading. Do not flatten out the mounds of mixture as they will flatten as they cook. Bake in a preheated oven at 150°C until a rich brown, about 20 minutes. Make sure they do not burn. Remove from the oven and leave on baking trays for a minute to set before placing with a spatula on a wire rack to cool.

A 'bickie' or a biscuit

IN MARY Gilmore's childhood a certain ritual surrounded the eating of biscuits:

The funny thing about it all was that it was customary to eat biscuits with wine. My own people had cracknels with port, arrowroot biscuits with sherry, and a 'plain' biscuit with sweet Madeira and Malaga.

Biscuits were reserved for visitors or special occasions:

Besides the removal of the bonnet, and the special seating of the visitor when she came, there was the glass of wine and a biscuit if your wealth ran so far, or cake if you could not afford 'stores' …

There were no bridge afternoons then; instead, the visitor would ask for a piece of sewing or some mending, or 'receipts' would be talked, and an orgy of cooking would be indulged in.

By the end of the colonial period biscuits had lost their association with wine and instead became a convenient accompaniment to morning and afternoon tea. A neighbour dropping in for a quick 'cuppa' could always count on a 'bickie'.

Jerrawangala Honey Cakes

MAKES ABOUT 45

THE taking of tea in a bush setting is surrounded by a different set of practices than in the home, with the emphasis on informality. In *A Lady's Visit to the Gold Diggings of Australia in 1852–53* Ellen Clacy describes an outdoor tea party that took place on her way to the goldfields:

It was certainly the most curious tea-table at which I had ever assisted. Chairs, of course, there were none, we sat or lounged upon the ground as best suited our tired limbs; tin pannicans (holding about a pint) served as tea-cups, and plates of the same metal in lieu of china; a teapot was dispensed with; but a portly substitute was there in the shape of an immense iron kettle, just taken from the fire and placed in the centre of our grand tea-service, which being new, a lively imagination might mistake for silver.

Biscuits go well with billy tea as any other and it is possible to bake them in a camp oven but most bush recipes come from the kitchens of country homes, like these ones flavoured with honey and ginger from Jerrawangala near Sussex Inlet south of Sydney.

2¾ cups plain flour	¼ teaspoon bicarbonate of soda
¼ cup sugar	60 g butter, chilled and diced
1 teaspoon ground ginger	¾ cup honey

▪ Sift the flour, ginger and soda into a large bowl and stir in the sugar. Rub in the butter with fingertips until the mixture resembles breadcrumbs. Add the honey and knead in with your hand until combined.

▪ With a floured rolling pin roll out the dough 6 mm thick on a floured board. Cut into shapes with a biscuit cutter. Bake on greased flat baking trays in a preheated oven at 180°C for 16–18 minutes until cooked through. Place to cool on a wire rack with a spatula.

Crisp Lemon Thins

MAKES ABOUT 36

IN 1971 the universal acceptance of mechanical harvesting in the sugar industry put the last canecutter out of work, but before that cultivating and cutting the cane was one of the hottest, hardest and dirtiest jobs available. It was regarded as unsuitable for Europeans and so from 1863 South Sea Islanders were indentured, often under duress, to labour in the Australian cane fields. They were paid £6 a year, given an allowance of tobacco and soap, and a regulation daily ration of 500 g beef or mutton, 500 g bread, 1 kg sweet potatoes, 150 g sugar or molasses, plus 60 g salt per week and all the bananas, mangoes, pineapples and watermelons they could grow. An alternative to field work was domestic service, as cooks, maids, nannies and houseboys. Many white women in Queensland depended heavily upon their Islander cooks, often learning from them new methods of preparing tropical foods.

Blackbirding, as this enforced labour trade was called, ceased in 1904 and most island people returned home. One descendant of those who stayed is Gloria Arrow, for many years the housekeeper at Greenmount Homestead near the sugar town of Mackay. The following is one of the dishes frequently prepared at Greenmount during her period of service, collected by Miss Arrow in *Homestead Kitchen Recipes*.

190 g butter, softened	1 egg
½ cup sugar	¾ cup self-raising flour
1 tablespoon finely grated lemon rind	¾ cup quick-cooking oats
1 teaspoon lemon essence	½ cup finely chopped almonds

■ With electric beaters cream the butter with the sugar, lemon rind and essence until light and fluffy. Beat in the egg until combined. Beat in the flour, oats and almonds.

■ Drop heaped teaspoonfuls of the mixture onto greased baking trays and press flat with a floured fork. Allow room for spreading. Bake in a preheated oven at 200°C for 10 minutes until lightly browned. Remove from the oven and let set for 1 minute before removing to a wire rack with a spatula.

Fruit Slice

MAKES ABOUT 30

COOKERY skills are transmitted from one generation to the next in often fairly subtle ways, by children helping with small tasks or by unconscious observation of kitchen ritual. In my mother's kitchen there were canisters of home-baked biscuits and jars of chutney, pickles and marmalade, in winter a big pressure-cooker full of home-made soup and at Christmas hands of steaming pickled pork and fruit cake in the tin. As well as the usual baked dinners and topside pot roasts, richly flavoured casseroled chops and simple grills and offal dishes, there were macaroni pies and pizzas, Hungarian goulash and Indian curries, her own special fried rice, and fruity trifles like no-one else could make. Her kitchen was, and still is, a source of inspiration of what good food should be, what it symbolises, something more than mere bodily sustenance, but wholesomeness, honesty of flavour, a concrete expression of love and caring.

For me home-made biscuits are an essential part of any good kitchen, typifying what real food is all about. Fruit slice is full of goodness and flavour, which not only my mother but many other Australian mums have prepared over the generations to nourish and warm their children's hearts.

FILLING
1⅓ cups mixed dried fruit
⅔ cup currants
⅔ cup dates, chopped
¼ cup pecans or walnuts, chopped
30 g butter
2 teaspoons brown sugar
1 teaspoon mixed spice
Grated rind and juice of 1 lemon

⅓ cup water

DOUGH
125 g butter, softened
½ cup sugar
2 eggs
2½ cups self-raising flour
½ cup milk

■ Place all the ingredients for the filling in a saucepan and bring to the boil over a moderate heat. Simmer over a low heat for a few minutes until all liquid has absorbed. Let cool.

■ With electric beaters cream the butter with the sugar in a bowl until light and fluffy. Beat in the eggs, one at a time, until well combined. Beat in the flour alternately with the milk with the beaters on low speed.

■ Line a buttered rectangular tin about 20 x 30 cm with baking paper. Spread half the dough over the base, spread with the filling and then carefully cover with the remaining dough.

■ Bake in a hot oven at 200°C for 25–30 minutes. Cut into 4 x 5 cm squares and let cool in the tin. When cold remove to a sealed container.

Budgeree Meringues

MAKES ABOUT 22

THE art of the baker is seen to best advantage at the elaborate afternoon teas and suppers that form such an important part of country life. Fund-raising dances, tennis mornings and sports days all provide an excuse for a fine spread, with the local women each bringing a plate of whatever they do best. Patsy Adam-Smith, in *Hear the Train Blow*, describes the race ball back in the 1930s at the little town of Waaia set in Victoria's wheat belt:

Dancing stopped while supper was handed around, the men carrying big trays with the tea and coffee and the women and children carrying cakes and sandwiches.

'A real blowout,' was how Dad described the supper. There were sausage rolls and sandwiches, sponges four inches high filled with cream, sponge rolls, Napoleon cakes, custard slices, chocolate eclairs, meringues, sponge kisses, lamingtons, jelly cakes, and 'wheat-stacks' … big three-deckers of chocolate, vanilla and raspberry-coloured cake joined with whipped cream and iced all over with chocolate icing dusted with coconut.

The following cream-coloured meringues, delicately flavoured with macadamias and banana, come from the era portrayed by Patsy Adam-Smith. Budgeree is a Koori word meaning 'good'.

1¼ cups sugar	groceries)
2 tablespoons water	¼ teaspoon yellow food colouring
2 egg whites	¼ cup ground macadamias
¼ teaspoon banana essence (available at Indian	22 macadamia halves

■ Place the sugar and water in a small saucepan and bring to the boil. Simmer, uncovered, for 3 minutes. While the sugar is boiling, whisk the egg whites until stiff in a mixing bowl with electric beaters. Pour in the hot boiled sugar in a steady stream and beat for 5 minutes. Add the banana essence and yellow colouring to tint the meringue cream. Beat in the ground macadamias.

■ Place level tablespoonfuls of the mixture on flat baking trays lined with baking paper. Decorate each meringue with half a macadamia. Bake in a preheated oven at 130°C for about 1¼ hours until dry and crisp. Remove from the oven, peel off the paper and put on a cake rack to cool.

Wattle Cheese Straws

MAKES ABOUT 5 CUPS

THE following little gem I unearthed late one evening in the beautiful reading room of Sydney's Mitchell Library, handwritten on the endpapers of a Perth cookbook. Like most of the rich heritage of Australian cookery it was probably the contribution of some nameless woman, her talents unknown and unsung outside the circle of her acquaintance, presumably some West Australian housewife of another era. The one legacy from her now vanished kitchen is an excellent recipe for cheese straws, pale gold in colour as their name implies, easy to prepare and, since they contain no butter, low in fat.

1¼ cups plain flour

1 teaspoon salt

½ teaspoon cayenne pepper

1 cup tasty cheese, finely grated

1 egg

1 egg yolk

1 tablespoon water

■ Mix the flour in a bowl with the salt and cayenne pepper. Stir in the cheese. In another bowl lightly beat the egg with the egg yolk and the water. Pour over the flour and cheese mixture. Knead together in the bowl with your hand until thoroughly combined to produce a fairly firm dough. If your eggs are small add a little extra water.

■ On a lightly floured board roll out the dough 5 mm thick with a floured rolling pin. Cut into strips 8 x 0.5 cm and place on greased flat baking trays. Bake in a preheated oven at 180°C until cooked through, about 15 minutes. Remove with a spatula to cool on wire racks.

11

Lollies and lilli pilli jelly

The lemon-drinks that the little Japanese ladies brought me, shuffling along in their wooden slippers with many a bow, I shall remember every summer of my life. They were a foot long, all crushed ice and deliciousness, with a whole lemon and a syrup-secret from Osake.

ERNESTINE HILL,
THE GREAT AUSTRALIAN LONELINESS, 1940

Many a 1940s summer thirst was slaked by an economical draught of lemonade made with water and crystals.

Coconut Ice and Eucalyptus Lollies

BEFORE the advent of the lolly shop Australian children found their sweet treats in the bush. Apart from the many native fruits they could sip the nectar of flowers, nibble on lerp or sugar bread (sweet incrustations on gum leaves caused by an insect), or suck on 'bush lollies,' consisting of balls of sugary gum exuded by wattles, she-oaks and manna gums, enjoyed as much by white as by Aboriginal children. In the desert another sweet treat are honey ants, dug deep from the ground, their abdomens swollen to the size of grapes with honeydew and nectar.

During the colonial period Australians developed a reputation for being great lolly eaters. At home mothers would occasionally boil up toffees for their children or for sale at fêtes, but gradually in the twentieth century a number of easy, non-cook confections evolved, rolled into balls or pressed into tins. Coconut ice, well known since colonial times, the more recent white Christmas, apricot and rum balls, are typical and appear frequently at dinner parties and at Christmas time.

Most lollies are, however, manufactured outside the home. The most successful confectioner was Sir Macpherson Robertson, born in Ballarat in 1859 who began in 1880 to make sugar dolls, mice and horses in the family bathroom. Dressed immaculately in white, he presided until the 1940s over the Great White City at Fitzroy in Melbourne, where thousands of white-uniformed employees worked, loyal to their employer who took a keen interest in their welfare. Through hard work, a flair for new products and their skilful promotion he established MacRobertson's old gold chocolate assortments, cherry ripe bars, freddo frogs and columbine caramels as Australian favourites.

Other uniquely Antipodean lines include Jaffas, Fantales, Minties, Violet Crumble bars, Polly Waffles and Caramello koalas. Eucalyptus drops have always been liked, as much for their medicinal properties as for their taste, and a variety of rock lollies are produced, the oldest being Castlemaine rock from country Victoria. A range of excellent boiled lollies are made, including O'Brien's Bendigo sweets and Molly Bushell's.

Chocolates are an important part of the manufacturing sector. Foremost amongst Australian chocolatiers is Haigh's of Adelaide. Started in 1915 by Alf Haigh over a shop in King William Street, the family-run company is famous for its fruit centres, truffles and frogs which all begin with the importation of the cacao beans, roasting to specific requirements, and then the weekly preparation of the couverture which lasts three-and-a-half days. Ernest Hillier of Melbourne also turns out a fine range, including superb chocolate ginger; and Alpha's liqueur apricots and plums are to my mind the most scrumptious of any chocolates anywhere in the world. Pink Lady in recent years has become famous for their smooth milk chocolate bilbies and green tree frogs. In Sydney the tradition of Paddington liqueur creams begun by Russian emigré Walter Pulkovnik lives on, as does the Nut Shop with its nut and fruit clusters. In addition, the mass market is served by Darrell Lea and Cadbury.

Drinks—Drought breakers and spiders

IN A HOT, dry country like Australia water is critical to human survival. Traditionally where surface water, such as streams, lakes and pools, is absent knowledge regarding the location of hidden rockholes, soaks, wells and springs is vital and there are strict rules on their maintenance and taboos against sullying them. Aboriginal wells may be quite deep, sometimes six metres or more, and must be dug out and entered via ladders consisting of notched poles. Grass and sand are used to filter water if too fullbodied, particularly after prolonged drought. Tree stumps may be puddled, that is hollowed out by fire and the wood waterproofed with a layer of pebbles and clay before rain and dew are led in with the help of boughs and strips of bark strategically arranged around the mouth. Where sources are known to be far apart, water is carried in coolamons or skin water bags. Additional supplies can be obtained from plants: precipitation often collects in the forks of large trees; or sap can be drawn from incisions in the trunks, boles or surface roots; morning dew is collected from grass; succulent desert plants provide a source of moisture. The bloated bodies of frogs can also be squeezed to yield a thirst-quenching drink.

Apart from water, a palatable beverage called bool is provided by steeping the flowers of banksias, grevilleas, bottle brush, paperbarks and so on, in water. Mildly intoxicating brews can be obtained from the Tasmanian cider gum or from pounded pandanus nuts, soaked in water and mixed with sugar bag. The flower heads of grass trees can be fermented and a more potent drink, tuba, is concocted by Torres Strait people from the sweet juice of coconut-palm flowers. The mainstay for Islanders, though, is the innocuous milk of green coconuts.

The location of the first white settlement in Sydney was primarily determined by the presence of an adequate water supply, the Tank Stream. Settlers in the bush relied either on natural sources such as creeks or lakes, or on roof run-off collected in iron tanks, dams hand-dug into hill sides, or bores sunk to underground water supplies, such as the Great Artesian Basin.

The water so obtained was not always of the purest quality and to disguise the taste it was turned into tea, an ideal drink since the leaves were light to carry and could be boiled up quickly over the campfire, firstly in the quart pot and later in the billy. If unavailable, substitutes were made such as the fragrant leaves of some species of *Leptospermum* and *Melaleuca,* known to this day as tea-trees. Billy tea is made by throwing a handful of leaves into boiling water, giving it a stir with a gum twig, and then either tapping the side of the billy to settle the leaves or swinging it vigorously in a circular motion. Impregnated with the smoke of the fire and the scent of eucalyptus it contains a hint of the wild which makes it like no other tea on earth. In colonial times it was drunk strong and well sweetened but without milk.

Tea consumption was high through all ranks of society and the tea pot was normally present at all meals for the duration of the meal. In some parts of Australia, tea consumption per capita was more than double that of Britain. John K, in testimony given to Caroline Chisholm in 1845 for presentation to the House of Lords select committee on colonisation from Ireland, stated, 'we use 3 lbs. tea and 30 lbs. sugar a week; have seven in family; have tea and meat three times a day,—I like a pot of tea to be handy by my fire for any body travelling by'. White settlers on the land invariably offered this hospitality to passing strangers.

Tea, of course, was not the only beverage. Migrants from continental Europe and North America often preferred coffee, and grinders were to be seen nailed to trees outside diggers' tents on the goldfields, although it was still a minority taste unlike today. Alcoholic drinks were important, mainly rum, which was the centre of the lucrative trade controlled by the infamous Rum Corps up until 1809. The brewing of beer, the chief alcoholic beverage these days, was begun in 1795, originally a rich, dark ale. Known as shearer's joy, it only superseded rum in popularity when problems with its stability in hot weather were solved later in the nineteenth century. Some colonial drinks had colourful names like the nobbler composed of whisky or brandy; the spider of brandy and lemonade or ginger beer; bush champagne, a lethal mixture of methylated spirits and salvital; blow my skull, a combination of ale, rum and brandy watered down and flavoured with lime juice and sugar; the Paroo sandwich of beer and wine mixed; the Noonkanbah cocktail of lime juice, fruit salts and whisky; and bayan rum, a mixture of rum and salt, spiced with tobacco and stinging-tree leaves!

The Australian wine industry had its beginnings in 1788 when cuttings and seeds were included in the supplies of the First Fleet. By 1791 Governor Phillip had established a vineyard of three acres on the Parramatta River and some settlers planted vines as part of their mixed farms. By the early 1800s reasonable quantities of wine were being produced. James Busby is credited as the founder of the Hunter Valley industry: he collected cuttings in Europe, taught viticulture and published a treatise on the subject in 1825. Australia's second major area, the Barossa Valley, was explored in 1837 and settled soon after by Silesian Lutherans. Within two decades wine production there was firmly established. Vineyards were gradually set up in the Yarra Valley in Victoria, at Margaret River in Western Australia and in Tasmania and Queensland. Australia now makes some of the best wines in the world and consumption has risen greatly since the 1960s. Australia is now the third largest exporter of wine in the world, with exports of over 400 million litres per annum.

Soft drinks, or 'lolly water', have been drunk since the early days of white settlement, many of them originally home-made such as ginger beer, barley or oatmeal water, lemonade and fruit cordials. Tropical fruit punches for parties came in with the health movement of the 1930s; and consumption of milk shakes and fruit juices has increased enormously in the twentieth century under the impetus of greater nutritional information and improved packaging and marketing. The main trend during the post-war decades of increasing affluence has been a decline in the drinking of plain water and a tendency for most fluids to be flavoured. Soft drink consumption practically doubled in the 1960s with fizzy drinks such as lemonade, orangeade, cola, mineral water and Australia's own Passiona (invented in 1925 by Spencer Milton Cottee of Lismore) becoming commonplace items of everyday consumption.

By the end of the twentieth century American youth culture had firmly established Coca Cola as a major beverage; fitness fans had created a boom in fruit juices and energy sports drinks; and mineral water, herbal teas and Italian styles of coffee prevailed with trendy city dwellers. Light beer made inroads at pubs, while at home water filters became fashionable.

Rosella Jam to Choko Pickles

Australian cooks have always preserved foods in times of plenty, setting them aside for the inevitable shortages that occur during droughts or through the natural rotation of the seasons. Drying is traditionally used by Aboriginal women to preserve fruits and nuts. In the Western Desert green tomatoes are ground to a paste and shaped into a large ball about 25 cm diameter: the outer surface dries hard in the sun and may be stored up a tree almost indefinitely. In the Gulf country a fruit known as mundjutj is partially sundried, coated with red ochre and then left until brittle when it is wrapped in paperbark. Again in northern Australia slices of cycad kernel are dried and enclosed in paperbark in grass-lined trenches up to six metres long. The Torres Strait Islanders dry boiled slices of turtle and pearl oyster meat on long skewers in the sun for taking on lengthy voyages.

During the colonial period the drying of grapes, apricots and other tree fruits commenced. Vine fruits, particularly sultanas, are the most significant: the industry was set up in the Murray Valley in 1887 and expanded considerably after World War I when soldier settlers were allotted farms, the largest centre now being Mildura and the surrounding Sunraysia region. The exceptionally high quality of Australian dried fruits means that they are found in shops the world over, with the United Kingdom, Canada, New Zealand and Germany the leading importers.

Jam manufacture began in Hobart in 1861 although home bottling was already well established. In the eyes of English commentator Evelyn May Clowes, writing in the early twentieth century, 'The Australian—both child and adult—devours enormous quantities of jam, particularly up in the back blocks, where butter is almost an unknown luxury'. Australians still lay their jam on good and thick. Isabella Beeton recorded peach and pineapple marmalade and guava jelly as specifically Antipodean and, though jams are made from all sorts of fruit, those from native or tropical fruits are the most distinctive. Native fruit recipes from colonial times include lilli pilli, quandong, wild lime, Macquarie grape, cluster fig, Burdekin pepper vine, Herbert River cherry, native currant and tamarind. Of the tropical fruits passionfruit, rosellas, limes and cherry guavas are the best. Jams from melon are an old bush standby, particularly melon and lemon or ginger, and jam melons are grown for the purpose. Pumpkin is another bush ingredient, more frequently used in the nineteenth century than now, and dried fruits are an interesting feature of bush recipes, dried apricot being the most widespread. Macadamia nuts were an unusual addition to jams in the 1980s.

With the early establishment of citrus groves marmalade quickly became part of the colonial breakfast. Some colonial recipes feature bitter oranges like the poorman and the Seville but today most marmalade is sweet, thick and chunky, made from sweet oranges, grapefruit, lemons, cumquats, mandarins, and, in tropical areas, limes. A major trend is the inclusion of non-citrus fruits which add to the chunkiness and sweetness but also lend interesting undertones to the dominant citrus flavour.

Given the national consumption of meat there is a corresponding demand for accompanying pickles, relishes, chutneys and bottled sauces. Evelyn May Clowes concluded that 'one cannot live on boiled beef and damper alone, and as tomato sauce and jam are the cheapest relishes obtainable, every camping-place and hut is littered round with an inevitable medley of sauce-bottles and tins'. Despite the changes in fashion over time, tomato sauce has kept its place: poured over chops, steaks, sausages and meat pies, it was bottled at home in the early days, but factory production began in the second half of the nineteenth century. Today, the mushroom ketchup, anchovy sauce and pickled walnuts of the colonial larder have vanished in favour of spicier condiments from Asia with soy, plum and chilli sauces becoming very popular, not to mention curry pastes and sambals. Despite the availability of manufactured products, some home cooks continue to make their own pickles and chutneys and again, like jams, tropical and dried fruits figure prominently.

Eucalyptus and Honey Lollies

MAKES ABOUT 500 G

CHILDREN are inordinately fond of lollies and will use great ingenuity to obtain them. In *Unna You Fullas* Glenyse Ward recounts her expeditions into the bush as a child, nibbling on gumnut seeds and the sweet centres of mistletoe fruits:

There was also a tree with thick crusty bark and as we walked we could see the pale gum shining on it in big round lumps. We collected them in rusty jam tins. If they were too hard we knocked them off with rocks. Inside, the lumps were soft. We took the gum back in tins to the kitchen and while the nuns were at prayers, we found an old pot, sneaked into the storeroom and robbed a handful of sugar. Then we mixed the gum with sugar and water and boiled it up on the stove to make toffee.

Some girls couldn't wait for it to cool down and burnt their mouths. All the time we were nervous that the nuns might catch us.

Eucalyptus lollies preserve that great bush taste but are more usually made from the contents of the kitchen cupboard and medicine chest than from gathered ingredients.

2 cups sugar

½ cup water

2 tablespoons honey

1 tablespoon white vinegar

1½ teaspoonks eucalyptus oil (available from
    your local chemist

■ Care must be taken when making toffee as spills can cause terrible burns.
Put all the ingredients in a small saucepan and bring slowly to the boil over a
moderate heat. Boil, without stirring, for about 30 minutes until the toffee
reaches 150°C or the hard crack stage (a small quantity dropped into iced
water will be brittle and not stick to one's teeth when bitten). Wipe down
the inside of the pan occasionally with a wet brush to stop crystals forming.
■ Pour into small foil patty pan cases. When cold store in an airtight jar.

Coconut Ice

MAKES ABOUT 18

MOST people have memories of the lolly shop of their youth with its array of
snakes and freckles, licorice straps and licorice allsorts, milk bottles and jelly
beans, musk sticks, choo–choo bars, sherbert bombs, all-day gob suckers and
rainbow balls. Kathleen McArthur in *Bread and Dripping Days* remembers the
payment for running errands as a child:

*The reward was a penny for an ice-cream or only a halfpenny which would purchase
some 'gumboils' of the sugary sweet kind. A penny would also buy a Lamp-post,
which was a pyramid-shaped confection on the end of a stick. These came in red, green
and yellow and it would be interesting to know what the shopkeepers did with all the
leftover reds and greens which no child with worldly knowledge of such important
matters would buy, because the reds were made from Red Indians' blood and the green
were deadly poisonous. Gospel!*

Lollies were sometimes given to children as a token of goodwill. In *Muma's
Boarding House* Shirley Ball recalls the outings to the grocer's with her mother
and the encounter with the store manager once the bill had been paid:

*As he peered at me through the opening in the grille he always said the same thing
each week: 'There's one item a certain little lady will be able to carry, I'm sure.' This
was a white paper spill in the shape of a dunce's cap full of boiled lollies. He shovelled
these in from the bag beside his desk, and clutching this I happily moved on to more of
the day's pleasures.*

Stalls at school and church fêtes are another source of lollies, usually featuring home-made toffees, toffee apples and coconut ice, the latter always a favourite with children because of its pretty layers of pink and white.

3 cups icing sugar

3 cups desiccated coconut

125 g copha (white vegetable shortening)

2 teaspoons vanilla essence

2 egg whites

2 or 3 drops cochineal (pink food colouring)

▪ Line the base of a 20 cm square cake tin with foil. Sift the icing sugar into a large bowl and stir in the coconut. Melt the copha over a low heat and stir into the coconut mixture along with the vanilla. Mix well. Beat the egg whites in another bowl with electric beaters until frothy and mix in thoroughly with the coconut mixture.

▪ Press half of the mixture into the prepared tin, smoothing the surface with a spatula. Add some cochineal to the remainder to colour it pink. Stir until well blended. Smooth this evenly over the white layer and allow to set in the refrigerator, about 1 hour.

▪ Remove the coconut ice from the tin, discarding the foil. Cut into squares with a sharp knife. Store in a sealed jar in the fridge.

Apricot Balls

MAKES ABOUT 50

A NUMBER of colonial commentators remarked on the lavish addiction to lollies by Australians of all ages. Evelyn May Clowes, in *On the Wallaby*, notes the situation at the beginning of the twentieth century:

Everyone loves 'lollies'—as they are called out here, the word 'sweets' only being applied to what we generally call 'puddings'—and Melbourne and Sydney are the only towns where I have ever seen grown-up people gathered in absorbed and wistful groups round the windows of the confectioners' shops, both men and women, discussing the good things on show there as engrossedly as they would stocks and shares—or hats … while a young man here very rarely goes to call on a girl without an offering of a box of lollies.

Confectionery for adults now often takes the form of chocolates or home-made rum, sherry, whisky or apricot balls.

300 g dried apricots, finely chopped
3 cups desiccated coconut

1 x 400 g tin sweetened condensed milk
¼ cup icing sugar, sifted

▪ In a bowl, mix the apricots with the coconut and condensed milk with your hand until thoroughly combined. Roll lumps of the mixture between the palms of the hands to form balls about 3 cm diameter. Roll in the icing sugar to coat. Place in an air-tight container for 48 hours before eating.

Ginger Truffles

MAKES ABOUT 20

THE French have had a significant influence on Australian cooking which cannot be ascribed solely to the small numbers of immigrants from France, but comes in the main from the hegemony of French cuisine. The first licensed hotel in New South Wales, the Freemason's Arms, was opened in the 1790s at Parramatta and achieved a considerable reputation for the cookery of its Parisian chef. French cuisine was introduced to Melbourne in 1849 with the opening of the Union Hotel in Bourke Street where the chef was paid the exorbitant sum of three guineas a day. Under the impetus of gold many French restaurants flourished and French immigrants established wineries in the Goulburn Valley and Great Western districts of Victoria. Most high-class restaurants and most public banquets in the colonial era had menus written in French and featured dishes based on the haute cuisine of Paris; wealthy households such as the residences of the colonial Governors often employed French chefs; and food writers generally featured a small selection of French dishes in their books for home use.

However, the greatest impact on domestic cookery came from the 1950s onwards with the opening of French provincial bistros in the cities and the publication of books and newspaper and magazine columns on French cooking. The free use of garlic, olive oil, wine and herbs marked the new approach. French mayonnaise largely replaced boiled and condensed milk dressings while lettuce was not shredded but torn, and tossed with a vinaigrette. Cheeses based on French models, such as camembert and brie, have been manufactured on a wide scale from the 1970s and popular foods include garlic bread, pâté, quiche, pepper steaks, crêpes, crème caramel, chocolate mousse, fruit flans, croissants and baguettes. French culinary techniques have been widely promoted and Australian adaptations of French recipes have appeared, such as these chocolate truffles with ginger.

250 g dark chocolate

2 teaspoons instant coffee powder

2 tablespoons water

125 g unsalted butter, softened

2 tablespoons rum or brandy

80 g glacé ginger, cut in about 20 pieces

Dutch cocoa powder or desiccated coconut

▪ Break the chocolate into squares and place in a bowl sitting in a saucepan of simmering water. Stir in the coffee and water. Heat over simmering water until the chocolate is melted. Remove the bowl from the heat and beat in the butter gradually with an electric mixer until combined. Beat in the alcohol. Refrigerate for at least a couple of hours until firm.

▪ Using two teaspoons, break off lumps of the mixture. Push a piece of ginger into the centre and mould the chocolate around it. Roll into balls between the palms of your hands. Roll in cocoa powder or coconut. Place in paper patty cases and store in an airtight container in the refrigerator.

Red-back Spider

SERVES 1

EARLY in the colonial era some Australian men acquired the reputation of being hard drinkers, although the average national consumption of alcohol was not high. Danish bricklayer Emil Hall, working near Castlemaine in Victoria from 1859 to 1862, describes in his *Diary* a pretty rough, occasionally brutal goldfields existence where every bargain was sealed with a drink, every birthday or anniversary celebrated with punch, and most pay days ended in a trip to town to get 'gloriously drunk' on rum or beer. Sometimes he and his mates became so inebriated they could not walk home and frequently brawls resulted with injuries to men and property. The expense of alcohol was a constant source of complaint:

During these Christmas Days we amused ourselves with the only pleasure available, namely take a schnaps and play cards. I have almost ruined £5 during the holidays and I was not even drunk. Had I spent as much at home I would have enjoyed myself a hundred times better.

The 'spider' was one alcoholic drink popular at the time, a mixture of brandy and lemonade or ginger beer. By the 1920s, however, the term had come to mean an ice-cream soda. Named after one of Australia's lethal but fortunately timid arthropods, the following raspberry or strawberry spider is a bright lolly pink and sure to be a winner with any child.

1½ tablespoons raspberry or strawberry cordial   *About ¾ cup lemonade*
1 small scoop vanilla ice cream

▪ Place the cordial and ice cream in a tall glass and top up with lemonade. Serve with a long spoon.

Drought Breaker

SERVES 1

THE drunkenness common in certain sectors of colonial society awakened an interest in temperance issues from an early date, particularly within the churches. Yet an organised temperance movement aimed at control and eventual abolition of drinking was only formed in the 1880s. A number of societies were established about that time with the first Australian branch of the Women's Christian Temperance Union founded in Sydney in 1882. The movement was mostly Protestant, attracted many women and clergy but few members from the working class, and sided more with the Liberal than the Labor Party. It was an important political force at the turn of the twentieth century, never achieving prohibition but it succeeded in limiting hotel

In the 1930s, personal, over-the-counter service was the order of the day at William's grocery store at Bega on the south coast of New South Wales.

opening hours. Some of its victories were mixed, however, early closing introduced into New South Wales and Victoria from 1916 leading to the infamous six o'clock swill where patrons attempted to down as many drinks as possible between the finish of their working day and the 6 pm closing. This was abandoned in 1954 by New South Wales followed in 1962 by Victoria. Despite a decline, temperance issues still survive in government education campaigns, legal controls over alcohol consumption by drivers, and the establishment of 'dry' communities by some Aboriginal people.

For the teetotaller the following drink from Steabben and Corsar's *Australian Bartender's Guide to Cocktails* is a refreshing adult thirst quencher.

Ice blocks

4 drops Angostura bitters

1½ tablespoons lime cordial

About ¾ cup dry ginger ale

2 thin slices of lime or lemon

▮ Half fill a tall glass with ice blocks. Add the bitters and cordial. Top up with dry ginger ale. Arrange a slice of lime or lemon in the drink and another over the rim of the glass to decorate.

Pearl Diver's Lemon Squash

MAKES 2 DRINKS

PEARLING has always been a part of Australian life for the Torres Strait Islanders and Aboriginal people living near the sea who use mother-of-pearl in their jewellery and tools, as well as eating pearl oyster meat. However, it only became big business in the 1860s. The Japanese entered the industry in 1885 and gradually took over as captains, tenders and divers both in Broome, the main pearling port, and also on Thursday Island. At that time Australia supplied eighty per cent of the world's mother-of-pearl. During World War II the Japanese withdrew from the industry but later re-entered in limited numbers and now pearls are cultured in joint ventures with Australians.

During their heyday the Japanese operated a soy sauce factory on Thursday Island, and in Broome worked market gardens a few miles out of town. There at the cemetery they held their Bon-matsuri or Feast of Lanterns under the harvest moon, offering up tomatoes and biscuits, baskets of manju-rice-cakes and fish, sake and sweets, sending these across the waters of Roebuck Bay on tiny pearl luggers carrying the souls of the newly dead. Ernestine Hill describes this festival in *The Great Australian Loneliness* and also recalls refreshments offered to her by ageing kimonoed women:

The lemon-drinks that the little Japanese ladies brought me, shuffling along in their wooden slippers with many a bow, I shall remember every summer of my life. They were a foot long, all crushed ice and deliciousness, with a whole lemon and a syrup-secret from Osake.

PEARL DIVER'S LEMON SQUASH

½ cup sugar

1 cup water

1 tablespoon lemon juice

1 tablespoon sake, optional

2 small lemons, about 100 g each

Crushed ice

▪ Place the sugar and water in a small saucepan and bring to a rapid boil over a moderate heat. Boil, uncovered, for 5 minutes. Let cool and stir in the lemon juice and sake.

▪ Stab a lemon all over with a skewer, holding it above a tall glass (about 2-cup capacity) to catch the juice. Squeeze as much juice as you can out of the fruit with your hands, leaving the lemon whole. Put the lemon in the glass, fill with crushed ice and pour over half the syrup. Make crushed ice in the food processor or wrap it in a clean tea towel, place on the chopping board and crush it with a hammer. Repeat the process with the remaining lemon.

Custard Apple Milkshake

SERVES 2

THE first milk bars were opened in Sydney in the early 1930s and by 1937 there were four thousand operating throughout Australia. It would seem that Greeks, arriving from the United States, brought the idea with them, adapting the American drugstore soda-fountain to local needs. For many years milk-bar ownership was dominated by Greeks and other new Australians who saw the opportunities for making money by hard work and long hours.

Some of the early milk bars were especially beautiful with elaborate wood panelling and decoration, booths for seating, and the bar itself where the milkshakes were whisked to a stiff froth in their tall aluminium beakers and then poured into a glass for serving. Milkshakes were promoted as a health drink and cookbooks of the 1930s and '40s encouraged housewives to prepare them at home using fresh fruit instead of the syrup flavouring ladled in by the milk-bar proprietor. Bananas make a particularly thick, filling milkshake, but custard apples go well in this type of drink, too.

1 small custard apple, about 500 g
1½ cups milk, chilled

2 teaspoons honey

▪ Cut the custard apple in half, scoop out the flesh and carefully discard all the seeds. Purée the flesh in a blender or food processor with the milk and honey on high speed until smooth and frothy. Pour into glasses and serve.

Passionfruit Jam

MAKES ABOUT 6 X 250 G JARS

JAMS and pickles are seasonal creations, mirroring their time of making, stored away in the pantry like bottled memories of days vanished, only later to jolt the taste buds with a flash of flavour from the year past. They follow the annual rhythm of nature and the succession of harvests from one month to another as most good cookery has always done. In *My Australian Girlhood* novelist Rosa Caroline Praed recalls the seasons at Marroon Station in southern Queensland, giving the reader a garden calendar of fruits, flowers and ever-changing culinary delights:

Lying in the hammock on a drowsy spring afternoon, with its strange September dreaminess, one can easily fancy oneself back into youthful springtime, rocking in a hammock—now on the verandah, with the cool evening breeze blowing on one's face and bringing the scent of orange flowers from the big mandarin tree in the garden. That garden! What a contrast to the fat-hen and pumpkin patch at Naraigin! ...

Next month, the wild jasmine shrubs on the track to the Springs will be covered with yellow and cream flowers ... a pomegranate, in bud now, will be hanging out balls of vivid red ... But in November the cool, soft shades have gone ... The passion fruit is ripe and so are the Cape mulberries and flat-stoned peaches ...

Then comes December, when the thermometer ranges 100° in the verandah; when the grass is brown and scorched, the creeks dry, and lean kine lift pleading eyes from their insufficient pasture. The fruit becomes juiceless from want of rain ...

Intense sultry heat weighs upon the world, wrapping it as in a steamy grey blanket. One day maybe, at about four of the afternoon, the blanket turns to the colour of coal smoke, and through it, fiery shafts dart down, rebounding against an ironstone ridge in zig-zag coruscations. The thunder growls like a beast before it springs ... Hailstones make a clatter on the roof ...

When it is over, the whole earth, with all upon it, lifts up its voice in rejoicing. Hailstones are gathered in buckets, and wrapped in blankets to ice butter and drinks for the morrow ... It is January: and every morning the grapes are gathered in a big

milk-pan and put in the verandah for all persons to eat … the water-bags drip
moisture … the watermelons are ripe, and the snakes enjoy life.

In February we fight the satin birds by legions for the last bunch of grapes, and
make jam from figs and pie melons. The quinces come in in March—they grow inside
the high fence, which is a mass of prickly pear …

In April, out-of-door life begins and goes on through the winter … It is on these
days that new chums go and shoot ducks on the lagoons, and fish in the creek, and eat
oranges under the mandarin trees. In June, the west wind … puffs a gale which tears
the bark off the hide-house, and sends oranges whirling …

Passionfruit are one seasonal fruit that have since Rosa Caroline Praed's
time formed the basis of a great Australian classic jam in which both the pulp
and purple skin are used. 'Wattle Blossom', who lists this recipe in her 1916
cookbook *Off the Beaten Track*, describes it as 'a delicious jam of very beautiful
appearance—bright, clear red, with black seeds, and the consistency of a firm
jelly'.

PASSIONFRUIT JAM
_____

2 dozen passionfruit *About 1¼ kg sugar*
8 cups water

■ Twist the stalks off the passionfruit and discard. Wash the fruit and scrub off
any mould. Cut in half and remove the pulp with a teaspoon and reserve.
■ Place the skins in a large, heavy-based saucepan with the water. Bring to the
boil and simmer, covered, for 1 hour until the inside of the skins is quite soft.
Uncover the pan and let cool until the skins are cold enough to handle.
Scrape out all the soft interior with a teaspoon, discarding any hard lumps
and the outermost layer of tough skin. Reserve the liquid.
■ Combine the soft interior of the skins with the passionfruit pulp and
weigh: add an equal weight of sugar. Put in the cleaned saucepan with the
reserved liquid in which the skins were cooked. Boil rapidly until it reaches
jam set, about 1 hour. To test, deposit a teaspoon of jam on a saucer which
had been chilled in the freezer. Place near an open window to cool for a
couple of minutes. Gently push the jam with your finger: the surface should
crinkle noticeably. Spoon hot into hot, sterilised jars and seal immediately.

Lilli Pilli Jelly

MAKES ABOUT 5 x 250 G JARS

ONE of the most entertaining and at the same time practical books written in
colonial Australia was surely Mina Rawson's *Australian Enquiry Book of
Household and General Information* in the pages of which there was 'something
about everything and for everybody', its object being 'to help people to help
themselves'. It included information on all domestic matters including how
to cut down a kerosene tin for a cooking vessel, instructions on wattle-work
embroidery or the making of cushions out of pelican down, how to create
furniture from barrels and packing cases, or carpets from rags. With Mrs
Rawson as guide you could remedy unpleasant perspiration or warts, tell the
age of a cow, tame the wildest horse, tan koala and platypus skins and, 'a
favourite amusement of many ladies in the bush', skin and stuff birds.

There were, of course, many excellent recipes and advice upon native
foods. Regarding the lilli pilli she writes that 'While rather acid to eat raw,
they have a very pleasant sharpness when properly preserved'. Of all colonial
recipes for lilli pillies, lilli pilli jelly must have been the most common, a
sparkling cerise-coloured preserve, wonderful with scones and cream. This
recipe suits the small-leaved lilli pilli. Double the quantity of fruit if using the
blue lilli pilli *Syzygium oleosum* or the creek lilli pilli *S. australe*.

1 kg lilli pillies   1 kg sugar
4 cups water

- Discard any stalks and place the lilli pillies in a saucepan with the water.
Bring to the boil over a moderate heat and simmer, covered, for 20 minutes
until soft. Let cool.
- When the fruit is cool enough to handle, strain through a jelly bag or 2
layers of muslin lining a sieve. Squeeze out as much liquid as you can.
- Place the liquid in a large saucepan and bring to the boil over a high heat.
Stir in the sugar. Bring to a rapid boil, stirring, and skim off any scum that
forms on the surface. Boil until jam set, about 20–30 minutes. To test, deposit
a teaspoon of jam on a saucer which had been chilled in the freezer. Place
near an open window to cool for a couple of minutes. Gently push the jam
with your finger: the surface should crinkle noticeably. Pour into hot,
sterilised jars and seal.

Passionfruit Cheese

MAKES 2 x 250 G JARS

THE art of the home cook receives its test of fire at the local agricultural show and at the Royal Shows held in the state capitals. The first show in Australia was the Parramatta Fair, run by the Agricultural Society of New South Wales on 7th October 1823. This was eventually replaced by the Sydney Show, which shifted to the Common at Moore Park in 1882, acquiring its 'Royal' prefix from Queen Victoria in 1891. A century later it moved to the site of the 2000 Olympics.

In addition to the sections for individual exhibitors there are always magnificent displays of the bottler's art in the district exhibits. Here the emphasis is on appearance. Jennifer Isaacs, in *The Gentle Arts*, proclaims Beryl Mills the grand champion bottler of Australia, designing the whole Southern District exhibit at the Royal Easter Show over a number of years, and making up a total of 8,542 bottles between 1950 and 1985, winning 378 prizes at both Melbourne and Sydney. For Western District bottling duo Norma Maxwell and her husband, 'Mrs Mills was always the one we set out to beat'.

For champions like these, meticulous care in cooking and cutting is as essential as the judicious choice of produce:

We have to go with the fruits and the seasons. The good old fruits are the best; for example, the Williams pear, which is not on the market anymore, holds its colour best. We have to get them now from old orchards, but have managed to grow a couple of trees ourselves so we have a ready supply. New fruits such as Kiwi fruit and tamarillos bottle well, but the berries are hard to make 'look anything'—they're too soft. Most people use the metal biscuit cutters. Plastic ones are replacing them on the market, but these are useless for bottling.

Passionfruit cheese, or butter, is a regular feature of the show displays. It makes an exquisite filling for cakes and a good spread for hot buttered toast.

---

2 eggs	*¼ cup lemon juice*
1 cup sugar	*60 g butter*
¼ cup passionfruit pulp	

▪ In a bowl beat the eggs lightly with the sugar. Place the bowl in a saucepan of simmering water over a low heat. Add the remaining ingredients. Cook, stirring constantly with a wooden spoon, until it thickens and coats the back of the spoon, about 10–15 minutes. Don't overcook or the eggs will curdle. Pour the passionfruit cheese into hot, sterilised jars and seal.

Pineapple Chutney

MAKES ABOUT 6 X 350 G JARS

CHUTNEY for most Australians is part of an Anglo-Indian heritage, adapted from the days of the Raj to suit the palate of the British Empire, an accompaniment to cold meat dinners and cold meat sandwiches and the occasional curry. For some Australians, descended from the Indian hawkers, the making of chutneys, and the curries and preserved chillies that go with them, is an important ritual. Mena Abdullah, in *The Time of the Peacock*, describes how she and her sister helped their mother Ama in the kitchen:

The smell of spice was everywhere; Ama was making curry. She was roasting the seeds of cumin, coriander, black pepper. She was softening them for the grinding, when they could be blended with clove, cardamon, chilli, cinnamon, and mace.

Rashida was cutting mangoes and lemons into quarters, ready to be turned into chutney. I was too young to be allowed a knife and I sat at the table by her and stalked the chillies, so that they could be salted and set in trays on the roof, to dry in the sun.

The sun was everywhere in the kitchen, in Rashida's singing and in the rows of new-washed bottles that were waiting for Ama's curry powder.

Apart from mango chutney, both green and ripe, chutneys made from other tropical fruits are also favourites with many Australians, such as tomato, pawpaw, rosella, banana and pineapple.

1 pineapple, about 15 kg	1½ cups malt vinegar
2 Granny Smiths	2 birds-eye chillies, chopped
2 onions, finely chopped	2 teaspoons salt
125 g sultanas	½ teaspoon mixed spice
80 g chopped glacé or crystallised ginger	450 g sugar

▪ Peel and core the pineapple and apples and chop finely. Place in a large saucepan with all the remaining ingredients except the sugar. Simmer, covered, for 20 minutes until the fruit is soft.

▪ Add the sugar and simmer, uncovered, stirring occasionally for about another 20 minutes or until thick. Spoon into hot, sterilised jars and seal.

Choko Pickles

MAKES ABOUT 8 X 350 G JARS

JAM making and pickling are part of the domestic frugality practised by all good housewives, maximising their families' comfort without incurring undue expense. They can save money by utilising the backyard harvest or by taking advantage of cheap seasonal produce on the market. Bottling is a pre-refrigeration, pre-freezer art since, apart from drying, it was the only satisfactory way of dealing with sudden gluts.

In the old days most housewives did their own bottling. It was of greatest benefit to isolated country households but during World War II the government provided an extra sugar ration to all housewives who made their own jam. For Shirley Ball's mother, running a Brisbane boarding house during the Depression, preserving helped feed all the mouths:

When other fruit in season was cheap Muma would bottle pears, peaches and apricots and make melon and lemon jam, my favourite sweet tomato conserve, and huge jars of vegetable pickles and pickled onions.

Bottling was an event in which we all had a hand—peeling fruit and vegetables, stirring the thick savoury mixtures, cutting brown paper for the lid covers, and mixing plain flour and water paste to stick the covers to the jars. Our pantry shelves were stacked with bottled fruits and other preserves. To see them lined shoulder to shoulder, fat, opulent and inviting, promising to do battle against need and hunger was extremely satisfying.

Many people's hunger in the Depression was assuaged by the humble choko from the back fence and choko pickles were then an economical accompaniment to cold meat.

1.5 kg chokoes	⅔ cup plain flour
500 g onions	3 teaspoons dry mustard
125 g green beans	3 teaspoons turmeric
⅔ cup salt	3 teaspoons curry powder
8 cups water	3 cups white wine vinegar
2 cups sugar	

▮ Peel the chokoes if they are large or thick skinned and cut them into 1 cm dice. Peel and slice the onions. Top and tail the beans and cut diagonally into 2.5 cm lengths. In a large bowl dissolve the salt in the water. Add the vegetables and soak overnight to draw out the excess fluid.

▪ The next day put the water and vegetables in a large saucepan and bring to the boil over a moderate heat. Turn the heat down and simmer the vegetables for 5 minutes. Drain. In a mixing bowl mix the sugar with the flour and spices. Gradually stir or beat in the vinegar until smooth. Cook this mixture in the cleaned saucepan over a low heat until it boils and thickens, stirring constantly. Add the vegetables, bring to the boil again over a moderate heat and simmer for 5 minutes. Pack into hot, sterilised jars and seal.

Beekeeper's Chutney

MAKES ABOUT 4 x 250 G JARS

HONEY, or sugarbag, is one of the most highly esteemed of all Aboriginal foods. It is a food for sharing, a special food for feasts and ceremonies, an article of gift and trade. Sugarbag is eaten comb and all, perhaps with hot, freshly-baked damper or mixed with mashed figs or other fruit.

Different bees make different kinds of honey, some sweeter than others, some runnier, some easy to collect from ground hives, some located high in trees. Botanist Daniel Bunce, in *Travels with Dr. Leichhardt*, narrates how a child discovered a tiny black bee sipping nectar from a banksia:

The little fellow was caught and marked by the boy with the feather-like seed of a composite plant, and followed to its home in a neighbouring gum tree; thus betraying the little industrious community of which it formed a member. The boy returned to the camp, and communicated the result of his discovery, when two large hollow sheets of bark were procured, thus forming bowls, which were carried to the tree and speedily filled with pure honey.

Most honey now is produced by Italian bees, including the famous leatherwood honey from Tasmania. In 1894 a whole book of honey recipes was published in West Maitland north of Sydney, *The Economic Housewife's and Beekeeper's Guide to Cookery*, from which is taken this excellent chutney.

250 g tomatoes, peeled	*1⅔ cups stoned dates*
250 g onions	*1 cup honey*
125 g capsicum, deseeded	*2 cups vinegar*
1½ cups dried figs	*2 teaspoons salt*

▪ Cut the vegetables up roughly and then finely chop in a food processor with the figs and dates. Place in a large bowl and stir in the remaining ingredients. Leave for 24 hours, covered with cling wrap.

▪ Pour the contents of the bowl into a large saucepan and bring to the boil over a high heat. Cook, uncovered, until it has thickened, about 30 minutes. The chutney will tend to spit as it thickens, so turn the heat down gradually and stir to prevent it catching. Spoon into hot, sterilised jars and seal.

Bush Pickle

MAKES 1 CUP

A RIVER of recipes and food memories surges forward uninterrupted. Where to conclude? Perhaps it is fitting to end where all cookery inevitably ends, with the banal ritual of washing and wiping up. Mary Gilmore, that fine historian of the everyday, tells in *Old Days: Old Ways* that when she was young tea towels had first to be beetled with a mallet or waddy to make the linen 'kind':

When the kitchen towels had been done enough they were put away to be brought out as required, the fine ones for the fine china and the silver, and the coarser ones for the delf and the big dishes. And it was in washing-up that the quality of your breeding showed … In great houses china was washed-up as carefully as a baby, and sets came down intact, uncracked and unchipped, generation after generation, to be the pride of later times, and the desire of the collector. So I remember with what pride (and I had learned my lesson well) that I would hear my mother call from the next room, 'Isn't it time you washed up?' and I would answer, 'I have; and the things are all put away'. Not one cup had chinked upon another, not one plate clicked against the next, not one dish bumped in going up on the dresser where it belonged; for noise in movement was 'a sign of a poor bringing up,' and a gentlewoman handled china as a gentlewoman should.

More sauce is washed off plates than almost anything else in Australia, usually tomato sauce or, for some bushmen, a simple concoction of Worcestershire sauce and jam.

¾ cup plum jam   *2½ tablespoons Worcestershire sauce*

▪ Place the jam and sauce in a small saucepan and heat gently over a low heat. Stir until combined. Pour into a small serving bowl and let cool.

List of sources

Grateful acknowledgment is made to the owners of copyright for permission to use quoted material. Every effort has been made to contact all copyright owners; the publishers would appreciate notification of any omissions or corrections of sources wrongly attributed for inclusion in future editions.

Abbott, Edward. *The English and Australian Cookery Book.* Sampson Low, Son & Marston, London, 1864.

Abdullah, Mena and Mathew, Ray. *The Time of the Peacock.* ETT Imprint, Sydney, 1992.

Adams, Phillip. *The Age.* 30 July 1977.

Adam-Smith, Patsy. *Hear the Train Blow.* Nelson, Melbourne, 1987.

Alexander, Stephanie. *Stephanie's Australia.* Allen & Unwin, Sydney, 1991.

Alexander, Stephanie. 'Barbecued Yabbies' in *Australian Food.* Lansdowne, Sydney, 1999.

Alliston, Eleanor. *Escape to an Island.* Heinemann, London, 1966.

Aronson, Zara Baar. *XXth Century Cooking and Home Decoration.* William Brooks, Sydney, 1900.

Arrow, Gloria and Tyerman, Margaret. *Homestead Kitchen Recipes.* Mackay Historical Society & Museum, Mackay, 1990.

Arthur, J. K. *Kangaroo and Kauri.* Sampson Low, Marston & Co., London, 1894.

Austin Palmer, Joan. *Memories of a Riverina Childhood.* UNSW Press, Sydney, 1993.

Australasian Cookery Book. Ward, Lock & Co., London, 1913.

Australian Technical Journal. I, 7, 30-8-1898, pp. 228–232.

Backhouse, James. *A Narrative of a Visit to the Australian Colonies.* Adams Hamilton, London, 1843.

Baker, Sidney. *The Australian Language.* 2nd Ed. Currawong, Sydney, 1966.

Ball, Shirley. *Muma's Boarding House.* Rigby, Adelaide, 1978.

Barker, Lady Mary. *Station Amusements in New Zealand.* William Hunt, London, 1873.

Barraba Pre-School Centre Association. Gunyah Gabba. Barraba, NSW, 1967.

Bean, C. E. W. *On the Wool Track: Pioneering Days of the Wool Industry.* Angus & Robertson, Sydney, 1985.

Beckett, Richard. *Convicted Tastes.* Allen & Unwin, Sydney, 1984.

Blay, Rosslyn. *A Living History of Parramatta.* Soroptimist International of Parramatta, Sydney, 1992.

Boothby, Mary. 'Memories of My Bush Life' in *Journal of the Historical Society of South Australia.* No. 12, 1984, pp. 123–134.

Boswell, Annabella. *Journal.* Angus & Robertson, Sydney, 1987.

Brown, Ruby and McCarthy, Marion. *'Explorer's' Country Kitchen.* Brown and McCarthy, Yass, 1986.

Bunce, Daniel. *Travels with Dr. Leichhardt.* Oxford University Press, Melbourne, 1979.

Chisholm, Caroline. *Comfort for the Poor! Meat Three Times a Day!!* John Ollivier, London, 1847.

Chisholm, Caroline. 'Pictures of Life in Australia' in Household Words. Vol. I, 22-6-1850, pp. 307–310.

Chisholm, Caroline. 'Bush Cookery' in Eneas MacKenzie. *The Emigrant's Guide to Australia.* Clarke, Beeton & Co., London, c.1852, pp. 111–113.

Civil Service Store. *Twentieth Century Cookery Book*. H. Pole, Brisbane, 1899.

Clacy, Ellen. *A Lady's Visit to the Gold Diggings of Australia in 1852–53*. Lansdowne, Melbourne, 1963.

Clowes, E. M. *On the Wallaby through Victoria*. Heinemann, London, 1911.

Cohen, Israel. *The Journal of a Jewish Traveller*. John Lane, London, 1925.

Conway, Jill Ker. *The Road from Coorain*. Heinemann, London, 1989. Reprinted by permission of The Random House Group Ltd.

Courier-Mail. *The Courier-Mail 100 Prize Winning Recipes*. Brisbane, c.1939–1945.

Coustas, Mary. *The Food Programme*. Radio National, Australian Broadcasting Corporation, 1994.

Crawford, Evelyn as told to Chris Walsh. *Over My Tracks*. Penguin, Ringwood, Vic, 1993.

Curr, Edward M. *Recollections of Squatting in Victoria Then Called the Port Phillip District (From 1841–1851)*. George Robertson, Melbourne, 1883.

Daly, Harriet W. *Digging, Squatting and Pioneering Life*. Sampson Low, London, 1887.

Davey, Lois et al. 'The Hungry Years: 1788–1792' in *Tucker in Australia*. Ed. Beverley Wood. Hill of Content, Melbourne, 1977, pp. 24–46.

Davis, Jack. *A Boy's Life*. Magabala Books, Broome, 1991.

Devanny, Jean. *Travels in North Queensland*. Jarrolds, London, 1951.

First Australian Continental Cookery Book. Cosmopolitan, Melbourne, 1937.

Ford, Margaret. *End of a Beginning*. Hodder & Stoughton, Melbourne, 1963.

George, Elisabeth. *Two at Daly Waters*. Georgian House, Melbourne, 1945.

Gilmore, Mary. *The Worker Cookbook*. The Worker Trustees, Sydney, 1919.

Gilmore, Mary. *Old Days: Old Ways*. Reproduced with permission of Gilmore's publishers, ETT Imprint, Sydney 2002.

Goobalathaldin. *See* Dick Roughsey.

Hall, Emil. *Diary*. Trans. Renee Holscher. W.H. Hall, Wellington, 1969.

Hammond, Dorothy C. (ed.). *Calendar of Cake and Afternoon Tea Delicacies: A Recipe for Each Day of the Year*. 4th ed. Country Women's Association of NSW, Sydney, 1931.

Hanrahan, Barbara. *The Scent of Eucalyptus*. University of Queensland Press, St Lucia, 1973.

Harris, Alexander. *Settlers and Convicts or Recollections of Sixteen Year's Labour in the Australian Backwoods*. Melbourne University Press, Melbourne, 1964.

Harris, Patricia. *Accept with Pleasure*. Angus & Robertson, Sydney, 1969.

Hatfield, Jean. *Good Cheap Cooking*. Rigby, Adelaide, 1979.

Henning, Rachel. *The Letters of Rachel Henning*. Angus & Robertson, Sydney, 1986.

Hill, Ernestine. *The Great Australian Loneliness*. ETT Imprint, Sydney, 1995.

Holthouse, Hector. *S'pose I Die: The Story of Evelyn Maunsell*. Angus & Robertson, Sydney, 1973.

Housewife's Cookery Book. James Inglis, Sydney, 1896.

Isaacs, Jennifer. *Bush Food*. Ure Smith, Sydney, 1987.

Isaacs, Jennifer. *The Gentle Arts*. Ure Smith, Sydney, 1991.

Jenkins, Joseph. *Diary of a Welsh Swagman 1869–1894.*, W. Evans (ed.). Macmillan, Sth Melbourne, 1975.

Kennedy, Marnie. *Born a Half-Caste*. AIATSIS, Canberra, 1985.

King, Annie. J. (ed.). *Australian Missionary Cookery Book*. Marchant, Sydney, 1915.

Kirkland, Katharine. 'Life in the Bush' in *The Flowers of the Field: A History of Ripon Shire*. Hugh Anderson. Hill of Content, Melbourne, 1969.

Lady Victoria Buxton Girl's Club. *The Kookaburra Cookery Book*. E. W. Cole, Melbourne, 1917.

Langford Ginibi, Ruby. *Don't Take Your Love to Town*. Penguin, Ringwood, Vic, 1988.

Langford Ginibi, Ruby. *Real Deadly*. ETT Imprint, Sydney, 1992.

Laurel Recipe Book and Household Guide. Vacuum Oil Company, Melbourne, c.1940s.

Leichhardt, Ludwig. *The Letters of F. W. Leichhardt Vol. II*. Trans. M. Aurousseau. Cambridge University Press, Cambridge, 1968.

Lloyd, George. *Thirty-Three Years in Tasmania and Victoria*. Houlston & Wright, London, 1862.

Macarthur, Elizabeth. *The Journal and Letters of Elizabeth Macarthur 1789–1798*. Introduced and transcribed Joy N. Hughes. Historic Houses Trust of NSW, Elizabeth Farm Occasional Series, Sydney, 1984.

McArthur, Kathleen. *Bread and Dripping Days*. Kangaroo Press, Kenthurst, NSW, 1981.

McCrae, Georgiana Huntly. *Georgiana's Journal Melbourne 1841–1865*. Angus & Robertson, Sydney, 1966.

McGowan, Henrietta C. *The Keeyuga Cookery Book*. Thomas Lothian, Melbourne, 1911.

McLean, Linda. *Pumpkin Pie and Faded Sandshoes*. APCOL, Sydney, 1981.

Maclurcan, Hannah. *Mrs Maclurcan's Cookery Book*. George Robertson, Melbourne, 1899.

Mathew, R. H. 'Rock-holes Used by the Aborigines for Warming Water' in *Journal and Proceedings of the Royal Society of NSW 1901* Vol. XXXV, pp. 213–216.

Maunsell, Evelyn. *See* Hector Holthouse.

Melville, Henry. *Australasia and Prison Discipline*. Charles Cox, London, 1851.

Meredith, Louisa Anne. *Notes and Sketches of New South Wales*. John Murray, London, 1849.

Mitchell, Blanche. *Blanche. An Australian Diary 1858-1861*. John Ferguson, Sydney, 1980.

Mitchell, Mary. 'Receipes'. M.S., Mitchell Library, Sydney.

M.M. *The Economic Housewife's and Beekeeper's Guide to Cookery*. E. Tipper, West Maitland, 1894.

Mundy, Godfrey Charles. *Our Antipodes*. Vol. I. Bentley, London, 1852.

Muskett, Philip E. *The Art of Living in Australia*. Eyre & Spottiswoode, London, 1893.

National Trust (Victoria). *Cork Fork and Ladle*. Comp. Penny Smith and Heather Hidder. Macmillan, Sth. Melbourne, 1975.

Noonuccal, Oodgeroo. *Stradbroke Dreamtime*. Angus & Robertson, Sydney, 1982.

Parents and Friends of Moriah College. *Secrets from Our Kitchens*. Capricorn, Sydney, 1993.

Pearce, Henriette. *See* Elisabeth George.

Pearson, Margaret J. *Cookery Recipes for the People*. Hearse, Melbourne, 1894.

Peirce, Augustus Baker. *Knocking About*. Yale University Press, New Haven, 1924.

Pell, Flora. *Our Cookery Book*. 2nd ed. George Robertson, Melbourne, 1916.

Phillips, Arthur A. *The Australian Tradition: Studies in a Colonial Culture*. Longman Cheshire, Melbourne, 1980.

Polishuk, Nancy with Douglas Lockwood. *Life on the Daly River.* Robert Hale, London, 1961.

Praed, Rosa Caroline. *My Australian Girlhood.* Fisher Unwin, London, 1902.

Queensland Presbyterian Women's Missionary Union. *W.M.U. Cookery Book.* 22nd ed. Jolly Book Supplies, Brisbane, 1981.

Raven-Hart, R. *The Happy Isles.* Georgian House, Melbourne, 1949.

Rawson, Mina. *Mrs Lance Rawson's Cookery Book and Household Hints.* W. Hopkins, Rockhampton, 1886.

Rawson, Mina. *The Australian Enquiry Book of Household and General Information.* 1st ed. Paper & Knapton, Melbourne, 1894.

Rawson, Mina. *The Antipodean Cookery Book.* 5th ed. George Robertson, Melbourne, 1907.

Rotary Club of Broome. *Broome Shinju Matsuri Cook Book.* Broome, c.1990.

Roughley, T. C. *Fish and Fisheries of Australia.* Angus & Robertson, Sydney, 1966.

Roughsey, Dick (Goobalathaldin). *Moon and Rainbow.* A. H. & A. W. Reed, Sydney, 1971.

Rousselet Niau, Marie. *Souvenirs d'une Parisienne aux Antipodes.* Angus & Roberston, Sydney, 1930.

Rowan, Ellis. *A Flower-Hunter in Queensland and New Zealand.* John Murray, London, 1898.

Rutledge, Jean. *The Goulburn Cookery Book.* Edwards, Dunlop & Co., Sydney, 1899.

Schauer, A. & M. *The Schauer Cookery Book.* Edwards, Dunlop & Co., Brisbane, 1909.

Simpson, Maureen. *Australian Cuisine.* ABC Books, Sydney, 1990.

Sing, Helen (ed.). *Recipes from Tropical Queensland.* Tully Nursing Home Committee, Tully, c.1990.

Steabben, Russell and Corsar, Frank. *Australian Bartender's Guide to Cocktails* 4th Ed. Hospitality Press, Sydney, 1999. Reproduced with the permission of Pearson Education Australia Pty Limited © Russell Steabben and Frank Corsar.

Stokes, Agnes. *A Girl at Government House.* Ed. Helen Vellacott. Currey O'Neil, Melbourne, 1982.

Story, Fanny Fawcett. *Australian Economic Cookery Book and Housewife's Companion.* Kealy & Philip, Sydney, 1900.

Tench, W. A *Narrative of the Expedition to Botany Bay.* J. Debrett, London, 1790.

Tester, Richard. 'Wombat Wallaby, or Reminiscences of a Trip Overland to Melbourne and the Gold Fields'. M.S. Mitchell Library, Sydney.

Tonkinson, Robert. *The Mardudjara Aborigines: Living the Dream in Australia's Desert.* Holt, Rinehart & Winston, New York, 1978.

Trollope, Anthony. *Trollope's Australia.* Ed. Hume Dow. Thomas Nelson, Melbourne, 1966.

Twopeny, R. E. N. *Town Life in Australia.* Elliot Stock, London, 1883.

Ward, Glenyse. *Unna You Fullas.* Magabala Books, Broome, 1991.

Ward, Glenyse. *Wandering Girl.* Magabala, Broome, 1987.

Waterhouse, F. C. *Childhood Memories of Life on a Sheep Station.* Adelaide, 1986.

Wattle Blossom. *Off the Beaten Track.* Bloxham & Chambers, Sydney, 1917.

Wentworth, W. C. *Statistical, Historical, and Political Description of the Colony of New South Wales and its Dependent Settlements in Van Diemen's Land.* Whittaker, London, 1819.

Wessa & Lummo. *A Guide to Aussie Bush Cooking.* Rabbit on a Shovel, c.1980s.

White, Mirtle Rose. *No Roads Go By.* Rigby, Adelaide, 1932.

Wicken, Harriet F. *The Kingswood Cookery Book.* 6th ed. Whitcombe & Tombs, Melbourne, 1890s.

Wicken, Harriet F. *Useful Recipes.* Websdale, Shoosmith & Co., 1890s.

Wicken, Harriet F. *The Cook's Compass.* J. G. Hanks, Sydney, 1890 or 1891.

Wicken, Harriet F. *Fish Dainties.* Mutual Provedoring Co., Melbourne, 1892.

Wicken, Harriet F. *Recipes of Lenten Dishes.* Angus & Robertson, Sydney, 1896.

'Woman's Mirror' Cookery Book. The Bulletin, Sydney, 1937.

Wood, Thomas. *Cobbers.* 3rd ed. Rigby (Seal Books), Adelaide, 1978.

Wright, Judith. 'Bullocky', from *A Human Pattern: Selected Poems.* ETT Imprint, Sydney, 1996.

Further Reading

Absalom, Jack and Reg. *Outback Cooking in the Camp Oven.* Five Mile, Hawthorn, Vic., 1982.

Addison, Susan and McKay, Judith. *A Good Plain Cook: An Edible History of Queensland.* Boolarong, Brisbane, 1985.

Blainey, Geoffrey. *Triumph of the Nomads: A History of Ancient Australia.* Macmillan, Melbourne, 1982.

Bligh, Marjorie A. W. *At Home with Marjorie Bligh.* 3rd ed. Richmond & Sons, Devonport, 1982.

Darwin Garden Club. *Darwin Gardeners' Gourmet Guide.* Darwin Garden Club, Darwin, 1978.

Dorrigo High School P&C. *Popular Recipes from the Dorrigo Plateau.* Dorrigo, NSW, 1967.

Fulton, Margaret. *The Complete Margaret Fulton Cookbook.* Paul Hamlyn, Sydney, 1974.

Gollan, Anne. *The Tradition of Australian Cooking.* ANU Press, Canberra, 1984.

Gye, Eve. *Woman's Tested Recipes.* Woman, Sydney, 1939.

Hayes, Babette. *200 Years of Australian Cooking.* Nelson, Melbourne, 1970.

Howe, Robin. *Cooking from the Commonwealth.* André Deutsch, London, 1958.

Irvine, A. C. *Central Cookery Book.* 17th ed. St. David's Park, Hobart, 1992.

Low, Tim. *Bush Tucker: Australia's Wild Food Harvest.* Angus & Robertson, Sydney, 1989.

Mason, Anne. *A Treasury of Australian Cooking.* André Deutsch, London, 1962.

Pan, Hanna (ed.). *The Australian Hostess Cookbook.* Nelson, Melbourne, c.1968.

Pembroke School. *Green and Gold Cookery Book.* Rigby, Adelaide, 1983.

Port Augusta Women's Auxiliary Royal Flying Doctor Service. *Mantle of Safety Cookbook.* Hyde Park Press, Adelaide, c.1980s.

St. Michael's Women's Auxiliary. *Recipes from my Grossmutter.* St. Michael's Lutheran Congregation, Hahndorf, 1979.

Walker, Robin & Roberts, Dave. *From Scarcity to Surfeit: A History of Food and Nutrition in New South Wales.* UNSW Press, Sydney, 1988.

Wylie, Margaret A. et al. *The Golden Wattle Cookery Book.* 28th ed. Wigg, Perth, 1989.

Sources of Illustrations

Front Cover: Captain John Hunter, 'Go-mah', (King Parrot, *Alisterus scapularis*), in *An Album of Birds and Flowers of New South Wales*, c.1788-1790, watercolour: 22.6x18.3 cm, RNK, NK2039/33; p. 1 'Pumpkin Scones', from *The Cook's Treasure House*, c. 1940s, Simpson Bros, Brisbane; p. 2–3 S. T. Gill, "'The Kitchen of Monsieur Henri Noufflard", a wool merchant in the 1850s', courtesy of HHTNSW; p. 5 The Port Jackson Painter, 'Method of Climbing Trees', © the NHM; p 5 G. F. Angas, 'Bethany, A Village of German Settlers', Plate 60, in *South Australia Illustrated*, ML, X983/2; p. 9 The Port Jackson Painter, op. cit.; p. 17 'Black Lubra Cooking Dampers', ML, SPF Australian Aborigines—Missions—North Australia; p. 29 Sydney Parkinson, 'Kangaroo', in 'Hawkesworth's Voyages of Captain Cook', Vol 3, p.157, NK 2851, by permission of the NLA; p. 34 'A miner's hut—Lithgow Valley, NSW, 1899,' by permission of the NLA; p. 38, S. T. Gill 'Stockman's Hut, Victoria.' DL, Pd 121; p. 41 J. W. Lindt, 'Fernshaw. The Maiden all Forlorn', c. 1890–92, LTPC, H85,40/1; p. 49, Joseph Lycett 'Aborigines Spearing Fish', in 'Hawkesworth's Voyages of Captain Cook', Vol 3, [plate XXVIII f. p. 134]. R5686, p122T, by permission of the NLA; p. 51 'Melville Islanders', ML, SPF Melville Islanders File No 763/70; p. 60 Henry King, 'Brewarrina Fish Traps', ML, PXA 434 No 11b: SPF Australian Aborigines—Hunting and Fishing; p. 69 'Picnic at Mrs Macquarie's Chair', 1855. DG, DG265; p. 73 'From the verandah of an Australian station showing river', watercolour. RNK, MK 1212, by permission of the NLA; p. 84 Joseph Lycett, 'View of the Nepean River at the Cowpastures', in *The Australian Bush*, ML, F980.1/l pl.17; p. 106 G. F. Angas, op.cit.; p. 119 Max Dupain, 'Crows Nest fruit market', c. 1950; p. 128 'House showing garden area, Hill End', Holtermann Collection, ML, PXA4999 Box 10 No. 70164; p. 133 'The corner store, Albury NSW, c. 1907', BCP, frame 0904; p. 137 Max Dupain, 'Fruit stall, Hume Highway', c. 1940s; p. 139 'Aspic Savoury Jelly', in Elizabeth Craig, *New Ways of using Custard*; p.58, Foster Clark (Aust.), Redfern, NSW, c. 1940s; p. 149 Alfred Chambers, 'The Kitchen', c. 1910. AGNSW; p. 175 Max Dupain, 'Black and White in Cairns', 1960; p. 179 Charles Kerry, 'Woman in Kitchen', c. 1895–1910, PHM; p. 196 'Greetings Fruit Cake', *The Cook's Treasure House*, op.cit.; p. 199 'Brockhoff's Federation self raising flour', in *Cookery Book*, Presbyterian Church of NSW WMA, c. 1900.; p. 204 Charles Kerry, 'Breakfast in a Drover's Camp', reproduced by courtesy of ACP; p. 221 'Eiffel Tower Lemonade Crystals and Fruit Cubes', in Elizabeth Craig, op.cit., p.31; p. 232 'Williams' shop, Bega NSW, c. 1930', BCP, frame 02248.

Index